A People's History of India

Volumes published:

1 Prehistory

2 The Indus Civilization

3 The Vedic Age

4 The Age of Iron and the Religious Revolution

5 Mauryan India

6 Post-Mauryan India, 200 BC – AD 300: A Political and Economic History

20 Technology in Medieval India, *c.* 650–1750

23 The Establishment of British Rule, 1757–1813

25 Indian Economy under Early British Rule, 1757–1857

28 Indian Economy, 1858–1914

36 Man and Environment: The Ecological History of India

General Editor: Irfan Habib

The Aligarh Historians Society, the sponsor of the project of *A People's History of India*, is dedicated to the cause of promoting the scientific method in history and resisting communal and chauvinistic interpretations.

A People's History of India 5

MAURYAN INDIA

Irfan Habib
Vivekanand Jha

Aligarh Historians Society

Tulika Books

Published by **Tulika Books**
35 A/1 (ground floor), Shahpur Jat, New Delhi 110 049

First edition (hardback) 2004
Second edition (paperback) 2005
Third edition (paperback) 2007
Fourth edition (paperback) 2009
Fifth edition (paperback) 2011
Sixth edition (paperback) 2013

Seventh edition (paperback) 2015
ISBN: 978-93-82381-62-4

Printed at Chaman Enterprises, Daryaganj, Delhi 110 006

Contents

Tables, Maps and Figures

Preface

In the present volume, which is No. 5 in the People's History of India series, we have tried to follow the style and approach aimed at in the first three published monographs of the series. Some factors have, however, made this text considerably longer than any of its predecessors. Some readers having complained that the style in the earlier monographs has sometimes been excessively concise, we have tried in this monograph to follow a more leisurely course, allowing a greater tolerance of explanatory statements and even repetition, and this naturally has led to greater expenditure of space. Moreover, the large amount of information available to us for the one-and-a-half centuries here studied cannot be very easily compressed. Greater space has also been taken up by excerpts from sources, which include translations of as many as ten edicts of Ashoka alone. We have also increased the number of maps and figures, in the belief that these will substantially supplement the textual information. We offer separate notes on Mauryan chronology, the date of the *Arthashāstra*, the science of epigraphy and Ashokan dialects, which have seemed to us to involve technical or controversial matters that deserve special attention.

As in *The Vedic Age*, the scheme of transliteration adopted departs from the conventional one in the following particulars: 'ch' and 'chh' are respectively used instead of 'c' and 'ch'; 'sh' and 'sh̲', instead of 'ś' and 'ṣ'; and 'ri', instead of 'ṛ'. We have not followed the scholarly custom of converting the words of Ashokan Prākrit into Sanskrit. Since, however, the forms of Prākrit words vary according to dialects, we have usually chosen the forms found in inscriptions using Ashokan Māgadhī, but replacing 'l' by 'r', wherever the corresponding Sanskrit forms or the forms in other dialects justify such an alteration. This hopefully preserves authenticity without sacrificing convenience.

While omitting, for reasons of space, detailed references to books and journals for individual statements, we have frequently given chapter-and-clause references to original texts, whereby the passages can be easily located in different printed texts and translations. Ashokan edicts are referred to by their full conventional designations, without troubling the reader with any abbreviations. The bibliographical notes are really select bibliographies and cannot, regrettably, include all the material that has been used in the making of this book.

The maps are drawn by Mr Faiz Habib with the collaboration of Mr Zahoor Ali Khan. Mr Ghulam Mujtaba photographed the originals for our figures, except the photograph of the pillar at Lauriya Nandangarh, which Mr Shamim Akhtar has given us. Mr P.N. Sahay has compiled the index.

Mr Muneeruddin Khan has processed the entire manuscript. Mr Arshad Ali looked after all the paper work, and Mr Idris Beg undertook the necessary xeroxing and 'courier-service' duties.

The libraries of the Centre of Advanced Study in History, Aligarh, and the Indian Council of Historical Research, New Delhi, have placed both of us greatly in their debt by their readiness to let us consult books and journals.

Professor Shireen Moosvi, Secretary, Aligarh Historians Society, has done everything to make things move fast, once our manuscript reached her, even if only in parts. Mr Rajendra Prasad and Ms Indira Chandrasekhar of Tulika Books have constantly made us feel, by their counsel and support, that the series occupies a special place in their regard.

December 2004

IRFAN HABIB
VIVEKANAND JHA

Note to the sixth edition:
Opportunity has been taken of this edition to make further corrections and update information. Sadly, Dr Vivekanand Jha passed away last year, and I have had to carry out the task alone.

June 2013

IRFAN HABIB

1
Alexander's Invasion and the Formation of the Mauryan Empire

1.1 People of Northwestern India at the Time of Alexander's Invasion

Of Alexander's invasion of India (327–325 BC) and attending events, no contemporary account, except a report of the voyage of his admiral, Nearchus, has survived. The Greek historian Arrian compiled, in *c.* AD 150, his *Anabasis*, a detailed and careful account of Alexander's career derived from a number of narratives left by the conqueror's companions and courtiers (notably Ptolemy), which he cites. Arrian's *Anabasis* and *Indica*, in which Nearchus's report is preserved, are supplemented, sometimes in significant ways, by other authors (such as Diodorus, *c.* 21 BC, Strabo, *c.* AD 23, and Plutarch, *c.* AD 119) who had access to the same or other early Greek texts and traditions. Drawing on these various narratives, we can reconstruct a picture of the conditions of life and culture of the people in the borderlands and the Indus basin on the eve of Alexander's invasion.

Though the Indians are often spoken of as 'barbarians' in the Greek accounts, it is clear that they were not thought by the invaders to have been primitive by any means. Living in villages, they cultivated the soil with numerous and excellent cattle. In the Swat valley, Alexander is said to have seized as many as 230,000 (!) oxen, the best of which he wished to send to his native Macedonia (north of Greece, in southeastern Europe) for working on the land there. Probably, being humped, the Indian bullock ('zebu') was expected to be more efficient in drawing the plough than the native Macedonian ox. Strabo (XV.1.18) tells us that both Nearchus and Aristobulus, who also came with Alexander, found that much of the cultivation in the Indus plains depended on floods. Aristobulus added that rice was sown in enclosed beds, where it could stand in water. Another writer from Alexander's entourage, Onesicritus, referred to 'bosmoran', a grain smaller than wheat, peculiar to India – perhaps the bajra millet. Nearchus must have been referring to sugarcane when he wrote of honey-yielding reeds. From him, again, is quoted (Strabo XV.1.20; Arrian, *Indica*, XVI) the statement that the Indians made their clothing from cotton, which was collected from trees: the cotton plant was thus still a perennial bush and had not yet been developed into an annual plant. The earlier notion, popularized from Herodotus, that India produced much gold, is not now repeated. On the other hand, rock salt is referred to as being dug out in the Salt Range to be supplied to different parts of India, presumably by way of trade.

Both agriculture and trade were sufficiently developed to sustain an urban economy of some size. Cities and fortified towns are frequently mentioned, and some of them are named as well, notably the city of Taxila. Archaeological excavations at the Bhir Mound at Taxila have indeed revealed, with fairly consistent carbon dates (calibrated), that this city had been established before *c.* 400 BC, with some Achaemenid influence traceable in its silver-bar punch-marked coins, as also Gangetic influence in its imitation Northern Black Polished Ware. After defeating Porus, Alexander moved eastward towards the Chenab and took some thirty-seven towns, "the smallest" of which, according to Arrian, had "not less than 5,000 inhabitants, and many of them more than double that".

There were undoubtedly some communities on the margins of the settled zone, in forests and deserts and on stretches of coast, that were still in the 'gathering' stage and so quite primitive. In his remarkable account of his voyage along the Baluchistan coast, Nearchus tells us that beyond the Indian tribe of Arabies, inhabiting the plains along the Arabis (Porali) river, people were found who were still living in the stone age ("for iron they had none"). They lived by fishing around the estuary of a seasonal torrent, the Tomeros (modern Hingal), and used their finger-nails and stones for tearing and cutting. They were an isolated community, for the 'Oritae' in the interior, though not Indians, dressed like Indians and used similar (presumably iron) weapons.

In the Indus basin, the territorial states were based in most cases on the dominance of particular tribes, the kings or chiefs often bearing tribal designations as in the case of Porus and Absares (Pūru and Abhisāra). That kingship had sometimes rendered such tribal affinities largely nominal was probably true in the case of Porus, but not, perhaps, in that of the 'Malloi' (Mallas), where different chiefs appear to have shared authority with one another. No trace of the earlier Achaemenid (Persian) suzerainty over the region seems now to have remained.

In none of the narratives of Alexander's expedition is the caste system directly touched upon. It is possible, however, that the tribes that are mentioned were really composed of ruling clans, and so were potentially Kshatriya communities, if not yet always so recognized. To Brahmans ('Brachmanes'), there are explicit references. They were 'Indian teachers of philosophy', and some of them also acted as advisors to princes. Alexander had groups of them hanged in Sindh on the accusation that they had successively induced two local rulers, Musicanus and Sambus, to oppose him.

Slavery existed at least in parts of the region. Onesicritus noticed it in the territory of Musicanus in Sindh (Strabo, XV.1.54); and Aristobulus saw poor people publicly selling their daughters at Taxila (Strabo, XV.1.62).

We have also in these records the earliest evidence of the practice of widow-burning. Aristobulus observed it at Taxila; Diodorus noted its prevalence among the 'Cathaei' (Kāṭhis? Khatrīs?) between the Ravi and the Beas. Diodorus also tells us that when an Indian captain, Keteus, was killed in the first battle of Gabienne (near Isfahan in Iran) in 316 BC, his younger wife mounted the funeral pyre with him: the description given of the event vividly conforms to the *sati* ritual known to us from later times. The practice, reminiscent of Iranian Magian (and Zoroastrian) custom, of exposing dead bodies to vultures was also in vogue at Taxila.

The narratives do not mention the use of writing among Indians. Strabo (XV.1.67), who notes this, also tells us, however, that Nearchus had observed (in the portion of his account not now extant) that Indians write their letters on "linen [cotton] cloth, that is closely woven". It is possible that under Achaemenid rule a familiarity with Aramaic had developed among Indians, and that the Kharoshṭhī script, created out of Aramaic, was already in use, though there is as yet no known example of Kharoshṭhī writing earlier than Ashoka's edicts. As to language, Nearchus, in his account of the Baluchistan coast, distinguishes the people of a tribe there from the Indians generally by "their language and customs". This can hardly be taken to mean that all the Indian communities subjugated by Alexander spoke the same language; the universal presence of a lingua franca used by officials and in the market-place is more plausibly to be inferred. This could well have been the northwestern or Gāndhārī Prākrit, used in Ashoka's Mansehra and Shahbazgarhi inscriptions. Names like Taxila and Sandracottus in Greek, one may note, were obviously derived from the Prākrit forms of the names, Takhasilā and Chandagutta (Gāndhārī *Chandragutta), not the Sanskrit ones (Takshashilā and Chandragupta).

Of the sciences, only medicine is mentioned. Nearchus (as quoted by Arrian, *Indica*, XV) says that Alexander, failing to find remedies for snake-bites from Greek physicians, gathered Indian healers, and "these very same men were able to cure other diseases and pains also". This would seem to be the first case of a foreign recognition of Āyurveda.

In respect of religion, the general absence of references to deities' images and temples (which are of frequent occurrence in the same accounts of Alexander's campaigns in Egypt, Mesopotamia and Iran) is surely not without significance: these apparently played no great part yet in Indian priestly practice. Brahmans were thought to be philosophers; Diodorus tells us of a Brahman in Sindh who spoke of the need to both live and die nobly – a strain of thought that has reminded some modern scholars of an anticipation of the teachings of the *Bhagavad Gītā*. Another incident suggests the presence of Jain ascetics. In Taxila, we are told, there were ascetics who went naked. Their leader, Dandamis (or Mandanis), refused to join Alexander's service, for he looked forward to leaving his earthly body, "my unseemly housemate". Another 'philosopher', Calanus (Kalyān?), accompanied Alexander back to Persepolis in Iran, where he decided to commit suicide by publicly setting up a funeral pyre. He was also presumably a Jain or an Ājīvika monk. The religious revolution in Magadha of the sixth and fifth centuries BC had thus by now acquired votaries in northwestern India, although it is curious that Buddhism should pass unnoticed in these Greek narratives.

1.2 Alexander's Invasion

Alexander's invasion brought India into direct contact with the Greek civilization that, in the fifth and fourth centuries BC, with its philosophers, historians and dramatists, its art, and spirit of reason and enquiry, constituted one of the great achievements of mankind. The Greek-speaking peoples ('Hellas') lived in the territories of modern Greece, western Turkey and southern Italy. The western part of Asian Turkey was called Ionia (whence the Prākrit 'Yona', Sanskritized into 'Yavana', for Greek). Politically, the Greeks were hopelessly divided: the Ionian cities and principalities were brought under subjection by the Achaemenid Empire of Iran, and the city-states of European Greece (with large slave populations) remained engaged in unrelenting conflicts with each other.

To the north of Greece, Macedonia was peopled by different tribes and clans who spoke dialects of their own. The Macedonian ruler Philip II (reigned 359–336 BC) forged a new kind of army out of the local aristocracy and peasantry. The infantry had protective shields and long pikes, and was arranged in 'phalanxes' or close formations, in squares and other shapes, trained to quickly open or close or change shape. The infantry was reinforced by light cavalry, made up of skilled riders (including mounted archers) who had to do without saddle, stirrup, and iron-shoe (none of these being yet known). In addition, large wooden catapults throwing stone missiles, mobile wooden towers and battering rams enormously improved the power to spread slaughter among the besieged and to pierce fortifications. Equally importantly, Philip introduced such a high degree of battlefield discipline and training in military skills that older armies appeared to be composed of mere rabble when confronted by his troops.

The effect of this revolution in warfare was dramatic. Philip became the master of Greece; and his son Alexander the Great (336–323 BC) crossed over to Asia Minor to challenge the huge Achaemenid Empire, extending from Egypt to Transoxiana. After three major battles (334–331 BC), of which two were fought with the ill-fated Iranian emperor Darius III (336–330 BC) himself, the Achaemenid Empire lay prostrate under the feet of the invader.

Alexander's campaign in the eastern parts of the defeated

Empire began in 331 BC. He entered Afghanistan when he occupied Aria (Herat); he then marched south into Zarangia (Zarang or Seistan). Leading his forces up the Helmand basin, he subjugated Arachosia (Harakhvaiti or the Arghandab basin). Its capital, Kandahar, hereafter contained both Iranian and Greek inhabitants, for in the next century the Indian emperor Ashoka set up at Kandahar inscriptions in Aramaic, the official language of the Achaemenids, as well as in Greek. Following the circuitous but easier route adopted by him, Alexander reached the valley of the Kabul river, where, near Begram, he founded yet another city named Alexandria. Crossing the Hindukush, he drove away Bessus, the ruler of Bactria (Balkh), who had murdered the fugitive Darius, and then, in further pursuit, began his conquest of Transoxiana.

Upholding Macedonian claims of overlordship over Greece, Alexander had stood forth as a representative of Greek culture and an avenger of wrongs that the Greeks had allegedly suffered at the hands of the Iranians. Now master of the Iranian heartland, another ambition beckoned to him, of being the 'Great king', an heir to the Achaemenid line. The apparatus of the Iranian Empire was bodily taken over with many of its official designations and customs kept largely intact. The Iranian title of provincial governor, *khsatrapa(wan)*, was retained in the Greek form of 'satrap'; and though the incumbents of this office were generally Macedonians, some of them were also drawn from the Iranian aristocracy. Reinforcements from Macedonia and Greece continued to arrive, but Alexander's forces were also simultaneously swollen by the influx of chiefs and soldiers from Iranian communities, including the semi-nomadic Saka ('Scythian') horsemen from north of the Oxus. These recruits rapidly learned to fight alongside Macedonian and Greek soldiery.

At the head of this diverse but disciplined host, Alexander began his march into India in the spring of 327 BC, after having completed his Central Asian campaign. He left Bactria (north Afghanistan), crossed the Hindukush Mountains ('Paropamisadae'), and strengthened his city of 'Alexandria' at Begram with new Macedonian and Greek settlers. Marching along the Kabul ('Cophen') river, his troops sacked Peucelaotis (Charsadda?), north of Peshawar. Perhaps to protect his left flank, he moved into the Swat valley, making slaves out of captives and seizing the much-admired local cattle. The major principality that

Map 1.1 Northwestern India, 325 BC: Alexander's Conquests

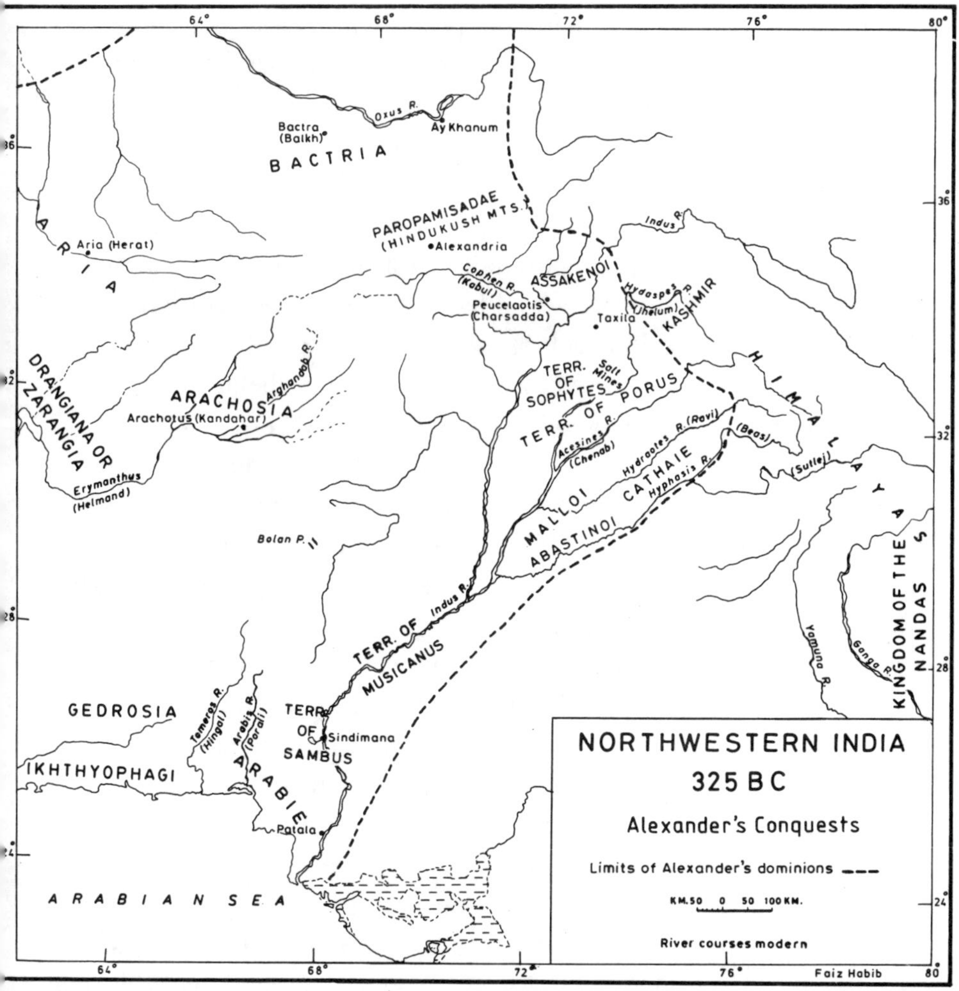

needed to be subdued was that of the Assakenoi (Assacenian) tribe, its chief known as Assacenus after the tribe. Their major town, Massaga (not located), fell before Alexander's siege engines, though only after spirited resistance. The rock of 'Aornas' (Varna?) was seized more apparently out of a spirit of adventure than because of any strategic value it possessed: the problem of its identification from the topographic details given has still defied satisfactory solution.

Accepting the submission of a town, 'Nysa', that allegedly claimed links with the Greek god Dionysus, Alexander crossed the Indus, possibly by a bridge of boats, and made for Taxila. Its ruler is given two names, 'Taxiles' (obviously from Taxila) and 'Omphis' (Āmbhi); he had already made his peace with Alexander and offered him allegiance. Across the next river, Hydaspes (Vitastā or Jhelum), were the principalities of two mutually hostile rulers, both called 'Porus', apparently after the name of a tribe (Pūru) that went back to the second millennium BC (see *The Vedic Age*, 1.5). The more powerful of these two princes barred Alexander's passage across the Jhelum. The battle that followed is an important one for the study of Indian military history in that it is the only actual battle in the entire history of ancient India that is described in such professional detail.

Alexander effected his passage over the Jhelum by deceiving Porus through a succession of feints; an attack by Porus's son with 120 chariots and some cavalry was easily crushed. Porus himself waited for Alexander on drier ground with reputedly 4,000 cavalry, 300 chariots, 200 elephants and 30,000 infantry. He formed them in a long front, placing his elephants in a line at intervals filled with infantry. On both flanks of this front were infantry and cavalry, the latter supported by screens of chariots. Alexander overthrew this apparently formidable array by creating chaos in Porus's army as, by well-directed cavalry attacks, he compelled Porus's cavalry to move now in one direction and then in the opposite. Since horses might shy away if brought face to face with elephants, Alexander let his disciplined infantry attack the beasts and their drivers. Cavalry was later used to attack the elephants from the rear (see *Fig. 1.1*). The chariots failed here against Alexander's troops, just as they had failed in the Iranian battlefields. Ultimately, Porus's troops were forced to crowd around the elephants, which then could not move without crushing their own soldiers. The Indian host was overthrown with much slaughter and Porus himself was captured.

Allowing Porus to keep his kingdom as a subordinate ruler, Alexander moved eastward to cross the 'Acesines' (Asiknī or Chenab) near the sub-Himalayan hills, and then, the 'Hydraotes' (Irāvatī, or Ravi). Thereafter, he stormed the fort of Sangala, a brick fort on a mound or hill with a lake nearby (not satisfactorily located), where the tribe of 'Cathaei' had gathered to defend themselves. He took 70,000 captives, to be profitably turned into slaves presumably. The next river to be reached was the Hyphasis (Vipāsh or Beas, possibly the joint

FIG. 1.1 Alexander's medallion, Babylon, *c.* 323 BC. *Obverse*: Macedonian horseman attacks Indian elephant. *Reverse*: Alexander holds the thunderbolt. (After A.B. Bosworth.) Note absence of saddle and stirrup on horse.

Sutlej–Beas). Further east lay the Gangetic basin, a country "rich and productive", possessed of more elephants than any other part of India. Alexander had by now clearly recognized the value of this animal in war. Despite his exhortations, Alexander's officers declined to go further: they were satisfied with the wealth they had won, and were exhausted by the long campaigning and awed by the distance from home.

In September–October of 326 BC, the return march began. Porus was rewarded for his assistance by letting him annex the territory up to the Beas. Coming back to the site of the battle with him on the Jhelum, Alexander resettled, with garrisons and local inhabitants, the two towns he had earlier established there. He accepted the final submission of Absares, the chief of the Abhisāra tribe in the lower Himalayas, and the allegiance of Sopeithes or Sophytes (Saubhūti), the ruler of the Salt Range. Arrangements were at the same time completed for a grand expedition down to the sea.

With the assistance of men from various communities of boat-builders brought from the eastern Mediterranean, Alexander had a very large flotilla prepared, the boats doubtless built out of timber from the hills floated down the Jhelum. Flanked by both infantry and cavalry on opposite banks, and accompanied by 200 elephants, he voyaged down the river with the flotilla. Past the confluence with the Chenab, he struck out across a waterless tract to surprise the 'Malloi' (Mallas). A fortified town being taken with much slaughter, the 'Malloi' retreated across the Ravi. Pursuing them, Alexander laid siege to their principal city, which might have been somewhere near Multan. (The Ravi used to flow past that city as late as AD 1400.) Impatient to capture it, Alexander led a storming party himself and, gravely injured, was rescued only with difficulty. In reprisal, all the town's inhabitants, including women and children, were put to the sword. Alexander took the surrender of the remaining Malla chiefs and of their allies, the 'Oxydracae', accepting a 'gift' of 500 chariots. He had to make just a short voyage now to reach the junction of the Ravi with the Chenab; and thereafter he voyaged down to the junction of the united river with the Indus. Near here, the 'Abastanoi' (Ambaṣhṭhas) were subjugated; and Alexander founded yet another settlement at the point where the two great streams met.

Alexander was now approaching Sindh. Musicanus, ruler in northern Sindh, being surprised by Alexander's rapid movements, submitted, but then revolted. He was captured and executed, and his subjects sold into slavery. The principality of another chief, Oxycanus, was seized and sacked. Further to the south was the territory of Sambus: he was a ruler of the hill tribes, and the hills must be those of the Kirthar Range. His capital, Sindimana, has therefore been plausibly identified with Sehwan. Sambus fled, and Sindimana capitulated peacefully.

Finally, Alexander and his flotilla reached the Indus delta. At the town of Patala, the great river divided into two arms. Alexander explored the delta and rode out to sea, and had a first-hand experience of observing the tides of the Indian Ocean.

Alexander had for some time been contemplating his return westward to Iran and Mesopotamia, and so made certain arrangements for the administration of his Indian conquests. The entire Indus basin was divided into two provinces. The northern portion, extending south to the Indus–Chenab confluence, was placed under Philip; and the area from that point to the sea was to be governed as co-satraps by Alexander's Bactrian father-in-law Oxyartes (presumably only nominally, *in absentia*) and Peithon. Philip and Peithon were Macedonians, commanding miscellaneous assemblages of troops of Macedonian, Greek and Iranian extraction, along with those of subordinate Indian princes. Such a situation, though unavoidable, was bound to breed disturbance

Soon after Alexander left India, there was a conspiracy by (Greek?) mercenaries, resulting in Philip's murder, probably at his headquarters, Taxila; but his Macedonian guards foiled the coup and executed the conspirators. Alexander ordered Eudemus (a Macedonian) to take charge of the province with the Indian prince Taxiles as his colleague, an arrangement indicative of Alexander's anxiety to retain local support.

When in lower Sindh in the autumn of 325 BC, Alexander decided that, leaving aside such troops as were needed to garrison strategic towns in the conquered territories, one part of his army, together with elephants obtained in India, should march to Carmania (Kirman, eastern Iran), through Arachosia (Kandahar) and Zarangia (Seistan). They could have gone through the Bolan Pass, but this is not clear. He himself decided to lead a large part of his forces through Gedrosia (Baluchistan), keeping close to the coast. A flotilla was sent under Nearchus to make a voyage along the coast so as to reach the Persian Gulf. The decision to take the land route through Baluchistan proved to be a rash one, and both men and animals perished in considerable numbers. Alexander ultimately paired Gedrosia with Arachosia into a single satrapy under Sibyrtius. In Carmania he received the troops that had been sent back from India through Arachosia. He arrived at Susa in southwestern Iran in April–May 324 BC. From here he proceeded to Babylon in Iraq, where he died suddenly in June 323 BC.

Conquered northwestern India was doubtless shaken by Alexander's invasion with its bouts of plunder and massacres. An unconcealed immediate object of Alexander was to secure booty on an immense scale in the form of treasure, goods and captives turned into slaves. The regime he established might use Indian princes and chiefs as intermediaries, but its real function was to extort enough tribute to maintain the foreign garrisons, and to provide wealth and luxuries to Alexander's own court, satraps and captains.

Although much suffering accompanied their progress, Alexander's conquests occupy a place of their own in history for the intercultural fertilization they brought about. In Egypt and Syria the Hellenistic civilization was firmly established with Greek as the language of government and science. Further eastward, the Hellenistic layer was more thinly spread, but Greek (and Macedonian) communities were settled in towns spaced at convenient distances, up to and including the Indus basin. One such town that archaeology has discovered for us is Ay Khanum on the Oxus in north Afghanistan, complete with a theatre and gymnasium, having been founded during the time of Seleucus I (311–281 BC), if not of Alexander himself. A striking find here has been that of aphorisms of Greek wisdom inscribed on stone in *c.* 275 BC by the philosopher Clearchus on a visit from Greece. Southward, at Kandahar, Ashoka's inscriptions, *c.* 250 BC, in excellent Greek with calligraphy suggestive of post-Alexandrian influences, similarly attest to contacts being maintained between the centres of the Greek world and these outlying settlements. Ashoka's own references to 'Yonas' within his Empire and to the five Yona rulers of West Asia, North Africa and Greece proper (Rock Edict XIII: *Extract 1.4*) are indicative, again, of communications (and commerce) between India and the Hellenistic world. The possible cultural and political effects of such a development on India could be many; and some of these will be touched upon later in this monograph, such as the use of eras, the efflorescence of sculpture and stone work, and the influx of Hellenized elements into the bureaucracy of the Mauryan imperial administration. The diffusion of scientific knowledge from the Greek world to India that came later could also be regarded as a long-term unintended consequence of Alexander's limitless ambition.

1.3 The Nandas and the Rise of Chandragupta Maurya

The early Purāṇas, compiled in the fourth century AD, probably from earlier popular versified Prākrit lists of dynastic rulers (as suggested by F.E. Pargiter), place the Nanda dynasty as immediately preceding that of the Mauryas (see *Extract 1.1*). According to them, the Nandas ruled for just two generations, the founder and his eight sons ruling one after another. The classical (i.e. Greek and Latin) accounts (Diodorus, XVIII.93; Curtius Rufus, IX.2), which apparently go back to a report of Alexander's time, also assign two generations to the dynasty, but mention only two rulers, father and son. The Buddhist tradition preserved in Sri Lanka (*Mahāvaṁsa*, V, 14–17) speaks of 'nine' Nandas, but all the nine are said to have been brothers who ruled successively. Practically all traditions speak of the Nandas as of obscure or low birth (or, if descended from a king, only from his Shūdra consort, according to the Purāṇas). The Greek report and a tradition that comes to us through the Jain polymath Hemachandra (AD 1088–1172) strangely agree in alleging that the first Nanda ruler was himself a barber or the son of one. On the names of Nanda rulers, our sources diverge inexplicably. The Buddhist tradition supplies the names of all the nine rulers, from Uggasena (Ugrasena) to Dhanananda; the Purāṇas give only two names, those of the founder, Mahāpadma, and his eldest son, Sukalpa. The Greek report gives the name of the ruler contemporary to Alexander as Agrammes or Xandrames, of which the first could conceivably be a corruption of Augrasainya (son of Ugrasena).

The period of the rule of the Nandas in the Purāṇas is set at 100 years, with an incredibly long reign of 88 years attributed to the founder. The Buddhist tradition assigns a more plausible period of twenty-two years to the Nandas, which, given 322 BC as the probable year in which Chandragupta Maurya supplanted them (see *Note 1.1*), would put the period of their ascendancy from *c.* 344 to 322 BC.

In the Sri Lankan Buddhist and Jain traditions, and in Vishākhadatta's Sanskrit play *Mudrārākshasa*, the capital of the Nandas is said to have been Pāṭaliputra (in Pāli also called 'Pupphapura'), modern Patna; and they were, therefore, the rulers of Magadha. The Purāṇas, too, by linking Mahāpadma Nanda with the last Shishunāga ruler (see *Extract 1.1*), make the Nandas the rulers of Magadha. The Greek report tells us that Agrammes was the king of the 'Gangaridae' and the 'Prasii'. Of these, the Prasii must be Prāchyas (Sanskrit for 'easterners'); and Megasthenes (*c.* 300 BC) puts Pāṭaliputra ('Palibothra') in the country of the Prasii. 'Gangaridae' seems to be a Greek name for people settled along the lower stretch of the Ganga. It would appear that Agrammes's territories came up to western Uttar Pradesh, for it was his opposition that Alexander is said to have been expecting if he himself went further east than the Punjab. Khāravela's Hathigumpha inscription (first century BC) has two references to Nanda ascendancy over Kalinga (Orissa): 'the Nandarāja' is said to have excavated a canal to bring water to the Kalinga capital 'over three hundred years' earlier.

With so extensive a territory, the Nanda king could maintain a very large army. It was reported to Alexander that Agrammes possessed 20,000 cavalry, 200,000 infantry, 2,000 four-horse chariots, and 3,000 or 4,000 elephants (figures given by Diodorus and Q. Curtius

Rufus; Plutarch has highly inflated numbers for all arms other than the infantry). The same Greek report adds that Porus told Alexander of king Agrammes's father's disreputable profession and treachery in seizing the throne through intrigue with the former ruler's queen. The ruler, he said, was therefore very unpopular among his subjects. The avarice and oppressive taxation attributed to the Nandas in tradition (especially the Buddhist) could also have played a part in making the Nandas unpopular.

These sources of unpopularity were possibly exploited by Chandragupta Maurya in his effort to overthrow the Nandas. 'Maurya' seems to be a clan name. Though it does not occur in the Greek accounts, including the surviving fragments of Megasthenes's *Indica*, or in Ashoka's inscriptions, Rudradāman's Junagarh inscription of AD 150 prefixes 'Maurya' to the names of both Chandragupta and Ashoka. The Purāṇas (no later than the fourth century AD) also assign the same name to the dynasty. The Buddhist tradition tells us that Chandragupta belonged to the Moriya clan of the Buddha's tribe of Shākyas which lived in a tract full of peacocks (*mora*), and the Jain tradition makes him a son of a royal superintendent of peacocks (*mayūra-poshaka*), both incapable of proof but less improbable than the claim in late Sanskrit literature that Chandragupta was the son or grandson of a Nanda king.

An important passage from Justin, the Roman historian who summarized a Greek history of the Macedonian monarchy, no longer extant, provides us the best source for the early career of Chandragupta (see *Extract 1.2*). He was of a "mean origin", we are told. Presumably, as a military captain he offended 'Nandrus', or the Nanda king, and, fleeing for life, went into rebellion. A modern editor's reading substituting Alexander for Nandrus has been shown to be erroneous, so that Chandragupta's earlier struggle was not at any point with Alexander but was entirely with the Nanda ruler. Plutarch remarks that 'Andracottus' (Sandracottus or Chandragupta), while a youth, had met Alexander, and was prone later to declare that the Nanda ruler was so unpopular among his subjects that Alexander could easily have taken possession of the country. Whether true or not, this also shows that Chandragupta's hostility was believed initially to be directed towards the Nandas alone. He ultimately assembled sufficient forces to try to overthrow the

Nandas. Both the Buddhist and Jain traditions refer to early reverses suffered by Chandragupta; and the Buddhist text *Milindapañho* (IV.8.2.6) mentions an extremely bloody encounter between Chandragupta's troops and those of the Nanda general, Bhaddasāla.

Every Indian (including Sri Lankan Buddhist) tradition assigns to the Brahman Chāṇakya, or Kauṭilya, a key role as a mentor and minister of Chandragupta in his struggle with the Nandas. He is presented to us as a bitter foe of the Nandas but steadfast in his support of Chandragupta's interest. In this cause he was recklessly cruel, unscrupulous, and quick to resort to plot and trickery. For Chandragupta, he is said to have coolly betrayed another protégé of his, Parvata, a Nanda prince or a ruler from the northwest or the Himalayas (so varied are the statements about this ill-fated ally). Of Chāṇakya himself, the only thing that can be said is that he probably is a historical figure and was, as minister of Chandragupta, the author of much cruelty. But most of the details about him, in the story of plot and counterplot in Vishākhadatta's *Mudrārākshasa* (composed in the fifth century AD or later), or in the various traditional accounts, are plainly fictitious. Whether he was really the author of the *Arthashāstra*, the famous treatise on statecraft, is discussed in *Note 1.2*.

1.4 The Reign of Chandragupta Maurya (*c.* 322–298 BC)

By the chronology that the Ashokan inscriptions enable us to reconstruct (see *Note 1.1*), Chandragupta's occupation of the throne of Magadha can be dated to around 322 BC. All traditional accounts agree that the seizure of the throne from the Nandas was the primary object of Chandragupta in his early career, and there is no mention in these of any enmity towards the 'Yavanas' or 'Yonas' ('Ionians', used for Macedonians or Greeks) on the part either of Chandragupta or Chāṇakya. It is only in the passage from Justin (*Extract 1.2*) that the subsequent ambition of Chandragupta to seize northwestern India from Alexander's successors is touched upon. To discover how this might have come about requires us to consider in some detail what we know of the events in Alexander's Indian dominions after his death and during the struggle for power among his generals.

When Alexander died in 323 BC, his 'Companions', or main commanders, acting in the name of the Macedonian army, sought to seize control of the Empire. First, Perdiccas practically became the regent (323–321 BC), ruling in the names jointly of Alexander's half-brother, on the one hand, and his posthumous son, on the other. Perdiccas controlled the Asian parts of the Empire, and his eastern satraps (including those in India) furnished reinforcements for an expedition he sent to suppress a revolt of the Greek mercenaries in Bactria. After Perdiccas's murder in Egypt in 321 BC, Antipater, who was in command in Macedonia, became the regent. He made fresh arrangements for the Indian territories. We are told by Diodorus (XVIII.39) that, since he could not remove the local princes without a military expedition, he recognized the authority of Porus over the territories along the Indus and of Taxiles over the Hydaspes (Jhelum). Peithon, who had held Sindh under Alexander, was given charge over 'India' below the Paropamisadae (the Hindukush); but, apparently, Eudemus, Alexander's satrap in the Punjab, continued to hold on to power there, since he is said to have subsequently put Porus to death by treachery.

After Antipater's death in 319 BC, the struggle among the factions of Alexander's Diadochi (successors) assumed a more bitter form. Quite significantly, elephants taken from India were recognized as a major asset in these wars. Antipater's successor in Macedonia, Polyperchon, was credited with a notable advantage in possessing as many as 67 elephants – this use of elephants in Europe, let it be noted, preceded by a hundred years that by Hannibal against Rome.

The Macedonian satrapies in India come into known history again when we have descriptions of the war carried into Iran between Antigonus, who entertained ambitions to possess the whole of Alexander's Empire, and Eumenes, Alexander's Greek secretary, determinedly loyal to his master's house. To his aid Eumenes called Sibyrtius, satrap of Arachosia (Kandahar district), who, however, deserted him. But Eudemus, from the Punjab, brought with him 114 elephants and some Indian troops, in time to join in the first (drawn) battle of Gabienne in Iran in 317 BC. In the second battle of Gabienne the next year, Eumenes was defeated, and both he and Eudemus were executed by the victor. Antigonus rewarded Peithon, satrap of Sindh, with the satrapy of Babylon, retained Sibyrtius in Arachosia and changed the satrap of Aria (Herat). Antigonus's control over the satrapies of the Indus and the Indian borderland was shaken by a reverse in 312 BC at the hands of

Ptolemy of Egypt in Gaza (where his son Demetrius, opposing Ptolemy, had forty-three elephants), which enabled Seleucus, one of Alexander's generals, to seize his chance and occupy Babylon. This effectively breached Antigonus's links with the eastern parts of Alexander's Empire. Though Seleucus celebrated his coup by establishing an era with its epoch in 312 or 311 BC, he himself had his hands full in consolidating his position around Babylon and defending himself from Antigonus, still entrenched in Asia Minor and Syria.

It was probably during this period that the Macedonian satraps in the Indian borderland became increasingly isolated and weak. Sibyrtius, satrap of Arachosia, was now cut off from his patron, Antigonus. In the Punjab Sophytes (Saubhūti), king of the Salt Range in Alexander's time (see 1.2 above), issued a silver coin which has his bust with a helmet on the obverse, and a cock with the legend 'Sophytou' (Sophytes) in Greek on the reverse (*Fig. 1.2*). The coin is probably an imitation of a type issued by Seleucus, and so should be of post-312 BC mintage. Sophytes gave himself no royal titles and thus presumably claimed to be no more than an independent Hellenized satrap.

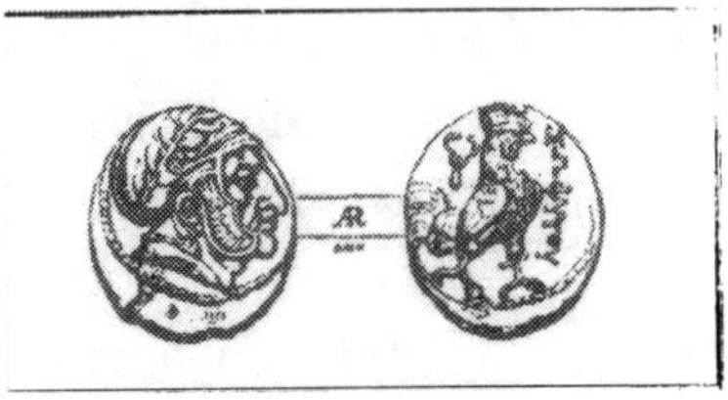

FIG. 1.2 Silver coins of Sophytes. *Obverse*: Bust of Sophytes, with cheek-piece of helmet in imitation of that of Seleucus. *Reverse*: Cock and Greek legend: SOPHYTOU. (After A. Cunningham)

With such decline of Macedonian power, the road was at last open for Chandragupta. It must have been while "Seleucus was laying the foundations of his future greatness" (Justin), that is, after 312 BC, that Chandragupta began his conquest of northwestern India, overthrowing the Macedonian "prefects", and also presumably such local Indian chiefs as Sophytes (see *Extract 1.2*). By then, Chandragupta had had time enough to consolidate his power in the dominions of the fallen Nanda dynasty. Going by Justin's statements, it would seem that the strictly Indian parts (i.e. the Indus basin) were directly occupied by Chandragupta, but it is possible that some of the borderland to the west of the Indus too came under his suzerainty.

Antigonus's increasing entanglements with Egypt and Greece at last gave Seleucus at Babylon the opportunity to subjugate the eastern satrapies. About the year 305 BC, he undertook a great expedition eastward to deal with Stasanor, the independent satrap of Bactria. Having subdued Bactria, he crossed the Hindukush (it is by no means certain that he also crossed the Indus). No battle seems to have occurred between him and Chandragupta, and a treaty was made by which Seleucus recognized Chandragupta's possession of a large part of the Indian borderland and Afghanistan. In a passage in Strabo (XV.2.9), the territories ceded are said to have been those of the Paropamisadae (Hindukush and Kabul region), Arachosia ('Arachotoi') (Kandahar) and Gedrosia ('Gedrosoi') (Baluchistan). All earlier doubts about Mauryan possession of these territories have been dispelled by the finds of Ashoka's Aramaic inscriptions at three sites near Kabul and his Greek and Aramaic inscriptions at Kandahar. 'Aria' (Herat), it may be noted, was not among the transferred territories.

In return for these territorial concessions, Seleucus obtained as many as 500 elephants from Chandragupta as gift. This was of immense importance to him, since he had soon to march westward in order to join battle with Antigonus at Ipsus in Asia Minor. In this battle (301 BC), the fact that Seleucus and his ally Lysimachus had 480 elephants, outnumbering the 75 possessed by Antigonus, proved decisive: Antigonus was defeated and killed, so closing one chapter in the violent history of the Diadochi.

To return to the treaty, a marriage alliance between Chandragupta and Seleucus was also concluded; but who married whom is not stated.

One result of the treaty was the despatch of **Megasthenes** by Seleucus as his envoy to Chandragupta's court. Megasthenes "spent much time in Arachosia with its governor Sibyrtius and tells us that he frequently visited the Indian king Sandracottus" (Arrian, *Anabasis*, V.6). This statement shows that Sibyrtius continued to be the satrap of Arachosia under the new regime; and his border territory, doubtless with its large body of Macedonian and Greek settlers, was a natural base for Megasthenes's journeys to Chandragupta's court, whether at Pāṭaliputra ('Palimbothra') or in camp elsewhere in India.

Megasthenes has done great service to Indian history by leaving behind an account of India, which was probably in four parts. This work, often called *Indica*, has disappeared, but portions from it have survived in quotations and summaries, chiefly in the works of Diodorus

Siculus (late first century BC), Strabo (early years of first century AD), Pliny the Elder (d. AD 79) and Arrian (*c.* AD 150). Of these authors, Pliny wrote in Latin, the others in Greek. Megasthenes endangered his credit with Hellenistic writers by his proneness to describe fantasies on hearsay, such as the stories of tribes of men without mouths, unicorns and other animals of fabulous form and habits, gold-digging ants, etc., merely, perhaps, in an effort to enliven his narrative. But there is much that is obviously creditworthy in his descriptions. He was the first Greek writer to note the presence of endogamy and fixed occupations in Indian social communities that we now call 'castes'; and his pairing of 'Brachmanes' and 'Sarmanes' as two classes of Indian 'philosophers' recalls to us the frequently paired 'Brahmans and *samanas*' [Gāndhārī *shramaṇas*] of Ashokan inscriptions. What, therefore, he says about Indian society, Mauryan administration and other matters of which he was himself a witness, deserves our careful attention (see especially 1.6 and Chapter 3 below).

Among other conquests of Chandragupta, the one certainty is Gujarat and Malwa. The Junagarh rock inscription of Rudradāman in Saurashtra (Gujarat), AD 150, says that the Sudarshana lake in its vicinity was created by "the Vaishya Pu<u>sh</u>yagupta", governor (*rā<u>sh</u>triya*) on behalf of "the Maurya king Chandragupta". The Girnar inscription of Ashoka happens to be on the same boulder. The possession of Gujarat by any power based on Magadha would naturally imply the previous subjugation of Avanti (Malwa).

Whatever uncertainty surrounds some other conquests that he possibly might have made, especially in the Deccan, Chandragupta's success in bringing the whole of northern India and much of Afghanistan under his control still represented an outstanding military achievement. Of the man himself, however, little is known. Megasthenes claims to have visited him and his court, obviously in his late years as king, but if he gave an account of his person, it has not been preserved in the extant fragments of his *Indica*. Strabo quotes him as reporting that, while in camp, Chandragupta used to be accompanied by some 40,000 people; yet, very good order was kept and thefts were rare. He was possibly a harsh ruler: Justin records a report that, while earlier claiming to overthrow the tyranny of his predecessors, he himself imposed, after his success, an equally oppressive form of servitude on the people (*Extract 1.2*). It was not surprising, then, that much vigilance needed to be exercised against possible plots. Strabo tells us, presumably with Megasthenes again as his source, that the king was constantly guarded by women slaves, and he frequently changed his bed-chamber at night to confuse plotters. He left his palace (except while on a military expedition) only on a few occasions: to go to court to dispense justice; to offer sacrifices; to take part in revels, where again he was well-guarded; and to go on hunt, surrounded by women guards.

According to the Jain legends, not only was Chandragupta's famous minister Chāṇakya a learned Jain (*shrāvaka*), but Chandragupta himself, shaken by a twelve-year-long famine, renounced kingship and, travelling south as a Jain ascetic, ultimately committed suicide in the prescribed way at a place in Karnataka. This is a possible, though implausible, story. Sri Lankan tradition and the Purāṇa lists give Chandragupta a reign of twenty-four years, whereafter he was succeeded by his son, Bindusāra. This event should have occurred in *c.* 298 BC.

1.5 Bindusāra and the Early Years of Ashoka (to *c.* 262 BC)

One of the few facts we know about Bindusāra is that he probably assumed the title of Amitraghāta (compare Ashoka's title, Piyadasi), and maintained friendly relations with the great Macedonian powers. Strabo (II.1.9) tells us that 'Amitrochades' was the name of the son and successor of 'Sandracottus' (Chandragupta); and that the Seleucid court sent to him, in succession to Megasthenes, an envoy named Deimachus, who too wrote an account of India that is not extant but is sometimes quoted by subsequent Greek authors. When Seleucus died, in 280 BC, he was succeeded by Antiochus I Soter (280–262 BC), and the latter received an embassy from the same 'Amitrochates' (so spelt), which brought requests for a supply of sweet wine and dried figs, and a sophist. The last request was not met, but the interest shown in Greek thought casts some credit on Bindusāra. Ptolemy Philadelphus of Egypt (285–246 BC), according to Pliny, also sent an ambassador, Dionysius, to India – but whether he was received by Bindusāra or Ashoka is not clear. These exchanges of envoys fit in with Ashoka's own despatch of missions to the principal rulers of the Hellenistic world, *c.* 260 BC (see *Note 1.1*).

It may be assumed from our knowledge of the borders of

Ashoka's Empire, as established from the sites and texts of his inscriptions, that Bindusāra not only retained the territories bequeathed to him by Chandragupta, but possibly also added to them. He might have subdued the "Aṁdhras" (modern Andhra), for they are mentioned in Ashoka's Rock Edict XIII as one of the peoples within the Empire. Assuming that Strabo has derived his information about them from Megasthenes, the 'Andarae' had held thirty well-fortified towns, and possessed 100,000 infantry, 2,000 cavalry and 1,000 elephants, so that they formed a powerful state in Chandragupta's time. Buddhist legends tell us of Bindusāra's control over Taxila and Ujjain. The *Divyāvadāna* says that he sent his son Ashoka to suppress a rebellion in Taxila; and the Sri Lankan *Mahāvaṁsa* (V.39) says that Ashoka was his viceroy at Ujjain when Bindusāra had his last illness.

According to the Purāṇas, Bindusāra ruled for twenty-five years; but the *Mahāvaṁsa* (V.18) puts the length of his reign at twenty-eight years. Adopting the latter (for a choice has to be made! – see *Note 1.1*), Bindusāra's death and Ashoka's accession should be placed in *c.* 270 BC.

The Buddhist legends tell us of much violence after Bindusāra's death. The Sri Lankan chronicles, *Dīpavaṁsa* (*c.* AD 400) and *Mahāvaṁsa* (V.18–20, 39–40), speak of Ashoka putting to sword his 99 brothers, including the eldest, Sumana. Less implausibly, the *Divyāvadāna* says that Ashoka seized Pāṭaliputra before his elder brother, Susīma (here so named), could return from Taxila, where he had been sent to put down a fresh rebellion; and that Susīma was killed when he returned to claim the throne.

Upon his accession, Ashoka used the title *Devānaṁpiya Piyadasi rāja*, which appears in his inscriptions. *Rāja*, of course, simply means king; and *Devānaṁpiya* ('beloved of the gods') appears to be the title of address for Mauryan emperors, since Ashoka's successor Dasharatha also uses it in his cave inscriptions. *Piyadasi* ('of gracious or pleasing appearance') was, then, Ashoka's distinct title as emperor, it being so applied to him also in the *Dīpavaṁsa*. Ashoka's own name (written 'Asoka') was first found only in the Maski inscription of Minor Rock Edict I, but now further inscriptions containing it have been discovered: at Gujarra, containing the same edict, and at Nittur and Udegolam, in copies of Minor Rock Edict II. The Minor Rock Edicts are probably the earliest inscribed edicts of Ashoka; on his subsequent edicts, his personal name never appears.

While the Buddhist legends, amidst their varied details, paint a picture of Ashoka as an especially wicked ruler until his conversion to Buddhism, there is little support for this in Ashoka's own inscriptions. Some of his brothers continued to enjoy an exalted position, since in his Rock Edict V he speaks of officials appointed to his brothers' and sisters' households. In his Pillar Edict V, there is a reference to the release of prisoners he ordered apparently once every year after his accession. The release of prisoners, whether as a regular measure or once only, is also recommended in the *Arthashāstra* (II.36.44; XIII.5.11).

It was with his conquest of Kalinga (Orissa) that the Mauryan Empire reached its maximum extent. Indeed, it is a signal commentary on the unreliability of our traditional sources for Ashoka that this event, which Ashoka considered to be crucial for his turning to *dhaṁma* and Buddhism, is not even mentioned in the Buddhist legends about him. We owe all our information about it to Ashoka's own Rock Edict XIII (*Extract 1.4*).

In this edict, Ashoka speaks as if he attacked the people called 'Kalingas' (in plural), but this was the natural way in which territories are named throughout in his edicts, and was the usual mode in earlier texts as well. If Strabo has drawn this particular piece of information from Megasthenes, the 'Calingae' (or Kalingas) in the time of Chandragupta had an army of 60,000 infantry, 1,000 cavalry and 700 elephants; and, therefore, Ashoka was faced by no mean opponent. Ashoka mentions no provocation that had been received: he implies that a desire for conquering the kingdom was for him, then, a sufficient justification.

The conquest took place in Regnal Year 8 or *c.* 262 BC, and involved much slaughter and enslavement. We are told that 150,000 were carried off as captives; 100,000 were slain; and as many died, apparently off the battlefield. The figures are probably rhetorical; but the reality was sombre enough to cause much remorse to Ashoka. Hereafter, he turned away from a policy of military aggrandizement to a policy of internal pacification. He even advised his successors in future not to consider any project of a 'new conquest'. As for himself, he promised to pardon all who could be pardoned. The new policy was one of striving for the conquest of *dhaṁma*, whose nature and evolution we shall consider in Chapter 2.2.

By this time the Mauryan Empire had reached limits that can be fairly well defined by the geographical references in Ashokan inscriptions and the actual sites of his inscriptions. Rock Edicts II and XIII make it clear that the northwestern frontiers of the Empire bordered on the Seleucid Empire, because Antiochus (I or II) is said to be Ashoka's immediate neighbour. Ashokan inscriptions at Kandahar, and in Laghman (in Afghanistan), and at Shahbazgarhi and Mansehra (in North Western Pakistan) establish that the Mauryan Empire extended deep into Afghanistan, justifying the reference to Yonas and Kambojas placed within the Empire in Rock Edict XIII (and also Rock Edict V). It is not certain that Kashmir was in Mauryan possession, but the inscribed rock at Kalsi (near Dehra Dun, Uttaranchal) and the Rummindei and Nigali Sagar pillar inscriptions in Nepalese Terai show that the Mauryan limits ran in the Gangetic plains along the base of the Himalayan Mountains. An official inscription at Mahasthan in Bangladesh suggests that much of Bengal had been subjugated. In the west, the Girnar rock inscription of Ashoka and the statements in Rudradāman's Junagarh inscription of AD 150 show that Gujarat was under Mauryan control. Within the peninsula, Ashoka's inscriptions have considerable spread; the one at Sopara near Mumbai is evidence that Konkan was included in the Empire. On the eastern coast, the inscriptions at Dhauli and Jaugada in Orissa fully confirm Ashoka's claim that Kalinga had been annexed. There are numerous Ashokan inscriptions on the Karnataka plateau and in southern Andhra. None has so far been discovered in Tamil Nadu and Kerala; and this accords with the fact that Ashoka, in Rock Edicts II and XIII, puts the territories of the Choḍas, Paṁḍiyas, Satiyaputas and Keralaputas, as well as Taṁbapaṁnī (Sri Lanka), outside the borders of his Empire. (See *Map 1.2.*)

We can easily agree with Ashoka that his dominions (*vijita*) were, indeed, "vast" (*mahālaka*) (Rock Edict XIV). We may now see how these vast dominions were administered.

1.6 Administrative Apparatus of the Mauryan Empire

Our major sources of information about the Mauryan administration are, in the order of reliability, (1) Ashoka's inscriptions, (2) the statements attributed to Megasthenes in ancient Greek and Latin works, and (3) the *Arthashāstra*, parts of which go back to the Mauryan or even pre-Mauryan times (see *Note 1.2*).

Because of its extent, we can justifiably use the word 'Empire' for the areas under Mauryan suzerainty. Ashoka himself seems to apply to it, in his Minor Rock Edict I, the name Jaṁbudīpa ('the Rose-apple [*jaṁbu*] Island'), one of the earliest names for India. Elsewhere, in Rock Edict XIII, he employs the terms *vijita* (conquered territories) and *rājavisava* (royal domain). But the association with the original kingdom of Magadha remained: in his Bairat edict he styles himself "the Magadhan King" (*rāja Māgadhe*). The Mauryan imperial seat was at Pāṭaliputra (the capital of Magadha); Megasthenes describes it under the name Palimbothra or Palibothra. In the Girnar copy of Rock Edict V, for the word "here" used by Ashoka is substituted the name "Pāṭaliputa", implying that Ashoka was held to be ruling from that city.

About how the **Mauryan king** conducted himself and his government before Ashoka changed at least some of its conventions after his turn towards *dhaṁma* (for which see 2.2 and 2.3 below), there are just a few hints in Ashoka's edicts. Formerly, he says (Rock Edict VIII), the kings went on pleasure trips, especially for hunting; and we have a description from Megasthenes (see 1.4 above) of how Chandragupta went out hunting surrounded by female guards. The kings did not permit business of state to disturb them when they were eating, or were in the harem, in the bed-chamber, in a public place (lit. cow-pen), in a carriage or on a journey (Rock Edict VI). Megasthenes is, however, quoted by Arrian as saying that Chandragupta used to devote full days for judging cases, and let some of his personal needs be simultaneously attended in public so as to avoid interrupting judicial business.

The emperor's own family occupied a crucial position in the control of the Empire. In Rock Edict V, Ashoka refers to his own households, and those of his brothers and sisters and other kinsmen, "here" (i.e. at Pāṭaliputra, as in Girnar copy) and in "outer" (distant?) towns, for looking after which special officials were appointed (*Extract 2.3*). From among such princes (as was the case with Ashoka himself during

Map 1.2 Mauryan Empire, *c.* 260 BC

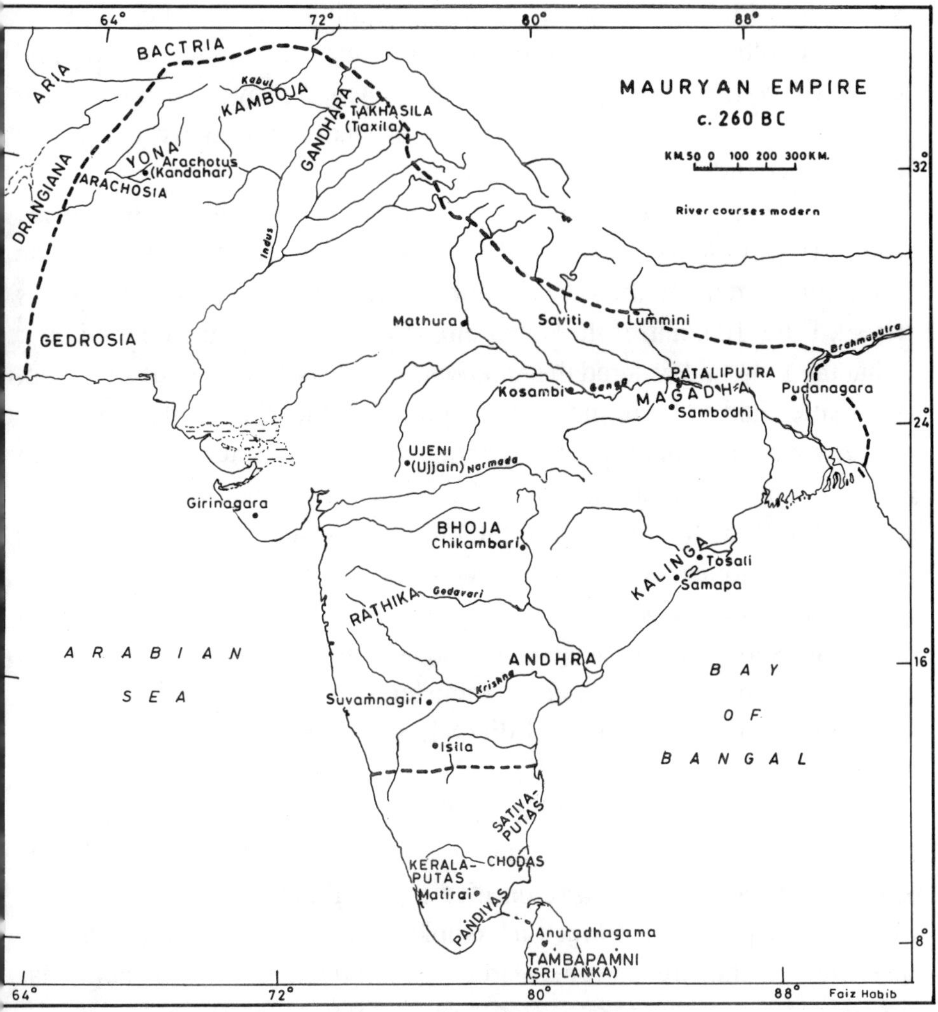

Bindusāra's reign) were appointed viceroys and governors of the provinces. According to Ashoka's Separate Rock Edict I (Dhauli copy), there was a *kumāra* (prince, especially son of the king) as viceroy at Ujeni (Ujjain) and at Takhasila (Taxila); the former, perhaps, is referred to in the Panguraria inscription as *kumāra* Saṁva. Separate Rock Edict II (Dhauli copy) is addressed to the *kumāra* at Tosali, presumably the governor of Kalinga. At Suvaṁṇagiri (near Maski?) an *ayaputa* (*ārya-putra*), 'the lord's son' or 'prince', was stationed as the viceroy (Brahmagiri group of Minor Rock Edict inscriptions). Thus, both at the capital and in the provinces, the imperial family kept a grip on the levers of control: its members also shared out among themselves the benefits that such control brought in terms of the good things of life. The wealth so gained could also be converted into property: Kāruvākī, the second queen (*devi*) of Ashoka, could give away mango-groves, retreats, alms-houses, etc., gifts that she wished to be proclaimed properly as her own ('Queen's Edict': Allahabad pillar).

There are two references in Ashokan inscriptions to a *parisā* (Sanskrit *pari<u>sh</u>ad*) or council. This council had the duty to formulate the king's orders as they were to be passed on to officers called *yutas* (Rock Edict III); and if there was any disagreement in the council over what the king had ordered the *mahāmātas* (Sanskrit *mahāmātras*) to do, the matter had to be immediately reported to the king (Rock Edict VI: *Extract 2.5*). In other words, the *parisā* was a committee entrusted with the carrying out of the king's orders, and so was neither an advisory council nor one that worked in the king's presence. There is, therefore, little correspondence between the Mauryan *parisā* and the *mantri-pari<u>sh</u>ad* of the *Arthashāstra* (I.12.6, 15.47–59, 19.13, etc.), which, in contrast, is to be a gathering of ministers summoned to advise the king. Curiously, the word *mantrī* or minister does not occur in Ashokan inscriptions, even, as in Rock Edict VI, where one would naturally have expected it.

From Ashoka's Pillar Edict I, it would seem that *pulisā* (= *purisā*; Sanskrit *puru<u>sh</u>a*, men?) was the general term for **administrative officials**, who were divided into high, middle and low ranks. The officials most mentioned in Ashoka's inscriptions, and undeniably assigned to the higher ranks, are the *mahāmātas*. It is to them that important matters were entrusted directly by the king (Rock Edict VI), so that they appear there as equivalents of ministers; and some scholars have assumed that they formed the membership of the *parisā* or *pari<u>sh</u>ad*. At Tosali (Kalinga) and Suvaṁṇagiri (Deccan), the *kumāra* or *ayaputa* (prince-governor) and the *mahāmātas* posted with him are addressed together by the king (Separate Rock Edict II: Dhauli; Minor Rock Edict I: Brahmagiri group), as if the *mahāmātas* were attached to each prince-governor as his ministers. At other towns, such as Samāpā in Kalinga and Isila in Karnataka, and Kosambi (Kaushāmbī) in Uttar Pradesh, the *mahāmātas* were in charge on their own and are so addressed (Separate Rock Edicts I and II: Jaugada; Minor Rock Edict I:

Brahmagiri group; and Schism Edict: Allahabad pillar). The Sohgaura bronze-plaque inscription of late Mauryan times shows the *mahāmātas* of Savati (Shrāvastī) making arrangements for storage of grain. *Mahāmāta* was thus seemingly a designation of a very large number of officials, including some of the highest in the Empire. In the *Arthashāstra* (I.10.7, 12.4; II.5.5, etc.), too, officers designated *mahāmātras* similarly appear generally as ministers and high officers.

In Ashoka's inscriptions, some of the *mahāmātas*, however, are also specified by the different tasks assigned to them. One set is designated in Rock Edict XII as *ithidhiyakha-mahāmāta* (Sanskrit: *stryadhyaksha-mahāmātra*), i.e. superintendents of women, seemingly concerned with grants or alms to women and thus not, surely, to be confounded with the *gaṇikādhyaksha*, superintendent of courtesans in the *Arthashāstra* (II.27.1). There were also *aṁta-mahāmātas*, posted on the border, with duties unspecified (Pillar Edict I). In towns, they could have judicial duties, for in the Separate Rock Edict I (Dhauli), the *mahāmātas* posted at Tosali are further designated *nagara-viyohāraka* or town magistrates. The corresponding designation, *pauravyāvahārika*, occurs in the *Arthashāstra*, V.3.7.

In the Sarnath pillar copy of the 'Schism Edict', the damaged portion may well contain a reference to the *mahāmātas* of Pāṭaliputra. For the organization of government of the **capital city**, we have, however, an account attributed to Megasthenes by Strabo (*Extract 1.3*). The city, we are told, was governed by six bodies composed of five officials each, with the following jurisdictions: (1) industrial crafts; (2) foreigners; (3) births and deaths, compiled for official information and taxation; (4) trade, weights and measures; (5) prevention of fraud in sale; and (6) collection of tax on the sale of goods. This description, as that of the army organization (see below), seems far too idealized; yet, it is not impossible that, under the Mauryas, bodies of officials were collectively made responsible for carrying out functions – a custom of which the *parisā* or *parishad* in Ashoka's Rock Edict VI might reasonably be held to offer another example. For the number five, we can refer to the prevalence in late ancient times of the *pañchakula*, the 'five' officials in whose presence all public transactions needed to be done.

On the **Mauryan army**, we not unsurprisingly find little in the Ashokan inscriptions, except for a mention of *koṭavishaya*, districts

FIG. 1.3 (a) Prince on horseback, North Gateway, *Stūpa* 1, Sanchi, first century BC. Note absence of saddle and stirrup. **(b) Horse head-harness, West Gateway, Sanchi** (After F.C. Maisey)

under forts, in the Sarnath Pillar Edict, suggesting that forts were established to keep garrisons for securing control of districts. We turn, then, to our Greek sources. Presumably drawing upon Megasthenes, Pliny and Plutarch put the size of Chandragupta's infantry at 600,000, with Pliny putting the number of cavalry at 30,000 and elephants at 9,000. These numbers may be exaggerated, especially since we are also told by Diodorus that the infantry, horses and elephants were entirely maintained at the king's own expense.

Strabo, citing Megasthenes, furnishes further details of military organization. There is agreement between his account and the *Arthashāstra* (2.30–33) in making the army consist of four divisions: infantry, horses, chariots and elephants. The horses, he says (and so also

FIG. 1.4 Chariot, North Gateway, *Stūpa* 1, Sanchi. (After F.C. Maisey)

Arrian, *Indica*, XVI), did not have bits put in their mouths, a possibly severe disadvantage in riding. Sculptures at Bharhut and Sanchi, of the second and first century BC respectively, do, however, show an elaborate head-harness put on the horse (*Fig. 1.3*). Horses pulled the chariots in the battlefield, while oxen drew them on the march. The chariots contained two warriors besides the charioteer (see *Fig. 1.4*), while each elephant carried three archers and the mahout. These particulars, all from Strabo (XV.1.52), show that despite the poor performance of chariots during their encounters with Alexander's troops, trust in their usefulness continued to be cherished under the Mauryas. Perhaps, they were effective enough against other opponents. Later Tamil traditions contain a recollection of a large invading Mauryan army coming on chariots, for which the way had to be cut through the hills. In the *Arthashāstra* (X.5.36), there is a suggestion of independent action by a group of infantry (armoured men in front, archers behind), but not the remotest reference to the Macedonian–Greek 'phalanx' (for which see 1.2 above). One can imagine, however, that with mercenaries recruited from Greek and Hellenized communities from the northwest, the Mauryan army might also have used such formations in battle. Similar speculation may be offered about the presence of military "engines", like wooden siege towers and battering rams and giant stone-throwing slings, which formed so important a component of Alexander's military machine. To these there is no traceable reference in the *Arthashāstra*, even when mobile instruments of war are listed (II.18.6) or when it offers counsels about how one is to attack a fort (XVIII.4.25–53). But these might still have been introduced in the Mauryan army through the Greek levies, for Megasthenes (through Strabo) speaks of "military engines" transported by bullock-teams. He also mentions an "admiral of the fleet", but we may be certain that only a fleet of river boats is meant, as in the *Arthashāstra*, II.28, and not the kind of naval fleets used in contemporary eastern Mediterranean.

On the organization of the army, Megasthenes (through Strabo) and the *Arthashāstra* are at complete variance. While Megasthenes speaks of four committees of five members each having charge of infantry, cavalry, chariots and elephants, with two other committees cooperating respectively with "the admiral of the fleet" and "the superintendent of the bullock teams", the *Arthashāstra* has only individual superintendents for managing the various departments of the army and makes no reference at all to any committees. We have also no information on the command structure of the Mauryan army. The last Mauryan ruler, Brihadratha, is said in the Purāṇas (*Extract 1.1*) to have been overthrown by his army commander (*senānī*); but it is not certain whether under the earlier Mauryan emperors there was such a separate head of the army at all.

As for fortifications, the capital Pāṭaliputra probably had the most extensive defences. Megasthenes reports (if we combine the citations in Strabo and Arrian) that the city, extending 80 stadia (14.8 kilometres) along the river, with a width of 15 stadia (2.8 kilometres), was protected by a wooden wall with loopholes for archers, and with 570 towers and 64 gates. All around, apparently on the landward side, ran a ditch, given the impossible width of 600 feet and depth of 30 cubits. Archaeology has at least confirmed, in two sections, the existence of a heavy wooden palisade at Pataliputra. At Kaushāmbī (Kosam, Allahabad district, Uttar Pradesh) the Mauryan-period ramparts are built of rammed earth; and at Taxila, a mud fortification wall has been traced, which is ascribed to Mauryan times.

We can again take recourse to Ashokan inscriptions when we turn to the **provinces**. In his Separate Rock Edict I, Ashoka says that he would send *mahāmātas* on tour every five years; the *kumāra* at Ujeni (Ujjain) was to send such officials every three years, and so too from Takhasilā (Taxila). It is obvious from this that a special position belonged to the viceroys at Ujjain and Taxila, who, in their large territories, were to do what the emperor did presumably in his own personally governed domain. The 'forwarding note' on Separate Rock Edict II (Dhauli) refers to the *kumāra* at Tosali, Orissa, who must have been the governor of Kalinga. Similarly, the Brahmagiri group of Minor Rock Edicts (Karnataka), in the initial note, mention the *ayaputa* at Suvaṁṇagiri, who must have been the governor of a portion of the peninsula. Rudradāman's Junagarh inscription of AD 150, which shows signs of being based on some authentic record, speaks of the local governor (*rāshtriya*) of Chandragupta Maurya, who built the Sudarshana lake at Girinagara (Girnar), and then, of a succeeding governor under Ashoka Maurya, who improved the lake. This inscription, by giving us names and ethnic identities of the two governors, shows that, at least in this case, there was no hereditary succession of governors: Chandragupta's governor was a Vaishya, Pushyagupta; Ashoka's, a 'Greek chief' (*yavanarāja*), Tushāspha, whose name (Old Persian, Tushāsp) indicates that he was in fact a Hellenized Iranian.

Ashokan inscriptions also help us by their linguistic peculiarities to determine more precisely the territorial limits of these viceroyalties and governorates. The chance survival of a prefatory note in the Brahmagiri group of Minor Rock Edicts is of great importance in letting us know that the texts of those edicts were transmitted from the king, first, to the *ayaputa* (prince-governor) at his headquarters at Suvaṁṇagiri (probably near Maski), whence they were forwarded to the town of Isila (close to Brahmagiri). One must, then, infer that the texts of the other edicts were also sent similarly from the imperial court to the viceroys and governors, who had them distributed to officials under their jurisdictions for being engraved at various places. We will see (3.4 and *Note 3.1*) that Ashokan inscriptions, carrying the same edicts in Prākrit, have dialectal variations that allow us to assign them to four main dialects: A ('Māgadhī'), B ('Ujjainī'), C ('Western') and D ('Gāndhārī' or 'Northwestern'), with three sub-dialects, A^1 (Kalsi),

A^2 (Kalinga) and B^1 ('Southern'). It has been presumed that, except where inscribed in Dialect A (Māgadhī), the edicts underwent 'translations' or textual modifications to suit the dialectal peculiarities of Prākrit in official use at the different provincial headquarters. Since, in the king's own domain, where orders went from Pāṭaliputra to lower officials, no such 'translation' needed to occur, all sites of inscriptions in Dialect A from Bairat in eastern Rajasthan to Mahasthan in Bangladesh may be presumed to have been directly under the king's administration. Ashoka's reference to himself as 'King of Magadha' in the Bairat edict thus assumes a new meaning, as referring to his large domain personally governed by him from Magadha. One cannot satisfactorily account for Dialect A^1 (Kalsi) in terms of provincial jurisdictions; but the Orissa inscriptions in Dialect A^2 should represent the separate province of Kalinga.

The 'Dialect B' set of inscriptions extend from Gujarra in north Madhya Pradesh to Sopara on the western coast, near Mumbai. If all the texts here went from the *kumāra* at Ujjain, we can understand why that viceroyalty was so large and, therefore, so important. Dialect B^1, found in Karnataka, has traces of accommodation to the influence of Dravidian pronunciation, and we may suppose that all B^1 texts came from Suvaṁṇagiri. But this area is peculiar in that it has Ashokan texts also in Dialects A and B, and the texts of the Brahmagiri group are engraved by a scribe who uses Kharoshṭhī in his signature-line and so must have come from the northwest. Clearly, then, the Suvaṁṇagiri governorate was not just an extension of the Ujjain viceroyalty but had officials from all parts of the Empire serving in it.

Dialect C is solely represented by the Girnar rock inscription and shows that Saurashtra (or even Gujarat) formed a separate province under the Mauryas. As for the viceroyalty of Taxila in Gandhāra, we have Dialect D represented by two Ashokan inscriptions (Mansehra and Shahbazgarhi, in the North Western Frontier Province). Aramaic seems to have been the other official language at Taxila, for translations of Ashokan edicts in Aramaic have been found at Taxila itself, Darunta near Kabul, and Kandahar, at which last place inscribed Greek copies of Ashokan edicts have also been found. The Aramaic inscriptions, in writing Ashoka's title as 'Prydrsh', invoke the Gāndhārī form 'Priyadrasi' and not the Māgadhī 'Piyadasi', while the Greek texts have

'Piodosses', answering to the Māgadhī form. We may suppose that at least the Aramaic copies were sent off from Taxila, capital of Gandhāra, whose viceroy might then have exercised some degree of authority over the trans-Indus regions within the Empire. We can therefore say that, by and large, the scheme of provincial divisions we get from the Ashokan edicts is confirmed by the linguistic peculiarities of the inscriptions.

Quoting Megasthenes, the Greek historian Arrian explicitly, and Diodorus obliquely, refer to **autonomous territories** and cities which had their own "magistrates" and not king's officials governing them. Ashoka, in his Rock Edicts V (*Extract 2.3*) and XIII (*Extract 1.4*), actually mentions particular peoples (and regions) specifically, as if they occupied a position different from the regularly administered areas of his Empire. These are: (1) Yona, (2) Kaṁboja, (3) Gaṁdhāra (Gandhāra), (4) Raṭhika, (5) Pitinika, (6) Bhoja, (7) Nābhaka, (8) Nābhapaṁti, (9) Aṁdhra and (10) Pariṁda. Of these, (1) to (5) are described in Rock Edict V as being on 'the western border', looked at, of course, from Pāṭaliputra. Numbers (5), (7), (8) and (10) cannot be located; for the others, see *Map 1.2*.

Our information on the 'Yona' region may give us an inkling of what kind of relationship may have existed between the territories named by Ashoka and the imperial administration. The discovery of his Greek inscriptions at Kandahar leaves little doubt that by the 'Yona' region he meant Arachosia (see *Map 1.1*). We may recall (see 1.4 above) that Alexander's governor of Arachosia, Sibyrtius, probably continued to serve under Chandragupta. The fact that in neither the Greek nor the Aramaic inscriptions at Kandahar does Sibyrtius's successor let his own name or even office intrude into the texts, suggests that he was probably not allowed to have any pretensions to being a semi-independent satrap. Yet, it has been noted that in the Greek translation of Rock Edict XII at Kandahar, the last two sentences concerned with the functions of officials (*dhaṁma-mahāmātas*, etc.) have been omitted, as if these had no relevance to the local administration in Arachosia. It is possible that in Kaṁboja (Kabul region), too, the administration was similarly largely left to the local Aramaic-using Iranian officials. It is worthy of note that the governor (*skn*), mentioned in the Laghman Aramaic road inscriptions, bears a clearly Iranian name,

Wāshava ('Wḥśw'), 'Charioteer', as does his subordinate, the judge (*dyn*), Wakhshu-frita ('waḥśwprt'), 'favoured by god Vakhshu'. On the other hand, it is hard to explain why Gandhāra, which contained Taxila, the seat of so important a viceroyalty, should be listed among these special territories. It is possible that in its case, Ashoka had in mind only certain local cultural or ethnic peculiarities, such as the presence of Iranian communities, and not the existence of a semi-autonomous satrapy.

The listing of the special regions implies that in other areas the regular **provincial administration** was in operation. We have already seen above how the *mahāmātas* were placed at the governors' headquarters and important towns. In Rock Edict III, three classes of officials are mentioned, who, posted throughout the Empire, were enjoined to go on tours of inspection every five years: *yuta* (*yukta*), *rajūka* (*rajjuka*) and *pādesika* (*prādeshika*). About the *yutas*, we learn that they were to be instructed in the contents of the king's orders by messages formulated by the *parisā* or *pari<u>sh</u>ad*, and were, therefore, presumably sent off from the capital.

Both the *rajūkas* and *pādesikas* seem to have been officers posted in the provinces (for which Pillar Edict VII uses the term *disā*). In Minor Rock Edict II (Erragudi), the *rajūka* is expected to instruct the people of a *janapada* under him in the principles of *dhaṁma*. That it must mean a large territory is shown by Ashoka's statement in Rock Edict XIII that there is no *janapada* where there are no Brahmans and *samanas*, except the territory of the Yonas. In Rock Edict VIII, the phrase "people of the *janapada*" seems to have the sense of people outside the capital, the 'provincials', so to speak. The size of a *janapada* is also indicated by Ashoka's statement in Pillar Edicts IV and VII (*Extracts 2.6* and *2.7*), that his "*rajūkas* are occupied with people (*jana*), with many hundred thousands of men". We may assume, then, that a *janapada* was a province or a large sub-province. From the Pillar Edict IV it is also patent that the *rajūkas* exercised extensive powers to judge and punish those whom they ruled over.

Of the *pādesikas* and *raṭhikas* (the latter mentioned in Minor Rock Edict II [Erragudi]), little more can be said except that their names (from Sanskrit *pradesha* and *rā<u>sh</u>ṭra*) suggest their connection with territorial jurisdictions. It may be added in passing that these designations have no satisfactory counterparts in the *Arthashāstra*.

In the Sarnath version of the Schism Pillar Edict of Ashoka, we are introduced to two territorial sub-divisions, *āhāra* and *vishaya*, both terms used for districts in later inscriptions. The latter appears in the compound *koṭavishaya*, 'districts controlled from forts'. These districts were presumably under a sub-province, which in the present case was Kaushāmbī, whose *mahāmātas* had received orders from officials at Pāṭaliputra, capital of the king's own province of Magadha.

An important instrument for keeping the various parts of the Empire bound to the imperial capital was a serviceable network of **communications**. Megasthenes (through Strabo) says that there were officers who made roads, setting up pillars at every ten stadia. Ashokan pillars are too magnificent to have been merely set up to mark the highways, though they may well mark important points on them. Similarly, while rock inscriptions were most likely to have been engraved near roads, they too cannot be considered as road distance-markers. But that Megasthenes was not wrong has been shown by two Aramaic inscriptions from Laghman (Afghanistan), both of which give distances in 'bows' from particular spots on the '*krpty*' (*kārapathi*), Old Persian for 'army highways'. In his Rock Edict II, and again in Pillar Edict VII, Ashoka shows his concern for easier travel on the roads (*maga*, *paṁtha*) by having wells dug and shady trees planted along them (see *Extract 2.2*). The importance of roads is also underlined by the *Arthashāstra*: it lays down the widths of different kinds of roads (II.4. 3–5) and prescribes fines for encroachments on land assigned to roads (III.10.5–7). An intelligence network could be laid out along the roads. In his Rock Edict VI Ashoka calls on his "reporters" (*paṭivedaka*) to report to him all the time about the people's affairs, and in Rock Edict III and Separate Rock Edict I, requires his officials to make tours of inspection every five or three years. Megasthenes thought that the establishment of inspectors and spies was so large that it formed the sixth of the seven classes into which Indian society was divided (accounts in Diodorus, Strabo, and Arrian) (*Extract 3.1*). In the *Arthashāstra* (I.11–14), too, the department of spies occupies a very central position, the spies functioning not only as news-gatherers, but also as conspirators and agents provocateur.

With regard to the **fiscal system**, Megasthenes's basic statement is that the land belonged to the king and no private person could own land. Diodorus (II.40) quotes him as saying that peasants had to pay to the king a 'land tribute' or rent and, besides it, a fourth part of the produce. Strabo (XV.1.40), on the other hand, seems to have understood Megasthenes differently. He says that the peasants tilled the soil on "receiving as wages one-fourth of the produce". (As Romila Thapar points out, the sense of the same word *misthos* changes from rent to wages.) Now, in the *Arthashāstra*, as we shall see in Chapter 3.1, there is a distinction between the lands belonging to the king and other land. In the former, the text recommends (II.24.16) that the peasants (presumably equipped with their own cattle and implements) should part with half of the produce (*ardhasītikāh*). But those who provided personal labour only (*svavīryopajīvin*), or share-croppers, were just to take away only a fourth or fifth of the crop, and so surrender three-fourths or four-fifths to the king. There seems to be no separate charge in lieu of rent. There are references in the *Arthashāstra* (I.13.6 and II.15.3) to one-sixth (*shaḍbhāga*) as the king's share in the produce, but in contexts suggesting merely its conventional or ancient nature. Elsewhere (V.2.2), the *Arthashāstra* states it as a normal measure that the king should demand a third or a fourth part of the produce from a region (*janapada*), thereby leading one to infer that these were the standard rates for tax collected outside the king's lands. One can see now that between Strabo's interpretation of Megasthenes's statement and the *Arthashāstra's* prescription of exacting three-fourths or more from share-croppers on crown land, there is much correspondence; yet, Diodorus's version too corresponds to what the *Arthashāstra* says of the tax the king took from outside the crown land. Of Diodorus there is a possible confirmation also in Ashoka's Rummindei pillar inscription. There, at the Buddha's birth-place, Ashoka made the village "free of *bali*" (*ubalike*), and reduced what is presumably to be deemed a separate produce-tax to *aṭha-bhāgiya*, a "one-eighth part" (of the produce) (see *Extract 3.3*). The former (*bali*) could have been a kind of 'rent-tax'; and the latter, at the privileged rate of one-eighth, would result from a reduction by half of the standard tax rate of one-fourth of the produce, set by both Diodorus and the *Arthashāstra*.

The *Arthashāstra*, II.24.18, provides for a "water[-based] share" (*udakabhāga*) of produce as tax, ranging from one-fifth to one-third of the crop, if the land was irrigated by various means by the peasant himself (for which see Chapter 3.1). These need not be taken as rates specifically confined to the king's personal estate where, given that half the produce was already taken from peasant-tenants, a share further taken at any of these rates would be an impossible addition. If this is a maxim which was to be applied to ordinary land tax, it may be taken to represent one way of fixing the different rates of it, a more general statement being made in the *Arthashāstra*, V.2.2, already cited.

As a passage in Strabo (XV.1.50) derived from Megasthenes, and Rudradāman's Junagarh inscription of AD 150 show (see Chapter 3.1 below), the Mauryan administration also undertook the construction of some irrigation works on its own. A recommendation to this effect also occurs in the *Arthashāstra* (II.1.20–22). We have, however, no means of knowing how extensive such work was; and whether the administration recovered its expenditure by means of any extra tax.

The taxes being set at particular shares of the produce imply that these were primarily collected **in kind**. The produce, then, often needed to be stored in state granaries. Two inscriptions, assigned on palaeographic grounds (see *Note 2.1*) to the late years of Ashoka or immediately afterwards, namely, the Mahasthan stone-plaque inscription from Bangladesh (fragmentary) and the Sohgaura bronze-plaque inscription from northeastern Uttar Pradesh (text well-preserved, but not yet fully understood), contain official instructions with regard to granaries (*koṭhāgāla/koṭhagala*), some of which could be three-

FIG. 1.5 Granaries shown on Sohgaura copper plate, with text.
(After D.D. Kosambi)

storeyed (see *Fig. 1.5*). Paddy and other grain were apparently stored here to guard against future scarcities.

Taxes were also collected from all other possible sources. Megasthenes (Strabo's version) tells us that the artisans paid taxes as well as rendered labour services; in the capital city taxes were levied on occasions of births and deaths, and there was a tax amounting to one-tenth of the value of all goods sold. Limitations of space prevent us from going into the details given in the *Arthashāstra* (II. 21 and 22) on customs and similar duties. Presumably, the taxes on crafts, trade and persons varied a great deal in different areas of the Empire.

Taxes must have been collected at least in part **in money**; and the numismatic evidence now shows that at least from the sixth century BC, 'punch-marked' silver coins (with no written legends) were in use in India; the crucial find of a hoard datable to *c.* 320 BC at the Bhir Mound, Taxila, has enabled numismatists to distinguish the Mauryan from the pre-Mauryan issues. A statement in the *Arthashāstra* (II.12.24) shows that the punch-marks (*lakshaṇa*) were struck at the state mint; and this is of importance in showing that these coins were issued by the state. The *Arthashāstra*'s further statement that these had a quarter-alloy of copper is corroborated by the debasement of Mauryan-period punch-marked silver coinage – a point to be considered in Chapter 3.1. Numismatists note that in the Mauryan phase (after *c.* 320 BC), the coin types become fewer – an indication of the centralization of coinage – while the coins themselves become more numerous.

Clearly, to operate this vast apparatus of Empire, there needed to be a large **bureaucracy**. Up till now, no firm evidence has turned up of any writing in India between the Indus Civilization and Ashoka's time; and Megasthenes's firm statement that the Indians did not use writing deserves more respect than it has received (see Chapter 3.4 below). For us, it is naturally difficult to understand how the Empire functioned without written accounts and record-keeping. That this was not impossible, however, is shown by the way the Empires of the Aztecs of Mexico and of the Incas of Peru could work without the use of writing, as late as the fifteenth century. The Mauryas probably required an army of memorizers, committing oral 'records' to memory as the priests did with religious texts. If so, the introduction of writing in Ashoka's early years, or a little earlier, must have meant a revolution in the way the Empire was organized. It might also have been accompanied by an influx into the Mauryan bureaucracy of elements who came from northwestern areas, where writing had been in use for a long time in Aramaic (and derived from it, Kharoshṭhi) as well as Greek (see 1.1 above). We have only eight authentic (that is, epigraphically attested) personal names from Ashoka's time: his own, of his second queen, and of the son by her, of a prince (*kumāra*) Saṁva, and of four officials. Two of the latter were posted in Laghman in Afghanistan, both of whom, including the local governor, bore Iranian names (see above). This is not surprising. But what is remarkable is that the other two named officials, serving within India, also came from the northwest: Tushāsp, the Hellenized Iranian governor of Gujarat; and Chapaḍa, the scribe signing partly in Kharoshṭhī, though posted in Karnataka. Unless chance alone has shaped our evidence here, the infusion of the northwestern elements into the Mauryan bureaucracy must be deemed to have been very considerable. There could be important cultural and political consequences of this influx, which one must henceforth always keep in mind.

TABLE 1.1 Chronology

	BC
Installation of the Nanda dynasty in Magadha	*c.* 344
Alexander's conquest of northwestern India	327–25
Death of Alexander	323
Overthrow of the Nandas; accession of Chandragupta Maurya	*c.* 322
Chandragupta's annexation of northwestern India	*c.* 311–05
Treaty with Seleucus; Megasthenes sent as envoy	*c.* 305
Death of Chandragupta; accession of Bindusāra	*c.* 298
Death of Bindusāra; accession of Ashoka	*c.* 270
Conquest of Kalinga	*c.* 262

EXTRACTS

Extract 1.1
The Nandas and Mauryas: Passages from the Purāṇas

Nandas

As son of Mahānandin [the last Shishunāga ruler] by a Shūdra woman will be born a king Mahāpadma, who will terminate all Kshatriyas. Thereafter kings will be of Shūdra origin. Mahāpadma will be sole monarch, bringing all under his sole sway. He will be 88 [28 in some copies] years on this earth. He will uproot all Kshatriyas, being urged on by prospective fortune. He will have eight sons, of whom Sukalpa [or Sahalya] will be the first; and they will be kings in succession to Mahāpadma for twelve years.

A Brahman Kauṭilya will uproot them all; and, after they have enjoyed the earth 100 years (*varshashataṁ*), it [the earth] will pass to the Mauryas.

Mauryas

Kauṭilya will anoint Chandragupta as king in the realm. Chandragupta will be king twenty-four years. Vindusāra will be king twenty-five years. Ashoka will be king thirty-six years. His son Kunāla will reign eight years. Kunāla's son Bandhupālita will enjoy the kingdom eight years.

Version A
Matsya and *Vāyu* (var.)

Their (?) grandson Dashona will reign seven years. His [var.: Ashoka's] son Dasharatha will be king eight years. His son Samprati will reign nine years. Shālishūka will be king thirteen years. Devadharman will be king seven years. His son Shatadhanva [var. Shataṁdhanus] will be king eight years. Brihadratha will reign 70 [?7] years.

Version B
Vāyu and *Brahmāṇḍa*

Bandhupālita's heir Indrapālita will reign ten years. Devavarman will be king seven years. His son Shatadhanus will be king eight years. Brihadratha will be king seven years.

These are the ten [or, in Version B, nine] Mauryas who will enjoy the earth full 137 years. After them it [the earth] will go to the Shuṅgas.

Shuṅgas

Pushyamitra, the commander of the army (*senānī*) will uproot Brihadratha and will rule the kingdom as king 36 [or 60] years …

(Translation by F.E. Pargiter, slightly modified)

Extract 1.2

The Rise of Chandragupta: Justin

[Seleucus Nicator] waged many wars after the division of Alexander's Empire among his Companions. He first took Babylon, and, then, with his strength increased by this success, he subjugated the Bactrians. He then passed over into India, which, after Alexander's death, as if it had shaken off the yoke of servitude from its neck, had put his prefects to death. Sandracottus was the leader who secured them their freedom; but after the victory, the title to [being the author of their] freedom changed into that of [the author of their] servitude, since, having seized the throne, he oppressed with servitude the very people whom he had freed from foreign thraldom. He was a man of mean origin, but was prompted to aspire to royalty by a divine omen. For when by his insolence he had offended Nandrus, and was ordered by that king to be put to death, he sought safety by a speedy flight. As he lay down overcome with fatigue and fell asleep, a lion of enormous size approached the slumberer and having licked with his tongue the freely oozing sweat, and gently waking him, quietly departed. It was this prodigy which first inspired him with the hope of winning the throne and so gathering [a band of] robbers, he instigated the Indians to establish a new sovereign [i.e. himself]. When thereafter he was preparing to wage war against Alexander's prefects, a wild elephant of monstrous size approached him on its own, and, as if tamed, took him on its back and fought in front of the army and was conspicuous in the battlefield. Having thus won the throne, Sandracottus was in possession of India while Seleucus was laying the foundations of his future greatness. Seleucus having made a treaty with him and (otherwise) settling his affairs in the east, returned to prosecute the war with Antigonus.

(After translations by J.W. McCrindle and Thomas R. Trautmann)

Extract 1.3
Megasthenes's Account of Municipal Government [at Pāṭaliputra] (From Strabo, XV.1.51)

Those who have charge of the city are divided into six bodies of five each. The first have the inspection of everything relating to the industrial arts; the second entertain strangers, assign them lodgings, observe their mode of life by means of the attendants whom they attach to them, and escort them out of the country, or, if they die, send home their property, take care of them in sickness, and when they die, bury them. The third body consists of those who enquire at what time and in what manner births and deaths occur, not only for the purpose of imposing a tax, but also of preventing births and deaths, among the high or the low, from being concealed. The fourth body is concerned with retail and barter. Its members have charge of weights and measures, and see that products in season are sold by public notice. No one is allowed to deal in a variety of articles unless he pays a double tax. The fifth body supervises manufactured articles and sells them by public notice. What is new is sold separately from what is old, and there is a fine imposed for mixing them together. The sixth and last body consists of those who collect the tenth of the price of the articles sold. Fraud in the payment of this tax is punished with death. Such are the functions which these bodies separately discharge. In their collective capacity they have charge both of their special departments and of matters affecting the public welfare, such as the repair of public works, the regulation of prices, and the care of markets, harbours and temples.

(Translation by J.W. McCrindle)

Extract 1.4
Ashoka's Rock Edict XIII

Anointed eight years, King Devānaṁpiya Piyadasi conquered the Kalingas. One and a half times of a hundred thousand living persons were carried away [captive], a hundred thousand were slain [in battle] and almost as many died. After the Kalingas were subjugated, there arose in the Devānaṁpiya a striving after *dhaṁma*, a desire for *dhaṁma*, instructing in *dhaṁma*. There is now in the Devānaṁpiya remorse for having conquered the Kalingas. For the unconquered to be conquered means the killing, the death, and being carried away [captive], of people. This is considered very painful and very grave [a matter] by the Devānaṁpiya. Even more grave than this to the Devānaṁpiya is this: That those who live there, the Brahmans and *samanas* (*shramaṇas*), and other sects (*pāsaṁḍas*) and householders, among whom there is [found] obedience to those placed above, and obedience to mother and father; who are well disposed, among whom there is obedience to elders, kindness and firm attachment to friends, acquaintances, companions and kinsmen, and to slaves and servants, – such suffer injury and killing and separation from beloved ones. Or, if those who, [themselves] well provided for (*suvihitinaṁ*), have constant (lit. undiminished) affection for friends, acquaintances, companions and kinsmen, who are struck by misfortune, then they too suffer injury. This is a misfortune for all men; and to the Devānaṁpiya this is a grave matter.

There is no territory (*janapada*) except of the Yonas (Greeks), where there are no groups of Brahmans and *samanas*, and there is no place in any territory (*janapada*), where men are not attached to one or other sect, if not the [afore-]named sects. Therefore, when the Kalingas were subjugated, if only a hundredth or thousandth part of all those persons had been slain or had died or had been carried away [captive], it would still be considered a grave matter by the Devānaṁpiya.

Today, anyone who commits a harmful act, the Devānaṁpiya wishes to pardon, if he can be pardoned. Even [the people of] the forest (*aṭavi*) within the Devānaṁpiya's domain (*vijita*), he wishes to conciliate and induce to meditate. For they should be told of the remorse and [also] the might of the Devānaṁpiya, so that they may feel ashamed and not be slain. The Devānaṁpiya desires for all creatures non-injury, self-control, detachment and happiness. [Securing] this is considered the chief conquest by the Devānaṁpiya – the *Dhaṁma*-conquest.

This has been won, again, by the Devānaṁpiya here [in his dominions] and among all the [royal] neighbours as far as six hundred *yojanas* (leagues) where there is the Yona (Greek) king named Antiochus, and beyond this Antiochus, four kings, named Ptolemy, Antigonus, Magas and Alexander, and similarly, towards the other (lit. lower) direction, [where are] the Choḍas and Paṁḍiyas as far as Taṁbapaṁnī.

Similarly, here in the kings' dominions, among the Yona–Kaṁbojas, Nābhaka–Nābhapaṁtis, Bhoja–Pitinikas and Aṁdhra–Pariṁdas, everywhere they follow the Devānaṁpiya's instruction in *dhaṁma*. Even where the Devānaṁpiya's envoys (*dūta*) do not go, they, having heard of the Devānaṁpiya's decreed orders on *dhaṁma* and instruction in *dhaṁma*, conform to and are set to conform to the *dhaṁma*. What is thus won is a supreme conquest. Such supreme conquest brings joy – the joy obtained upon the *dhaṁma*-conquest. But this joy [by itself] is a small matter. The Devānaṁpiya thinks only what comes in the world beyond to be the great fruit.

For this purpose has this *Dhaṁma* Edict been written so that my sons and grandsons may not think of making a new conquest. Should a new conquest please them, let them be satisfied with [effecting it with?] mildness and light punishments. Rather, when they think of conquest, let it be the *dhaṁma*-conquest, which is for this world as well as the world beyond. All their joy should be in the pleasure of exertion – such as for this world as well as the world beyond.

[Fresh rendering, using translations of E. Hultzsch, B.M. Barua, R. Basak and D.C. Sircar (the last, of the Erragudi version), and taking into account comments by L. Alsdorf and K.R. Norman, Checked with texts of inscriptions containing R.E. XIII throughout. Prākritized names of Greek kings in the original restored to standard English forms (as in *Note 1.1*).]

Note 1.1
Mauryan Chronology

We all know how important a date is for us. In ordinary matters of life the day of the week will often serve us – "I will see you next Tuesday", we say. But where the distance of time is more than a week, we find it more convenient to mention the date, which is really a numbered day of the month. "I will return your book by the 15th", where "15th" means the fifteenth day of the current month. Months are called usually by their names, though in abbreviated references we use numbers for them also. For longer periods, however, the year is the most important; unlike the month, it has no name but is invariably numbered. If the current year is 2004, the next will be 2005. We consider this very normal, but there was a time when this was not the case. Each past year would be known by a well-known event that occurred in it and so in every locality the same year might be differently recalled. And as time passed, the order of sequence of such named years would be forgotten. It was only quite late that the practice of numbering the years began. In India, the earliest textual evidence for the use of numbered years comes from the Ashokan inscriptions of the third century BC.

A numbered year implies the use of an era, from whose epoch, or beginning, the numbers are counted: the first year may be numbered 1, the next year 2, and so on.

The epochs in early eras were usually set by the ruler's actual or ceremonial accession to the throne; this is the case with the numbered years in Ashoka's inscriptions. The custom was initiated by the Macedonian ruler of West Asia, Seleucus. He established the Seleucid era setting its epoch at his accession upon his occupation of Babylon in 312–311 BC.

In such ancient eras a variation of one year may occur depending on whether the number is that of the current year or the expired year. In the Christian era it is always the current year; that is, the year 2004 began when 2003 years had elapsed after the epoch (the birth of Christ). If the numbering was based on expired years, the first year would not be numbered one but zero, and the year 2004 would be written as 2003. The way Ashokan inscriptions refer to the number of the years – such-and-such event happened when Ashoka had been "anointed (king) (*abhisitena*) eight years" – suggests that the years are not current but expired years, in the way we count our age: "I am 73" means 73 years have elapsed since my birth. The phrase in one of Ashoka's two Greek inscriptions at Kandahar, viz. "ten years having elapsed", has reinforced this conclusion. On the other hand, in Pillar Edict V Ashoka says that "anointed twenty-six years" he had ordered the general release of prisoners twenty-five times. In case the release had been ordered on a particular date every year (which is probable but not certain), the year 26 must be the current year, that is, the year after twenty-five years since Ashoka's accession had elapsed. After weighing the evidence we have treated Ashoka's regnal years as "expired" years; but a margin of error of one year minus must be allowed all the time, owing to the uncertainty of the matter. That is, our equivalents in years before Christ would be those in which Ashoka's regnal years began, if they are expired years; but in case the regnal years are current years, the BC years we have given would be years in which the regnal years closed.

For establishing Christian-era equivalents in order to place Mauryan India in a universal time-frame, the key passage for us is contained in Ashoka's Rock Edict XIII (*Extract 1.4*), where he says that he sent envoys to "where (there is) the Yona [Greek] king named Aṁtiyoka (var. Aṁtiyoga) and, beyond this Aṁtiyoka, four kings named Tulamaya (var. Turamaya), Aṁtekina, Magā (var. Makā) and Alikasudara (var. Alikyasudara)". This action of despatch of missions to "the Yona king named Aṁtiyoka and the other kings who are the neighbours of this Aṁtiyoka" is implied in Rock Edict II, and that Rock Edict is immediately followed by Rock Edict III, which says specifically that it was issued when Ashoka was "anointed twelve years". In other words, the envoys to the five Yona or "Greek" (Macedonian) kings were sent not later than Ashoka's Regnal Year 12.

If we now determine the time when all the five named rulers were on the throne, we can establish the range within which Ashoka's Regnal Year 12 fell and, from this, also establish the range for the year of Ashoka's accession. The five names have been easily restored, respectively, to Antiochus, Ptolemy, Antigonus, Magas and Alexander. Antiochus was the name not only of Seleucus's son, who ruled from 280 to 261 BC, but also of his successor, Antiochus II, who reigned 261–247 BC. Ptolemy was part of the names of all the Macedonian kings of Egypt throughout the third century BC and later. Antigonus II ruled Macedonia from 283 to 239 BC. Magas of Cyrenaica (part of Libya bordering Egypt) reigned from *c.* 274 and probably died in or just before 258 BC. There are two possible Alexanders, namely, Alexander of Epirus, who reigned 272–*c.* 255 BC, and Alexander of Corinth, who reigned 253–247 BC. We can see that if the dates for Magas given above are right, these would exclude Alexander of Corinth; and the period when all the rulers were reigning together is thus narrowed to the years 272 to 258 BC. Allowing a year for the news of a king's accession or death to be received at Ashoka's court from such a distance, Ashoka's accession must then have taken place in or before 269 BC. The range is further reduced by our knowledge that Ashoka's grandfather Chandragupta could only have overthrown the last Nanda ruler after 326 BC, for in that year Alexander, having encamped on the Beas, was fed on reports about the power of the Nanda king then on the throne. Treating 325 BC as the earliest possible date for Chandragupta's accession, and given the lengths of the reigns of Chandragupta (twenty-four years in both the Sri Lankan texts *Dīpavaṁsa* and *Mahāvaṁsa*, and the Purāṇas) and Bindusāra (twenty-eight years in the *Mahāvaṁsa*, though only twenty-five in the Purāṇas), we can set the earlier limit of Ashoka's accession at either 277 BC (following the Purāṇas) or 274 BC (following the Sri Lankan Buddhist tradition). Conversely, Chandragupta's accession must be placed in or before 318 BC (269 + 49, by the Purāṇas' reign periods) or 321 BC (= 269 + 52 years, according to the *Mahāvaṁsa*). The date we have adopted for Chandragupta's accession, 322 BC, thus falls within both the wider (325–318 BC) and the narrower (325–321 BC) ranges, but a margin of error of two or even three years must always be conceded. Having adopted the year 322 BC for Chandragupta's accession and following the *Mahāvaṁsa*'s reign periods, Ashoka's accession should be placed at about 270 BC, but any year within as wide a range as 277–269 BC is possible.

Some historians would allow for an interregnum of four years on the basis of statements in the early Sri Lankan Pāli chronicle, the *Dīpavaṁsa* (and the later *Mahāvaṁsa*), that Ashoka had his coronation four years after he succeeded to the throne upon Bindusāra's death, and that, three years later, having converted to Buddhism, he celebrated yet another coronation. But according to Rock Edict XIII (*Extract 1.4*), Ashoka turned to the *Dhaṁma* and Buddhism only after the Kalinga War fought in Year 8 since his accession. The *abhiseka* (coronation), from which Ashoka counted his years, thus preceded his conversion by over eight years, and cannot therefore be identified with either of the coronations alleged in the Sri Lankan tradition. All allowances for any period of interregnum must therefore be disregarded.

The dull, complex details above treated provide the necessary pillars on which Mauryan chronology rests. In its turn, Mauryan chronology has supplied us with the foundations on which practically the entire edifice of early ancient Indian chronology has been raised. It is hard, therefore, to underestimate the extent of service Ashoka's Rock Edict XIII has performed for us in this crucial matter.

Note 1.2
Kauṭilya's *Arthashāstra*

About a hundred years ago, R. Shamasastry announced the discovery of this very important Sanskrit text found in a manuscript in the Mysore Government Oriental Library. *Arthashāstra* is the title given to the book in the treatise itself. *Artha* means, among other things, success in the world in terms of power and wealth. It is traditionally distinguished from three other objectives, namely, the fulfilment of sensual desire, or *kāma*; the operation of the prescribed moral law and ritual, or *dharma*;

and the aspiration to religious or spiritual fulfilment, or *moksha*. *Shāstra* means a rule, treatise, or branch of knowledge. Kauṭilya's *Arthashāstra* is a treatise restricted to a special aspect of *artha*, viz. the holding and enhancing of royal power, which is also the royal road to wealth. It contains counsels addressed to a king of a small or medium-sized kingdom about how to maintain his power, suppress plots against himself, succeed in his own plots, overcome rival kings by means of diplomacy, conspiracy and war, conduct administration, tax his subjects, and maintain social order (with profit to himself) through imposing punishments (mainly fines, but including imprisonment and capital punishment) for offences against the law. It deals with the science of polity in the broadest sense, but mainly with a view to securing whatever should be of advantage to the ruler, not the ruled. Few moral constraints bind the counsels: murder of innocent persons, including even one's own agent, the use of sexual allurements, the despoiling of the wealth of temples, are all coolly recommended, if they can serve the cause of the king's ambitions or interests.

The *Arthashāstra* is a prose-work in the *sūtra* form, that is, each sentence usually contains a separate counsel or statement, and explanations or reasons are given so concisely as to be often just simple dictums. There are, however, considerable elements of description too, as in the accounts of functions to be assigned to officials of various designations. Book III contains a code of laws for which, of course, the *sūtra* form is very suitable.

In the work itself the authorship is ascribed in four passages to Kauṭilya, who is once (near the end) explicitly identified with the one who overthrew the Nandas. In a possible later addition, the author is called Vishṇugupta; but the well-known name Chāṇakya never occurs. At many places, the opinion of Kauṭilya is cited, sometimes alone, but mostly in succession to the opinions of others: Kauṭilya's opinion is always taken to be final and definitive. All this, taken with the very logical arrangement of the work (including a detailed and accurate list of contents at the beginning), suggests a single author; and if the ascriptions within the text are correct, Kauṭilya must have been that author, though whether he wrote it before the accession of Chandragupta (*c.* 322 BC) or after would still not be clear.

Though several historians have adopted this view of its authorship and date, including V.A. Smith and D.D. Kosambi, there are many difficulties involved in accepting it. The *Manusmriti* (first century BC) is ascribed to Manu in the text, and Manu's opinion is also quoted within it on various matters, but it will be futile to argue that this famous Dharmashāstra text, as we have it, was actually composed by the primeval sage Manu. Rather, the name of Manu was used to lend authority to the text. We may then legitimately wonder whether for a text dealing with the science of worldly or political power, a figure like Kauṭilya, known in legend for political intrigue, could not similarly be invoked to give the *Arthashāstra* the necessary authority and credibility and to ensure its survival.

There is also evidence that the *Arthashāstra* has been compiled from certain earlier texts. Indeed, in its very first sentence it is acknowledged that it has been created by collecting treatises on the *artha*-science composed by ancient teachers. T.R. Trautmann's quantitative analysis of style-markers has suggested that each of the longest Books in the *Arthashāstra*, viz. Books II, III and VII, were originally separate texts composed by different authors, at presumably different dates. How much the final compiler interfered with the earlier versions, while incorporating them in the *Arthashāstra*, cannot be known, since the earlier texts are not extant.

Finally, there is much in the *Arthashāstra* that suggests different dates for the various parts within it, from practically the fourth century BC to the second century AD.

We may begin by considering the important fact that the main political unit in the *Arthashāstra* is a kingdom of very moderate size. The largest territorial division it notes (II.1.4) is that of 800 villages under a *sthānīya*, with sub-divisions at three levels of 400, 200 and 10 villages. Though there is a mention (IX.1.17–20), in the context of military expeditions, of the *chakravartikshetra*, 'sovereign's region', from the Himavat (Himalayas) to the sea, this is seen more as the area within which kingly wars take place and conquests are made, rather than what already constitutes an empire. There is no concern anywhere with the need to govern large territories through viceroys and governors, as would be requisite in an all-India empire like that of the Mauryas, or even in the extensive kingdom of the Nandas. It is, therefore, a plausible argument that the roots of the *Arthashāstra* tradition go back to a time before even that of the Nandas. When the *Arthashāstra* (XI.1.4–5) lists names of *saṁghas* or clans, this list, but for the inclusion of the Surāshṭras, reminds us of the non-monarchical states among the sixteen *Mahājanapadas* of Gautama Buddha's time. Other indicators of an early age include a mention in the *Arthashāstra* (II.12.24) of coarse silver (25 per cent copper) and copper coinage with *lakshaṇa* or mark, which can only refer to the punch-marked coins that were minted in northern India from about the sixth century BC, though a large copper component was introduced into the silver coins in only its last phase (third and second century BC). A hostile reference (III.20.16) to "Shākyas, Ājīvakas [so spelt] and other heretical monks" is also significant, since the Ājīvikas mentioned in Mauryan inscriptions (see below, Chapter 3.3) disappear from the epigraphic record immediately thereafter. The reference would then suggest, at least for this passage of the *Arthashāstra*, a date before the end of the Mauryan Empire. It is also clear that the *Manusmriti* (second century AD), in its portion on rules dealing with royal power and secular law (chapters VII, VIII and part of IX), manifestly draws on the more detailed treatment of certain matters in the *Arthashāstra*, thus suggesting for the latter a date in the second century AD or earlier. The permissive attitude that the *Arthashāstra* displays towards divorce and woman's remarriage is also good evidence that it contains a code of social law that probably belongs to a much earlier milieu than that of the *Manusmriti*.

But, at the same time, there is no doubt that the *Arthashāstra* has material that cannot possibly belong to the period of the Nandas or the reign of Chandragupta Maurya or even of Ashoka. There is no evidence of any use of writing in the Gangetic basin or the peninsula before *c.* 260 BC, when we have the first inscriptions of Ashoka. Yet, in Book II.10, the *Arthashāstra* not only describes the writing of royal edicts, but also puts the number of letters of the alphabet at 63. It uses for the royal edict the word *shāsana* rather than *lipi*, common in Ashokan inscriptions, though the word *sāsana* for order does occur in the Sarnath copy of Ashoka's Schism Edict. The *Arthashāstra* goes on to prescribe such precise formalities for texts of royal edicts as are totally absent in the Ashokan edicts. The *Arthashāstra* assumes that the royal edicts would be composed in Sanskrit, as its detailed instructions (especially II.10.18–22) show. Yet, beginning with Ashokan inscriptions, practically all royal inscriptions on stone are found to be in Prākrit, with one stray exception (Dhanadeva's Ayodhya inscription, early first century AD), until we come to Rudradāman's Junagarh inscription, which is in classical Sanskrit, and is dated AD 150. A general shift to Sanskrit in northern India and the Deccan does not actually occur until the fourth century AD.

Later dates for some portions of the *Arthashāstra* are also inferable from certain geographical references. Words like 'Chinese silk' (*chīnapaṭṭa*), obtained from 'China-land' (*chīnabhūmi*) (II.11.114), could have been in use only after the first Chinese empire under the Chin (Qin) dynasty (221–207 BC) made foreigners apply the dynasty's name to the country. From Alakanda (Alexandria), coral is said to be brought (II.11.42), but the coral trade across the Arabian Sea, for which Alexandria served as an emporium, developed only after the discovery of the monsoons in the first century BC. 'Pārasamudra' is the name the *Arthashāstra* uses for Sri Lanka (II.11.28, 59), not Tāmraparṇī (Ashokan 'Taṁbapaṁnī, Greek 'Taprobane'), which, in the *Arthashāstra*, is actually the name of a south Indian river (II.11.2). But 'Palaisimoundou' (corruption of Pārasamudra) is first used for Sri Lanka in Greek accounts only in the latter half of the first century AD, in the anonymous *Periplus of the Erythraean Sea*, with 'Taprobane' expressly recalled as its ancient name. Finally, 'Nepāla' is mentioned as the source of woollen cloth in the *Arthashāstra* (II.11.100); yet, the earliest other use of this name is as late as Samudragupta's Allahabad inscription of *c.* AD 350. One will, therefore, hardly be entitled to believe that the name 'Nepāla' could have been employed in any text before the beginning of the Christian era.

It is, therefore, not possible to contest the supposition that materials continued to be added to the texts that went into the making of the *Arthashāstra* until the second, or even the third century AD, when a compiler brought them together, and carefully arranged and edited them. But, while some parts of the work, such as chapters II.10 and II.11, can be pronounced quite late with some degree of confidence, it is difficult to fix the age of the bulk of the remainder of the material. Some of it might go back to pre-Mauryan times, as we have seen; and some (even a considerable portion) possibly reflects conditions in Mauryan times.

We must, however, remember that the *Arthashāstra*, even where (as in Book II) it describes the functions of different officials, does not consciously aim at being the manual of any single administration, whether Mauryan or non-Mauryan. Before we seek detailed corroboration in the *Arthashāstra* for either the accounts of

Megasthenes or the evidence of Ashokan inscriptions, we should take into account the wide expanse of time to which the *Arthashāstra* materials might belong, as well as the purpose of the text itself. Correspondences should thus not be forced on the text. Even in regard to social customs, where the *Arthashāstra* seemingly reflects a social order prior to the one prescribed by Manu, a similar policy of caution should still be pursued, with at least partial corroboration sought from other sources.

See Chapter 3.4 below for further remarks on the *Arthashāstra*.

Note 1.3

Bibliographical Note

G.M. Bongard-Levin, *Mauryan India* (New Delhi, 1985), is exclusively devoted to the subject of the present monograph: it uses an impressive amount of source material and secondary literature. Portions on Mauryan India in such general histories as *The History and Culture of the Indian People*, Vol. II, edited by R.C. Majumdar (Bombay, 1951), and *A Comprehensive History of India*, Vol. II, edited by K.A. Nilkanta Sastri (Bombay, 1957), need much revision and updating. D.D. Kosambi's brilliant chapter (7) in his *An Introduction to the Study of Indian History* (Bombay, 1956, pp. 176–226) would, however, always repay reading. The remaining part of this note discusses reading specifically for Chapter 1.

The best secondary account of Alexander's invasion, with a detailed reconstructed chronology, is still that of V.A. Smith, *Early History of India*, fourth edition, revised by S.M. Edwardes (Oxford, 1924), Chapters III and IV. For the history of Alexander's successors, see *Cambridge Ancient History*, VI, edited by J.B. Bury *et al.* (Cambridge, 1964) (Chapter XV, by W.W. Tarn). The entire phase is missed out in the (newly written) second edition of the same series, edited by D.M. Lewis *et al.* (Cambridge, 1994). The Greek sources on Alexander's invasion are collected together and translated by J.W. McCrindle's well-annotated *The Invasion of India by Alexander the Great, as Described by Arrian, Q. Curtius, Diodorus, Plutarch and Justin*, second edition (Westminster, 1893; Indian reprint, 1992).

For the political history of the Nandas and Chandragupta Maurya, one can with some caution recommend Hemchandra Raychaudhuri, *Political History of Ancient India*, with commentary by B.N. Mukherjee (New Delhi, 1996), Chapter IV, and pp. 591–617 from the commentary. Purāṇic lists of dynastic rulers (including the Nandas and Mauryas) have been edited and translated by F.E. Pargiter, *The Purāṇa Text of the Dynasties of the Kali Age* (London, 1913; Indian reprint, Varanasi, 1962). Legends about the Nandas and Chandragupta Maurya are critically analysed in Thomas R. Trautmann, *Kauṭilya and the Arthaśāstra* (for which see below), Chapter II.

The *Arthashāstra* has been edited and translated by R.P. Kangle: *The Kauṭilīya Arthaśāstra*, Part I (text), Part II (translation) and Part III ('Study') (Bombay, 1969, 1972, 1965). The translation supersedes the much-used translation by R. Shamasastry, third edition (Mysore, 1924), which has, however, a comprehensive index compared to Kangle's very brief one. On the compilation and date of the text,

Thomas R. Trautmann's *Kauṭilya and the Arthaśāstra* (Leiden, 1971) is the most important work. S.C. Mishra's *Evolution of Kauṭilya's Arthaśāstra* (Delhi, 1997) carefully explores epigraphic affinities, but perhaps the 'Conclusion' is still a little too confident in dating the different portions of the text on this basis.

Megasthenes's account as it survives in the pages of various Greek and Latin writers can be largely recovered from J.W. McCrindle's translation of these passages in *Ancient India as Described by Megasthenes and Arrian* (London, 1877) (revised by R.C. Majumdar, Calcutta, 1960). See also McCrindle's *Ancient India as Described in Classical Literature* (London, 1901). Many of McCrindle's translations, along with other translations of extracts from Greek and Latin texts, are conveniently collected by R.C. Majumdar in his *Classical Accounts of India* (Calcutta, 1960) (the annotation is slender and not always reliable, but there is a fairly good index).

On the punch-marked coins, the standard monograph is P.L. Gupta and T.R. Hardaker, *Ancient Indian Silver Punch-marked Coins of the Magadha-Maurya Karshapana Series* (Nashik, 1985).

Romila Thapar, in *The Mauryas Revisited* (Calcutta, 1987), considers the spread and depth of imperial authority within the Mauryan Empire, and critically reviews the Greek evidence on Mauryan India. See also Gerard Fussman, 'Central and Provincial Administration in ... the Mauryan Empire', *Indian Historical Review*, XIV, 1–2 (1987–88), pp. 43–72.

For Ashoka and his inscriptions, see the bibliographical note in Chapter 2. Texts and translations (or summaries) of late Mauryan inscriptions, and Rudradāman's Junagarh inscription of AD 150, important for Mauryan history, are conveniently gathered together in K.G. Krishnan, ed., *Uttankita Sanskrit Vidya Aranya Epigraphs*, Vol.II: *Prakrit and Sanskrit Epigraphs, 257 BC to 320 AD* (Mysore, 1989), Nos 37–46 and 135. For the Mahasthan inscription, see *Epigraphia Indica*, XXI, pp. 83–91; and for the Sohgaura plaque, *Annals of the Bhandarkar Oriental Research Institute* (Poona), XI, pp. 32–48.

2
Ashoka and the Later Years of the Mauryan Empire

2.1 Ashoka's Inscriptions

The inscriptions that Ashoka left behind him constitute unique monuments, important for a number of reasons among which it is hardly possible to give precedence to one over another. To date, there is no earlier acceptable example of writing in India, if we overlook the undeciphered ideograms of the Indus Civilization. Ashoka's inscriptions are written in as many as three absolutely different languages, viz. Prākrit, Irano–Aramaic and Greek, and in four scripts, viz. Brāhmī, Kharoṣhṭhī, Aramaic and Greek. Ashokan Brāhmī is the ancestor to the various scripts in which Hindi and most other Indian languages (including the Dravidian languages) are written today; and it is not beyond the realm of possibility that this script was created (or brought from Sri Lanka) in Ashoka's time itself or only a little earlier (see below, 2.5, and Chapter 3.4). The inscriptions are found on pillars and rocks (and, in two or three cases, on slabs) at over forty places in an area extending from central Afghanistan to Karnataka.

Their uniqueness increases when we come to their contents. Over three-fourths of them carry different sets of Ashoka's edicts (*lipi*), so that most of the edicts have come down to us in multiple copies. The edicts carry (except for a few prefatory notes or labels in individual inscriptions) Ashoka's own words either in the original Māgadhī dialect of Prākrit, or in partial renderings into other dialects of that language, or in translations or summaries, when engraved in Aramaic or Greek. Ashoka addresses his subjects (and officials) in a simple conversational style that stands in sharp contrast to the ornateness and hyperbole of inscriptions of later times. For this reason alone his edicts make an appeal to the modern reader, so long as one overlooks the numerous repetitions, omissions and scribal errors, which Ashoka himself so frankly acknowledges in his Rock Edict XIV. Since we do not know the context, many of the complexities behind the simple *dhaṁma* formularies (see *Extract 2.1*) can so easily escape us, and there could be, as we hope to show (2.2 below), a fairly serious social and even political message behind the apparent naivete of the formularies. Further, Ashokan inscriptions are the first dated texts in India, and these enable us not only to reconstruct Mauryan chronology (see *Note 1.1* above), but also to use them as reference points for fixing the period of other material (for example, the *Arthashāstra*: see *Note 1.2*). We have just said that, to appreciate the substance of Ashoka's *dhaṁma*, we need to know more about the context. The inscriptions themselves constitute invaluable sources of information about social, political, administrative and religious matters, and so help us, in part, to reconstruct their own context. Lastly, in these inscriptions, we encounter, for the first time in our history, a figure whom we know of as a person and not simply as just a name; and we know of him, too, not through legend or distant report but from what he is himself communicating directly to us – his cause as well as his anxieties, his self-commendations and also, most surprising of all, his self-criticisms.

Ashoka's inscriptions began to be deciphered in the nineteenth century (see *Note 2.1*), and as these were discovered and compared with each other, the different sets of edicts were distinguished and names given to them, with each edict numbered according to the sequence established from the positions it occupied in the inscriptions in relation to other edicts.

From their contents, the set of two edicts designated **Minor Rock Edicts** have been usually held to be the earliest of all known edicts of Ashoka. Minor Rock Edicts I and II are found inscribed at seven places within Karnataka and southern Andhra Pradesh; eleven other inscriptions, in an area extending in the north to Bahapur (Delhi) and Sahasram (southwestern Bihar), carry copies of only Minor Rock Edict I (see *Maps 2.1–2.3*). Compared to the series of Rock Edicts and Pillar Edicts described below, the copies of Minor Rock Edicts diverge very greatly; and it is possible either that there were variations in the originals sent to the different provinces, or that these went through some mode of oral transmission, with more emphasis on substance than on words. Some obscurities, like the figure 256 in Minor Rock Edict I, have taken long to be resolved, and not, perhaps, yet to the satisfaction of all (see 2.3 below); and this may be due to faults in transmission. Neither of the Minor Rock Edicts is dated, but it would seem that Regnal Year 10 (*c.* 260 BC) is the likeliest date, being that of the Kandahar Bilingual Edict (for which, see below), whose text appears to summarize Minor Rock Edicts I and II.

The **Fourteen Rock Edicts** have their copies on rocks and slabs at sites from the North Western Frontier Province to southern Andhra (see *Maps 2.1–2.4*). Two of these, at Shahbazgarhi and Mansehra (in the North Western Frontier Province), are the sole inscriptions of Ashoka written in Kharoshṭhī characters. The other sites are Kalsi (Uttarakhand), Girnar (Gujarat) and Yerragudi or Erragudi (Andhra). At Sopara, near Mumbai, and Sannathi (Karnataka), only fragments of the set have been found. In Orissa, the Dhauli and Jaugada inscriptions contain all the Rock Edicts, except Rock Edicts XI–XIII. It has been supposed that since Rock Edict XIII (see *Extract 1.4*) concerned the conquest of Kalinga, it was not thought politic to engrave it in Orissa, and so Rock Edicts XI and XII, with which it had presumably been issued, were also omitted there. Rock Edicts I–IV probably formed the earliest sub-set, having been issued in Regnal Year 12 (*c.* 258 BC), a date given in Edicts III and IV. Rock Edict V mentions a measure taken in Regnal Year 13, so that this edict and the subsequent edicts of the series must have been issued in this year (*c.* 257 BC) or a little later.

The pair of **Separate Rock Edicts** was found at Dhauli and Jauguda (*Map 2.1*), following upon the main series of Rock Edicts. It was thought that they were issued for Kalinga only and, therefore, have sometimes been called Kalinga Edicts. But the fact that the fragmentary slab inscription at Sannathi, far away from Orissa, contains portions of Separate Rock Edicts I and II shows that these were not meant for Kalinga alone. From the way these have been engraved at Jauguda and Sannathi, it is clear that Edict II of the pair was actually issued before Edict I.

Outside these two series, there is one rock edict surviving in a solitary copy, inscribed on a boulder at Bairat (near Bhabru, north-eastern Rajasthan), which is really a message addressed by Ashoka to the *Saṁgha* or Buddhist order. It is not dated. Of a different kind are the

MAP 2.1 Maurvan Empire: East

INDEX
FOR MAPS 2.1-2.4

Ashokan Edict on rock	△	Other Mauryan inscription on slab/brick ⊠
" " " pillar	○	" " " in cave ∅
" " " slab	▢	" " " on vase/copper ✕
" " in cave	⊚	Copper mine, Gold mine Ⓒ Ⓖ
Uninscribed pillar	⟲	Lead-silver-zinc mine Ⓛ⟨ˢᶻ⟩

Place names from sources in italics

Faiz Habib

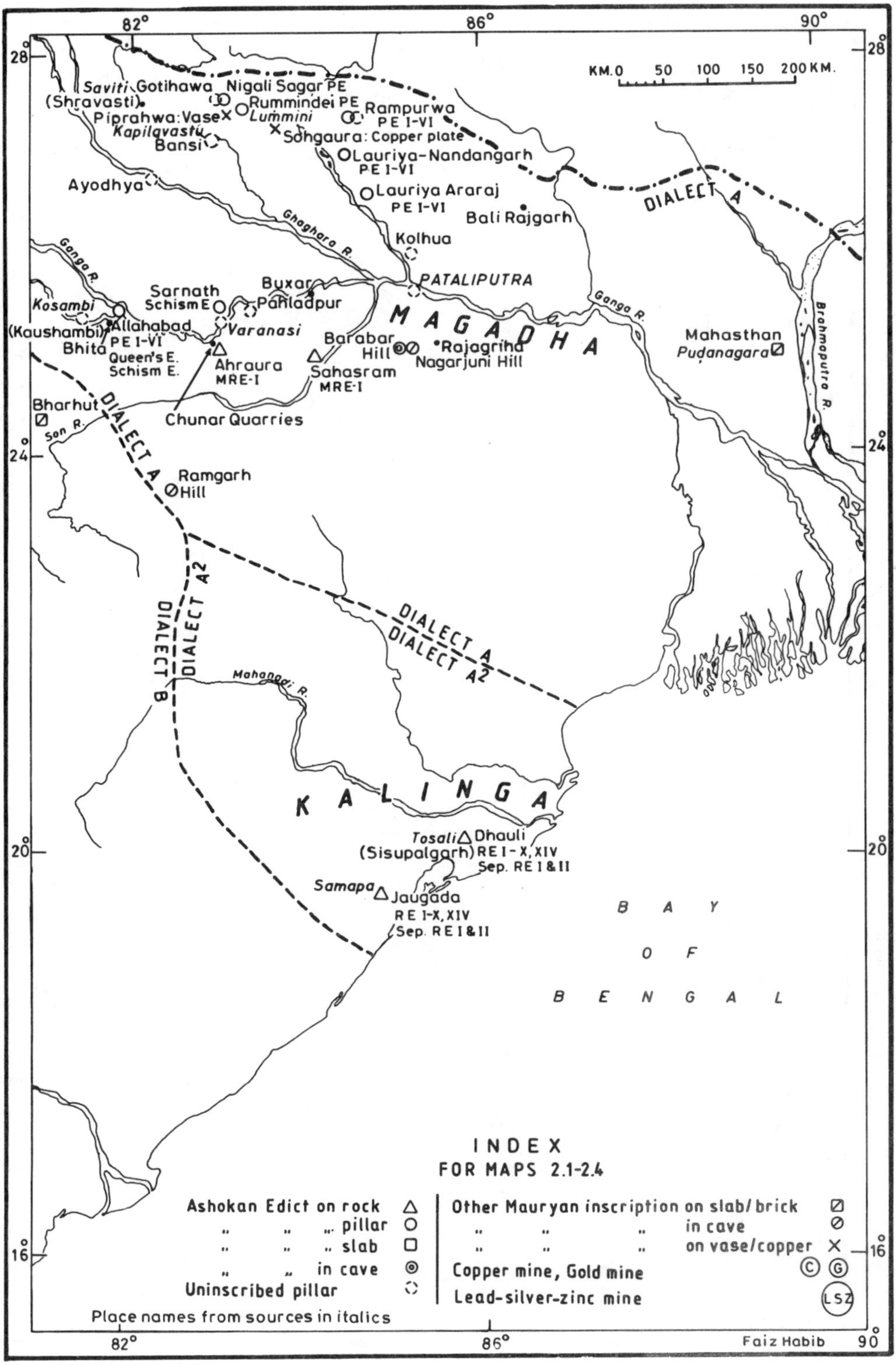

Map 2.2 Mauryan Empire: North

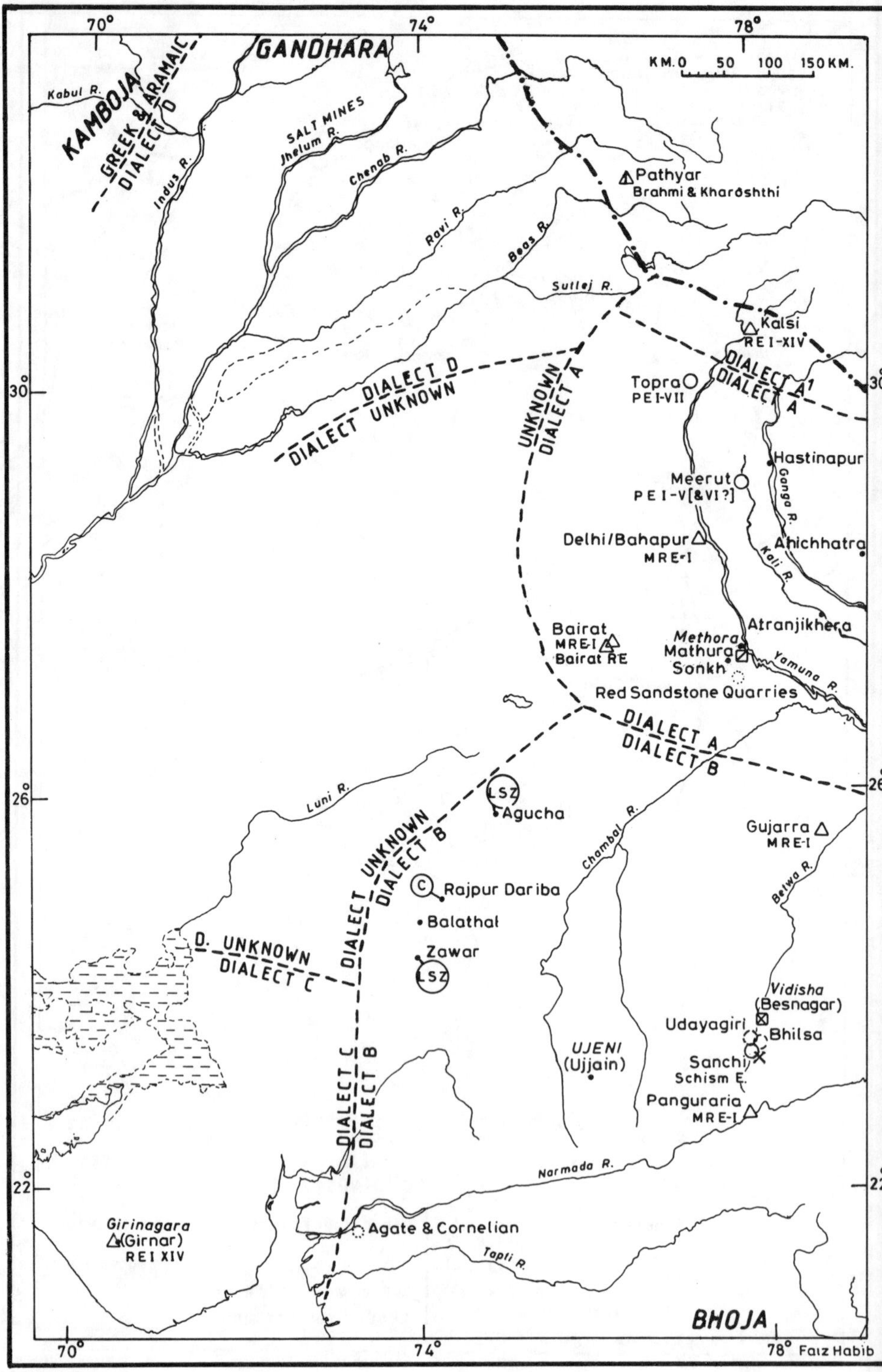

Map 2.3 Mauryan Empire: South

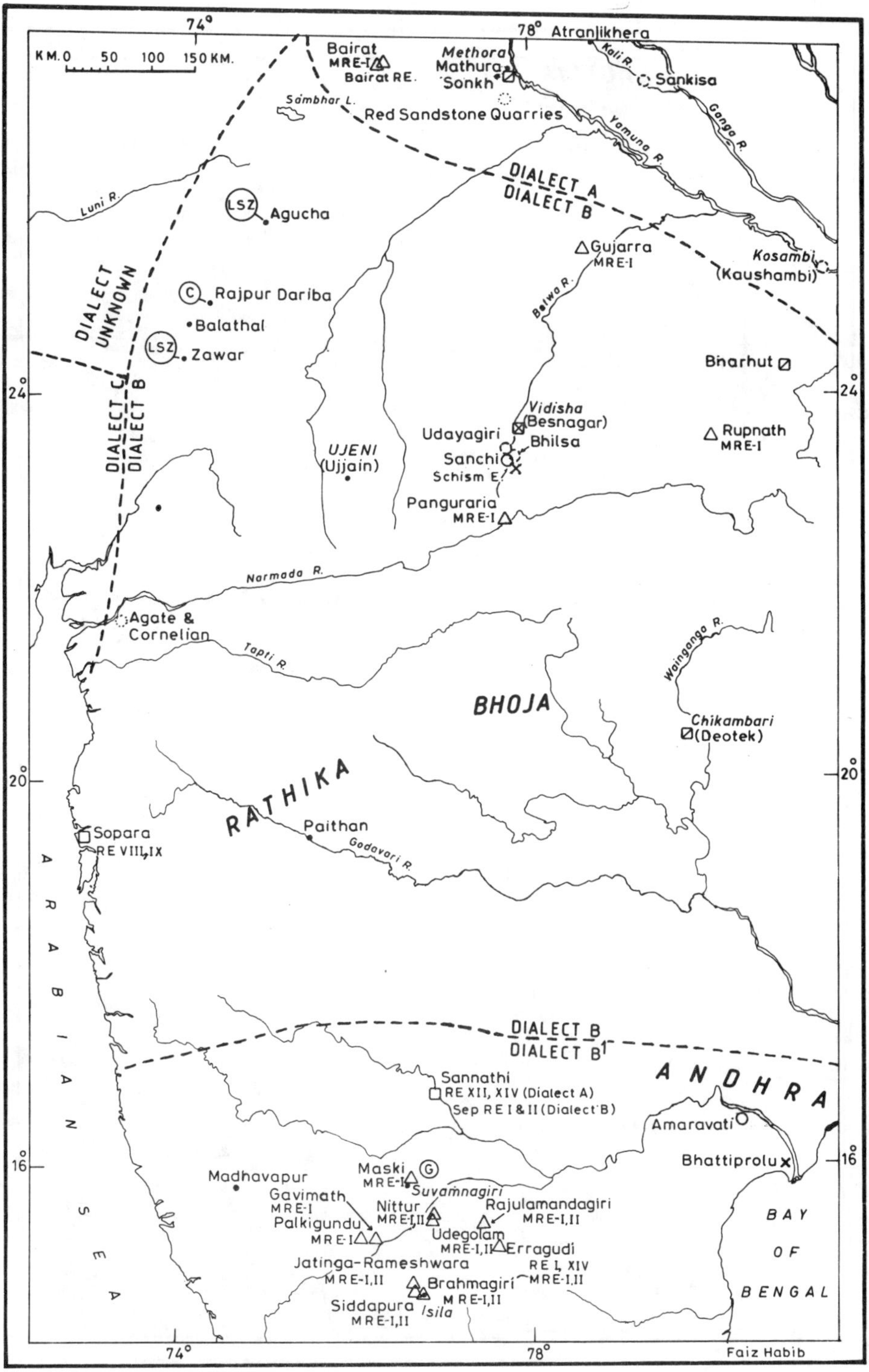

Correction: Read 'RE I–XIV' instead of 'RE I, XIV' under Erraguddi.

Map 2.4 Mauryan Empire: West

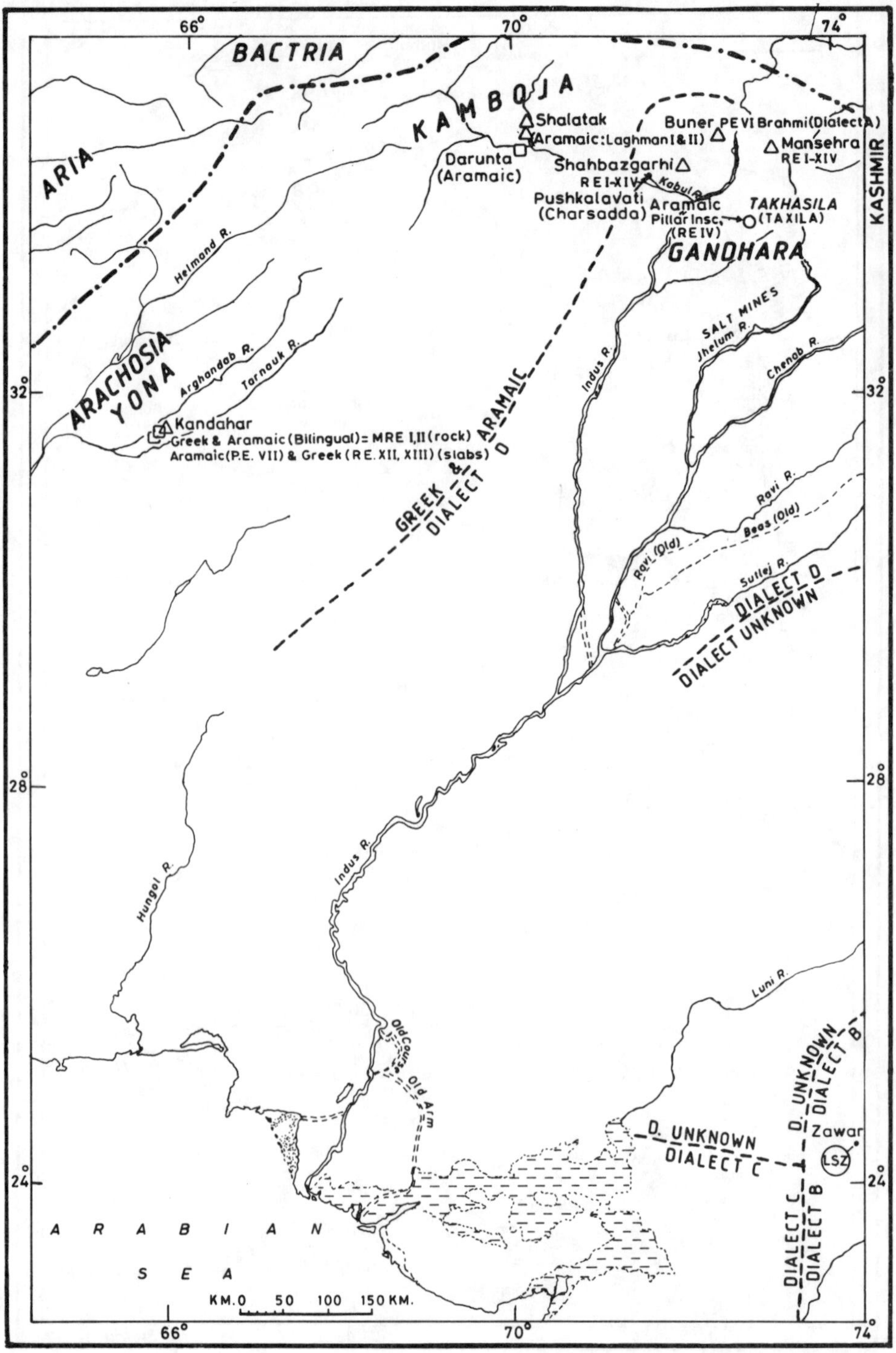

short donative inscriptions in three caves of the Barabar hills near Gaya in Bihar, which Ashoka made and gifted to the Ājīvikas. Two belong to Regnal Year 12 (*c.* 258 BC) and the third (with Ājīvikas not expressly identified as the donees) to Regnal Year 19 (*c.* 251 BC).

The series of **Pillar Edicts**, of which six (I to VI) have been found on pillars at six places, in Delhi, Uttar Pradesh and Bihar (see *Maps 2.1–2.2*), is consistently in the Māgadhī dialect of Ashokan Prākrit, the texts of all the inscribed copies agreeing very closely. The two Delhi pillars were not placed there originally, but one was brought there from Topra in Haryana and the other from Meerut in Uttar Pradesh by Sultan Firoz Tughluq (1351–1388). The Topra-Delhi pillar contains the very important Pillar Edict VII (*Extract 2.7*), not found anywhere else. This series of inscriptions may be among Ashoka's last. Pillar Edicts I–VI were issued in Regnal Year 26 (*c.* 244 BC), a date contained in Pillar Edicts I, IV, V and VI. Pillar Edict VII was issued subsequently and is dated Regnal Year 27 (*c.* 243 BC).

Another independent edict, known as the Schism Edict, was inscribed on pillars at Allahabad, Sarnath (near Varanasi) and Sanchi (the famous Buddhist site near Bhopal), but with the texts varying considerably. It bears no date, but on the Allahabad pillar it was apparently written after Pillar Edicts I–VI and so must have been issued later.

Two pillar inscriptions commemorate Ashoka's pilgrimage to holy sites in Nepalese Terai. The pillar at Rummindei (Lummini, the Buddha's birth-place) marks his visit to it in Regnal Year 20 (*c.* 250 BC); and the pillar at Nigali Sagar records his trip to the *stūpa* of the Buddha Konākamana in presumably the same year (surface damage obscures the year). A third inscription, designated the 'Queen's Edict', found on the Allahabad pillar, is undated: it records Ashoka's orders that the gifts of his second queen Kāluvākī (Kāruvākī) should be duly recorded. A rather surprising discovery has been that of a sandstone slab cut out of a pillar at Amaravati (coastal Andhra), which contains a very damaged text of a possible Ashokan edict; but the fragmentary text does not carry clauses found in any other known edict.

In his earliest known decree, Minor Edict I, Ashoka expressed his intention to inscribe his edicts on both rock (*pavata*) and stone pillar (*silāthambha*); and in what may well be his last edict, Pillar Edict VII, he speaks of inscribing his edicts on stone pillars and stone slabs

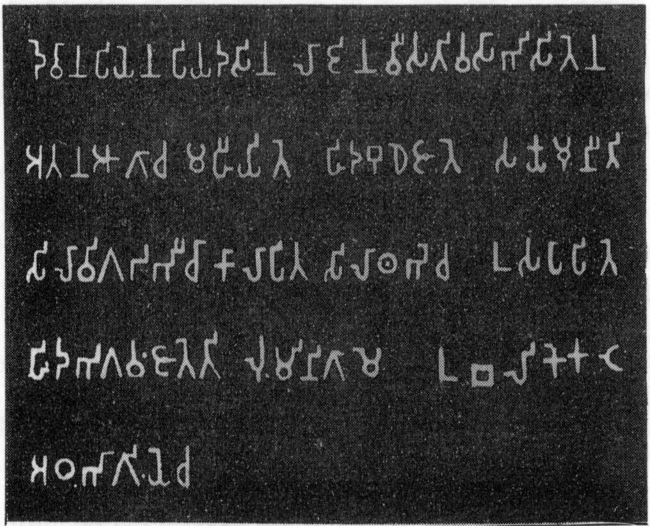

1 **(A) Devāna[pi]yena Piyadasina lājina vīsati-vasābhisitena**
2 atana āgācha mahīyite hida **Budhe** jāte **Sakyamuni** ti
3 **(B)** silā vigaḍabhī chā kālāpita silā-thabhe cha usapāpite
4 hida **Bhagavaṁ** jāte ti **(C) Luṁmini-gāme** ubalike kaṭe
5 aṭha-bhāgiye cha

FIG. 2.1 Facsimile of Rummindei Pillar inscription (V.A. Smith) with transliteration (E. Hultzsch). The character *pi* put within square brackets by Hultzsch is clear enough in Smith's reproduction.

(*silāphalaka*). Though there is no sanction for it in his own statements, it seems that when he issued his edicts these were inscribed either on rocks or on pillars, but never on both. This is a curious fact not easy to explain, but sufficiently established to form the basis for the conventional classification of Ashokan edicts into Rock and Pillar Edicts. This notion may be modified a little by the claimed recovery from Buner (North Western Frontier Province) of a boulder carrying in Brāhmī a fragment of Pillar Edict VI. The boundary between the two classes of edicts gets blurred also when we turn to Ashoka's Aramaic and Greek inscriptions.

These **Aramaic and Greek inscriptions** are found at Taxila and at four different sites in Afghanistan (see *Map 2.4*). By their contents these are divisible into two groups, according as they carry (1) direct translations of Ashokan edicts, originally issued in Prākrit, and (2) texts not directly attributable to any edicts in Prākrit known to us. To Group (1) belongs the bilingual inscription from Shahr-i Kuhna near Kandahar. Both its Greek and Aramaic texts appear to be translations of a common Prākrit original, which apparently modified the text of Minor Rock Edict I for an alien audience, and abridged Minor Rock Edict II. It gives Regnal Year 10 (*c.* 260 BC) as the date in the beginning (see *Extract 2.1 [B]*, for the Aramaic version). A slab from Kandahar contains a Greek version of Rock Edict XII (with some omissions), followed by the initial portion of Rock Edict XIII. It could well be a part of a panel of slabs on which the entire series of the Fourteen Rock Edicts was presented in Greek. A fragmentary Aramaic inscription on limestone, obtained from the Kandahar bazaar, is a close rendering of the corresponding portion of Pillar Edict VII, with some Prākrit clauses directly transcribed in Aramaic. At Taxila (Srikap), on the other hand, a slab from an octagonal marble pillar was found to contain a damaged text in Aramaic carrying a portion of Rock Edict IV.

To Group (2) we may assign the three Aramaic inscriptions from the Laghman province. A broken stone slab from Pul-i Duranta contains a fragment, which seems to contain elements (including Prākrit words and clauses) drawn from various inscriptions, such as Rock Edict V, and Pillar Edicts V and VII; and so its Prākrit original might have been especially compiled for local use. This may also be the case with the two highway inscriptions, where a prohibition of hunting and fishing dated Regnal Year 16 (*c.* 254 BC) (with no Prākrit original known) prefaces the distance indications.

It has often been suggested with some force that Ashoka had a model for his inscriptions in Achaemenid precursors, beginning with the grand Bisutun and Naqsh-i Rustam inscriptions of Darius I (522–486 BC). We know that copies were made of the Bisutun inscription to be sent out in other languages, such as Aramaic and Akkadian. With the deepened connections with the Iranian communities in the northwest, this Achaemenid tradition could well have come to Ashoka's knowledge. Indeed, the Old Iranian words *dipi* for written decree and *nipesapita* for writing, appear in the Shahbazgarhi inscription of his Rock Edicts (*dipi* also occurs at Mansehra). But there is a vital difference between the motives of Darius and Ashoka. Darius is concerned with proclaiming his military successes, gross power and capacity to punish. He, therefore, essentially addresses men of influence and potential rebels – in other words, the ruling classes. These could be reached by the inscribed word in different official languages in use within his Empire. But Ashoka sets out with a different message, that of *dhaṁma*, and his audience is also different – the small as well as the great men (Minor Rock Edict I and Rock Edict X), the people at large (*jana*, *loka*, etc.) (for example, Rock Edict VI: *Extract 2.5*). The question naturally arises whether such an audience could be reached by inscriptions alone, since any written text could be read by only a few persons. Even if the texts could be read out to them, it is doubtful if many in different parts of India would have been able to follow the royal Prākrit, however simple might be its diction and style, when the spoken tongues, even of Indo–Aryan derivations, must have been so very different in each locality. Even the dialect variations one sees in the Ashokan texts, after all, only represented differences in the dialects of the official language and not the common languages.

It seems that, given these limitations, there were still two motives that could underlie Ashoka's anxiety to put his words on stone. One was to make it long-enduring (Pillar Edict VII), so that generations of his successors might imbibe the message (Rock Edicts V and VI). Second, the inscriptions could serve as a kind of reminder (and the standard text) of what was to be conveyed to his subjects by his officials through widespread oral transmission (for which see 2.3 below). His hope for long duration has been fulfilled by the modern decipherment of his edicts; and there is still much that we can learn, to our profit, from his message, such as the one he gives of religious tolerance in his Rock Edict XII (*Extract 2.4*). His unique effort in leaving behind the record of his cause on stone has not, therefore, been entirely in vain, in terms of his own vision.

2.2 The *Dhaṁma* of Ashoka

Ashoka left behind his inscriptions, as we have just seen, so that his *dhaṁma-lipis*, or edicts propagating *dhaṁma*, might long endure. What, then, was the substance of the *dhaṁma* that he wished his contemporaries, especially his subjects, to imbibe, and so too the generations in future to come? The Prākrit word *dhaṁma* (Ashokan Gāndhārī: *dhrama*) corresponds to the Sanskrit *dharma*, literally meaning that which is to be held fast to, or kept, or is fixed and firm.

The word *dharma* (including its earlier form, *dharman*) appears in the *Rigveda* and subsequent texts in the sense of custom or law, whence the further sense of duty prescribed by such law. The late Vedic texts known as the Dharmasūtras, compiled from the sixth century BC onwards, contain statements of the *dharma* as law. In the Buddhist tradition, however, the term *dhaṁma* stands for the Buddha's doctrine or teaching, as in the well-known formula where one seeks refuge in the Buddha (Gautama), the *dhaṁma* (doctrine) and the *Saṁgha* (monastic order).

Ashoka's use of the term, except in two cases, conforms to neither usage. The first of the two exceptions is found in his Bairat Rock Edict, when he declares his faith in the Buddha, the *dhaṁma* and the *Saṁgha*, giving us thereby the earliest epigraphic evidence for this Buddhist article of faith. Rock Edict XII offers the second instance, when Ashoka calls on members of all religious sects (*pāsaṁḍa*) "to hear and follow each other's *dhaṁma*". In both cases, the sense of 'doctrine' alone will suit the context. As for established law or custom, the other sense of *dharma*, there is no passage in the inscriptions where this sense will at all serve. Nor does Ashoka use *dhaṁma* in the sense of duty specific to a particular class of persons, such as members of a caste or community. Ashoka's use of the word made his own contemporary translators render it differently. In the Kandahar bilingual inscription, the Aramaic translator renders *dhaṁma* as *qsyt*, or Truth, thus deeming it to carry the sense of doctrine. The Greek translator, however, takes it to stand for *eusebeia*, the Greek for piety or ethics. The latter is, indeed, precisely how modern translators, long before the Kandahar inscription came to be known, have been rendering the word, on the basis solely of the substance of *dhaṁma* as expounded by the Ashokan inscriptions themselves.

From Ashoka's statements in his inscriptions it is clear that the *dhaṁma* he propagates consists simply of a set of desired forms of conduct and attitudes of mind. (See *Extract 2.1* for a sample of *dhaṁma* formularies in his edicts.) Particular attention is invited to our *Table 2.1*, which offers a list of the major prescriptions of *dhaṁma* as given in the edicts, arranged by order of frequency of the references.

If we begin with the items of Ashoka's *dhaṁma*, as arranged in *Table 2.1*, we see that the most frequently mentioned principle is that

TABLE 2.1 The Practice of *Dhaṁma*

Items listed according to number of occurrences in Ashoka's Edicts

1.	Compassion towards, and avoidance of injury to, living beings	MRE II; RE III, IV, IX, XI; PE II, VII; Kandahar bilingual
2.	Obedience to mother and father	MRE II; RE III, IV, XI, XIII; PE VII; Kandahar bilingual
3.	Obedience, and reverence, to elders	MRE II; RE IV, IX, XIII; PE VII; Kandahar bilingual
4.	Liberality, etc., to Brahmans and *samanas*	RE III, IV, IX, XIII; PE VII
5.	Decorous behaviour towards slaves and servants	RE IX, XI, XIII; PE VII
6.	Liberality, etc., towards friends, relatives, associates, etc.	RE III, IV, XI, XIII
7.	Liberality	PE II, IV, VII
8.	Truth to be spoken	MRE II; PE II, VII
9.	Purity (especially of thought), compassion	RE VII; PE II, VII
10.	Self-restraint (especially in speech)	RE VII, XII
11.	Teacher to be honoured by pupil	MRE II
12.	Moderation in spending, moderation in possessing	RE III
13.	Respectful behaviour towards the aged	PE VII
14.	Decorous conduct towards the poor and the destitute	PE VII
15.	Obedience to those placed above	RE XIII
16.	Avoidance of fierceness, cruelty, anger, pride, envy	PE II
17.	Observance of fast	PE IV

Abbreviations: MRE = Minor Rock Edict(s); PE = Pillar Edict(s); RE = Rock Edict(s).

of compassion for living beings and avoidance of injury to them. This is what Rock Edict XIII (*Extract 1.4*) would naturally lead us to expect, since it was his remorse over the slaughter and suffering of people during his conquest of Kalinga that, according to this edict, induced Ashoka to spurn territorial conquest and turn to the pursuit of *dhaṁma-vijaya*, 'the *dhaṁma* conquest'. Initially, the remorse was over the human suffering brought about by his own action; but the attitude of compassion extended equally to animals, so that, depending on the context, the 'living beings', as objects of compassion, include animals as well. Ashoka himself tried to provide protection to animals from slaughter, to a somewhat limited degree, as we shall see below (2.3). The influence of Buddhism (and Jainism) in the adoption of this attitude is manifest, though this is not acknowledged in the edicts themselves.

The items that follow next in frequency of occurrence relate to relations between human beings at different levels. First come (No. 2) exhortations to render obedience to 'mother and father', invariably written in that order, which may seem strange for what was surely a male-dominated society. But, then, in current Hindustani too we have the same order in *mān-bāp*, without the phrase necessarily indicating much of a status for the mother in reality. The next item (No. 3), 'obedience to elders (*guru*)', may be seen similarly as an assertion of the ties of the community beyond the family, where 'elders' might be important upholders of community customs. Largely falling in the same class is the recommendation that liberality, etc., be shown to friends, relatives and associates (No. 6). There is nothing here that could be in opposition to the Brahmanical tradition; but it is significant that the edicts nowhere touch on caste: indeed, one looks in vain for the words *varṇa* or *jāti* in the entire corpus of the inscriptions. It may be argued that the exhortation to render obedience to elders may imply an expectation that customs of the community as set forth by its elders would need to be followed, and these could well be customs shaped by the norms of caste. This is possible; yet, this would again leave us with the question why such an indirect way of making concessions to the caste system should be adopted.

The modern reader will doubtless be attracted more by another item, fairly well-emphasized in the edicts, namely, "decorous behaviour" (such is the preferred literal translation) towards "slaves (*dāsa*) and servants (*bhaṭaka*)" (No. 5), and also towards "the poor (*kapana*) and the destitute (*valāka*)" (No. 14). Such concern for the poor and the enslaved, seldom seen in royal proclamations, is here supplemented by a denigration of excessive wealth, implied in item No. 12, which requires "moderation in expenditure, moderation in possessing".

These exhortations fall in line with some of Ashoka's aphorisms, which we may not, perhaps, dismiss as mere pious rhetoric. "All men (*savamunisā*) are my children", he says in both of his Separate Rock Edicts, "and just as I desire for (my) children that I may provide them with complete welfare and happiness here and in the next world, so do I desire for all men." In Minor Rock Edict I, he makes it clear that by "all men" he meant not only the great or high-ranking (*mahātpa*, *uḍālaka*), but also the lowly (*khudaka*), who too could progress in *dhaṁma*. In Rock Edict X, he goes further and pronounces that it was more difficult for the high-ranked person (*usaṭa*) to progress than for a lowly one: this amounts to a distinct inversion of the orthodox *dharma*, in which the higher ranks (*varṇas*) had correspondingly greater access to religious merit.

It is implicit in Ashoka's Rock Edicts VII and XII that his message of *dhaṁma* is addressed to followers of all religious sects (*pāsaṁḍa*). In Pillar Edict VII (*Extract 2.7 [C]*), he expressly proclaims his patronage of not only the *Saṁgha*, the Buddhist order, but also of the Brahmans, Ājīvikas and Jains. It is, therefore, natural that Ashoka should call for liberality towards Brahmans and *samanas*, the latter a blanket term for all non-Brahmanical monks, nuns and ascetics. This exhortation (item No. 4 in our table) occurs in as many as seven edicts. In three of these (Rock Edicts IV, IX and XI, except at Girnar and Sopara), the positions in the pair are reversed, the *samanas* being placed first; this is also the case with the pair in another context in Rock Edict VIII. The pairing of the Brahmans with the *samanas* shows that alms to Brahman priests (including ascetics) alone are being thought of, not alms to Brahmans in general. The reversed order ('*samanas* and Brahmans'), found in nearly half the references, shows that Ashoka had in mind a kind of parity between the two categories of religious men, and no intrinsic precedence to Brahmans was conceded. This is in obvious conflict with the prescription in the *Arthashāstra* (II.1.7), where land-grants (significantly called *brahmadeya*) are to be confined to Brahmanical "priests, preceptors, chaplains (*purohita*) and Brahmans learned in the Vedas", the *samanas* being thus excluded altogether.

In his Rock Edict VII, Ashoka proclaims his desire that "all (religious) sects (*pāsaṁḍa*) should settle everywhere". This promised freedom is in contrast to the stipulation in the *Arthashāstra* (II.1.32) that no "ascetic sect (*pravrajitabhāva*) other than the [Brahmanical] forest hermits" should be allowed to settle in a *janapada* (province, district), and (II.4.23) that (non-Brahmanical) sects – for which the word used is, significantly, *pāṣhaṇḍa* – along with the outcastes (*chaṇḍālas*), may not settle anywhere in the towns except near the cremation grounds. The enjoyment of freedom of settlement for all sects was part of a general environment of communal amity that Ashoka wished to foster. For such amity, he regarded self-restraint (*sayama*), especially in speech (*vachiguti*), to be a necessary condition (our item No. 10). In Rock Edict XII, he advocated a mutual dialogue by which the different sects should all prosper together (see *Extract 2.4*). The edict would not have been surely needed had there been no acrimony existing among the sects, and had mutual tolerance already prevailed.

The absence of any political demands in the name of *dhaṁma* is yet another surprising element of the Ashokan exhortations. Nowhere is there any call for his subjects to obey his orders as part of their *dhaṁma*. There is one item (No. 15), it is true, commending obedience to "those placed above" (*agabhuta*), from which one may infer that rendering obedience to someone placed higher in the hierarchical order was expected; but the phrase occurs only once, and other interpretations of *agabhuta* are possible. It is, on the other hand, remarkable that Ashoka twice considers himself as placed in debt to all human beings, a debt that he had to discharge (*ananiyaṁ*) by promoting their happiness (Rock Edict VI: *Extract 2.5*) and also by extending compassion to them (Separate Rock Edict II). One almost feels that he was moved here by a primitive sense of a 'social contract', in which the king, in receipt of taxes, needs to fulfil certain obligations in return. We are strengthened in this view by Ashoka's invocation of the same principle when, in Separate Rock Edict I, he calls upon his officials to discharge their debt to him by carrying out his orders. The 'debt' presumably consisted of the pay and other favours the officials received from the king.

Another aspect of Ashoka's *dhaṁma* consists of the demands he makes on the individual's inner self. As we can see from our *Table 2.1*, he demands that truth be spoken (No. 8); that self-restraint, especially in speech, be exercised (No. 10); that there be purity, especially of thought (No. 9); and that attitudes of fierceness, cruelty, anger, pride and envy be forsaken (No. 16). In Rock Edict IX, he concedes that some rites of good omen (*maṁgala*) may be performed – women, in any case, perform numerous such rites, he says. But he is, in effect, dismissive of the effectiveness of such ritual. Only conduct prescribed by *dhaṁma* would really bear fruit. He appeals to "the father, son, brother, husband (*suvāmika*), friend, acquaintance or even neighbour" to carry this message to each family. In Rock Edict I, he also denounces and prohibits the religious gatherings (*samāja*) where animals were slaughtered for sacrifice (*pajohitaviye*). These survivals of Vedic rites were obviously in conflict with the primary article of Ashokan *dhaṁma* (item No. 1), viz. non-injury to living beings. The only rite Ashoka seems to recommend is fasting (item No. 17), as a supplement to or substitute of alms-giving.

When Ashoka appeals to individuals to follow the *dhaṁma*, he often refers to its "fruit" (*phala*). He promises happiness here in this world (*hidaloka*), which, he admits, the rites of good omen also aim at; but the *dhaṁma* has fruits for the next world (*parata*, *paraloka*) as well (see Rock Edict IX; also Rock Edict XIII, both the Separate Rock Edicts and Pillar Edicts IV, VII). Ashoka even holds forth the promise of heaven (*svaga*) (Minor Rock Edict I, Rock Edicts VI and IX). Here, superficially speaking, Ashoka might have been invoking a common popular belief, recognized also in the *Arthashāstra* (I.3.14) when it says: "Fulfilling one's *dharma* leads to heaven (*svarga*) and endless bliss." It is another matter that Ashoka's concept of *dhaṁma* was quite different from Kauṭilya's idea of *dharma*. We may suppose, further, that Ashoka had in mind the determination of one's status in afterlife by the working of the *karma* system, since there is no place for God or deities or divine intervention in his own *dhaṁma*. The references to men commingling with *devas* (gods) in Minor Rock Edict I and to the exhibition to people of 'divine forms' (*diviyāni rūpāni*) in Rock Edict IV are obviously of a rhetorical or figurative kind. There is nothing about the soul (*attā* = *ātman*) either, partly perhaps because of the Buddha's denial of it (*anattā*). For communities that had different beliefs, the promise had naturally to be differently put. In the Greek version of the Kandahar bilingual inscription, no reference is made to afterlife, while in the Aramaic version, with an eye no doubt to the Zoroastrian doctrine, pious men are promised exemption from the (Day of) Judgement! (See *Extract 2.1 [B].*)

It is natural to expect that the principles of conduct that Ashoka propagates should sometimes coincide with those of other ethical systems. Even the *Arthashāstra*, I.3.13, has words that might well have come right out of Ashokan edicts: "Common to all men is [the *dharma* of] non-injury (*ahiṁsā*), truth, uprightness, lack of spite, compassion and forbearance." It may be argued that, given the long range of time over which the *Arthashāstra*'s text underwent compilation, this clause could be a post-Ashokan insertion. But even if such was not the case, there is still little common between the preceding eight clauses (I.3.5–12) in the *Arthashāstra* laying down the *dharma* of men by their caste (*varṇa*) and their four stages (*āshrama*) of life (*Extract 3.2*), on the one hand, and the prescriptions of Ashoka's *dhaṁma*, on the other. Partial coincidences may, therefore, be simply accidental.

There has naturally been greater readiness on the part of modern scholars to seek the source of Ashoka's ethics in the Buddhist tradition, given Ashoka's open acknowledgement of his own personal affiliation with Buddhism (see 2.3 below). Ashoka does not refer, it is true, to the Four Noble Truths. Yet, we have the use of the word *majhaṁ* (literally, middle) in Separate Rock Edict I in the sense of impartial, just, or good, thereby showing the influence of the use of the word as the approved appellation of the Eight-fold Path, a crucial component of the Buddha's Noble Truths. A large number of phrases have been detected in the Ashokan inscriptions that have their counterparts in early Pāli Canon, and this too establishes that Ashoka's formulation of many of his maxims and prescriptions was influenced by the lore about the Buddha's teachings that had been brought together by his time (on this, see Chapter 3.3 below). Especially significant for this connection is Ashoka's Bairat Edict, in which he lists seven "*dhaṁma* expositions" (*dhaṁmapariyāya*) of the Buddha himself, selected out of the many oral discourses by him. Some difficulty has all along been attached to the identification of these seven texts, since the titles of some have since altered or the same titles are borne by more than one passage. There has been a tendency, then, to choose the passage closest to what Ashoka must have seen as conformable to his own view of *dhaṁma*. There may be the danger of a circular argument here; but there is no doubt that a great part of counsel about the good moral life for laymen (*upāsakas*) or householders in utterances attributed to the Buddha in the Pāli Canon is fairly consistent with Ashoka's *dhaṁma*. The *Sigālovāda Sutta*, in the *Dīgha Nikāya*, might not have been included among Ashoka's seven selected texts, yet here we find the Buddha showing the lay householder Sigāla how he should discharge his duty towards (1) his mother and father, (2) his teachers, (3) *samanas* and Brahmans, (4) friends, relations, etc., and (5) slaves and servants – all of these are Ashoka's favourite categories.

While considering this evidence for a link between the Buddha's teaching suited to the laity and the *dhaṁma* of Ashoka, one must still remember that the former was only peripheral to Buddhism, a monastic religion aiming to lead one to *nibbāna*, or liberation from the cycle of births and rebirths, and so concerned more with the discipline of the *Saṁgha*, the order of monks and nuns, than with the upholding of the moral virtues of the laity. Ashoka's concern in the *dhaṁma* he preaches is the reverse of it: it is the ordinary man he appeals to and it is him, with all his worldly desires intact, that Ashoka wishes to bring under the umbrella of his *dhaṁma*. It is for this reason obviously that he invites his hearers to a moral path leading to *svaga* (heaven) and not a monastic one leading to *nibbāna* – the last word never occurs in his edicts. Ashoka probably drew on the ethics for the laity that the Buddha had on occasion preached, but this does not detract from his own originality. Even if we were to concede that his *dhaṁma*, in a large part, had its source in the Buddha's teachings, he yet carried out a notable act of selection in moving to the centre what was on the periphery in his source, and in underlining and enlarging it. Still more, he tried to make practice conform to preaching, so that he aimed, in his own light, at making both society and state answerable to the call of compassion. Whatever the degree of our scepticism about it, the undertaking would still seem to have been an enterprise of extraordinary vision. In the following sub-chapter, we shall try to reconstruct the story of this enterprise.

2.3 The Reign of Ashoka

The inscriptions of Ashoka form our principal source for his reign. Yet, however sincere and modest Ashoka might have been when he addressed his subjects through his edicts, we would still wish to have some independent evidence by which his statements could be verified or supplemented. The only other testimony we have, in fact, is in the shape of Buddhist traditions preserved in the Theravāda monasteries of Sri Lanka and in the literature of the Mahāyāna schools of the north. The Sri Lankan tradition is essentially contained in two Pāli texts, the *Dīpavaṁsa* (compiled, *c.* AD 400) and the much later *Mahāvaṁsa*, its initial portion composed in the twelfth century. Both of these are chronicles and often record the years in which particular events occurred; and the original kernel doubtless goes back to the time of Ashoka himself. However, the accounts in both have suffered from so much alteration, embellishment and insertions of fantasy, that it is difficult to credit anything that is said in them, unless it is corroborated by Ashokan inscriptions themselves. The same may be said with even greater force about the northern version of the Ashoka story, preserved in the *Ashokāvadāna*, which comes to us through the Sanskrit *Divyāvadāna*, the latter having been compiled over a long time within the first millennium AD. The two traditions might ultimately have drawn on the same body of oral recollections; but, with progressive additions and deletions, their divergences are now overwhelming. It is, therefore, not possible to use the bulk of these traditions for correcting or improving upon the information the Ashokan inscriptions supply us with. The narrative of Ashoka's reign that now follows will, therefore, necessarily be anchored to what we are told by the Ashokan edicts.

Our natural starting point here must be the Kalinga War of Regnal Year 8 (*c.* 262 BC), with which we had brought our survey of Ashoka's early years to a close in Chapter 1.5. The killing and other human suffering it brought about made a great impression upon Ashoka, who, in remorse, gave up all idea of further territorial conquest (*vijaya*) and made henceforth the *dhaṁmavijaya*, or '*dhaṁma* conquest', his principal object of endeavour. This required a lenient and merciful treatment of his subjects, and the active propagation of the principles of *dhaṁma*. (See Rock Edict XIII: *Extract 1.4*.) We have already discussed the principal components of Ashoka's *dhaṁma* (2.2

above), and have touched on the links between it and the conduct prescribed for the laity in Buddhism.

On what may be loosely called Ashoka's **conversion to Buddhism**, our primary source is his Minor Rock Edict I. The Kandahar bilingual inscription, which summarizes the two Minor Rock Edicts, shows that these must have been issued in Regnal Year 10 (*c.* 260 BC). Minor Rock Edict I tells us that Ashoka had been an *upāsaka*, or a lay follower, of the Buddha for over two-and-a-half years, that is, from Regnal Year 7 or 8; but that it was only for over a year, that is, since Regnal Year 8 or 9, that he had devoted much exertion in the cause of *dhaṁma*. This exertion consisted in part (by an interpretation of the figure 256 in Minor Rock Edict I, now generally accepted) of a tour of 256 nights. Rock Edict VIII too gives an account of this *dhaṁmayātā* (tour or pilgrimage of *dhaṁma*), made in Regnal Year 10, the high-point of which was Ashoka's visit to Saṁbodhi or the Bo-tree at Buddha Gaya (Bihar). The pilgrimage involved "visiting and making gifts to *samanas* and Brahmans, and visiting and giving money (*hiraṁṇa*) to old people, and visiting and preaching *dhaṁma* to the people of the *janapadas* (districts) and enquiring about *dhaṁma* from them". It was remarkably like a politician's meet-the-people programme of our own days, and not simply a conventional pilgrimage.

Ashoka's special relationship with Buddhism comes out notably in the Bairat Rock Edict, where he addresses the *Saṁgha* and commends seven of the dialogues or counsels of the Buddha to its attention. He repaired or enlarged the *stūpa* (*thuba*) of the Buddha Konākamana in the Nepalese Terai in Regnal Year 14 (*c.* 256 BC) (Nigali Sagar Pillar) and visited Luṁmini (Lumbini), the birth-place of Gautama Buddha, in Regnal Year 20 (*c.* 250 BC) (Rummindei Pillar: *Extract 3.3*).

In Pillar Edict VII, issued in Regnal Year 27 (*c.* 243 BC), the Buddhist *Saṁgha* is put first among the recipients of attention of the *dhaṁma-mahāmātas*. Finally, in the Schism Edict, found on pillars at Allahabad, Sarnath and Sanchi, issued after Regnal Year 26, Ashoka expresses his anxiety to maintain the unity of the *Saṁgha* and to secure the expulsion from it of all such monks and nuns as indulged in schism. The long note suffixed to this edict in the Sarnath inscription shows that the high officials (*mahāmātas*) were expected to spread the word of this

FIG. 2.2 Ashoka visits the *stūpa* of Rāmagrāma: story in *Ashokāvadāna* depicted in relief on South Gateway, *Stūpa* 1, Sanchi, first century BC.
(Reprod. and interpretation, J. Marshall and A. Faucher)

edict with a view apparently to getting it enforced. Ashoka thus, in effect, claimed to exercise a degree of authority over the affairs of the *Saṁgha*, but there are no grounds for supposing that he was ever the "head of the Buddhist church". The circumstances in which the Schism Edict was issued are referred to in the Sri Lankan tradition, which tells us that the *Saṁgha* was distracted by a large influx of undesirable elements wishing to share in Ashoka's lavish patronage of it (*Mahāvaṁsa*, V.228–230, 268–271). Another important measure where the inscriptions and Buddhist legends agree on the core, though little else, is the despatch of missionaries abroad by Ashoka, notably to Sri Lanka. But whereas Ashoka's Rock Edict XIII says that their purpose was to spread the message of *dhaṁma*, the Sri Lankan tradition implies that the object was the spread of Buddhism (*Mahāvaṁsa*, VII). In several other matters Ashokan inscriptions do not at all support the Buddhist legends even to a moderate degree, especially in respect of the fantastic claims made about the amount of his patronage to the *Saṁgha*. He is said, in both Sri Lankan and northern traditions, to have built 84,000 *ārāmas* or Buddhist monasteries. The Sri Lankan tradition also states that the third Buddhist Council was held in his reign. Of this, too, the edicts offer no explicit confirmation (but see below, Chapter 3.3).

We have also little reason to believe that through his growing commitment to Buddhism Ashoka at any time modified his **policy of**

tolerance towards other religious persuasions (*pāsaṁḍa*), as enunciated in Rock Edict XII (*Extract 2.4*). In what is his last major edict, Pillar Edict VII, issued in Regnal Year 27 (*c.* 243 BC), he repeats his assertion of goodwill for "all sects", and specifically mentions the attention paid not only to the *Saṁgha*, but also to the Brahmans, Ājīvikas and Jains (*Extract 2.7 [C]*). Even during his pilgrimage to the Buddhist holy of holies, the Bo-tree, in his Regnal Year 10, he did not forget to visit and offer gifts to Brahmans, as we have just seen. The case of the Ājīvikas is of particular interest, since in the Buddhist tradition there is fierce hostility towards this sect. Yet, Ashoka dedicated two and possibly three caves in hills near Gaya to them, so well cut that these deserve a place among the monuments left behind by him (see Chapter 3.5). Two of these were gifted in Regnal Year 12 (*c.* 258 BC) and the third in Regnal Year 19 (*c.* 251 BC), in each case long after Ashoka's 'conversion' to Buddhism had taken place.

One notable aspect of Ashoka's 'exertion' in pursuit of *dhaṁma* was its **propagation**. Writing being now in use, the written means are especially mentioned: the people could read the *dhaṁma* edicts as they were inscribed on rocks, stone blocks and stone pillars (Minor Rock Edict I, Pillar Edict VII). The large number of surviving inscriptions that carry his edicts is testimony enough that these were extensively inscribed on stone at places where people were likely to assemble or pass by. From Regnal Year 20 (*c.* 250 BC) onwards, inscriptions in Prākrit are only found on Ashoka's splendid pillars (with the single exception of a Brāhmī rock fragment from Buner, North Western Frontier Province), and their number is naturally much smaller than that of the rock inscriptions. It is possible to suppose that the enthusiasm for displaying the edicts at sundry places waned in course of time, and the inscribed word began to be restricted to the more respectable space of pillar surfaces.

Stone was naturally not the only medium of writing at the time. Nearchus tells us of the practice of writing on cloth; and palm-leaves too were probably used to convey Ashokan edicts to far-off places for scribes or engravers to copy on stone. Many variations in different versions of the same edicts can be best explained by envisaging the miswriting of certain letters of the alphabet in the originals on cloth or palm-leaves. Such written texts were probably also necessary for the spread of *dhaṁma* by oral means, since officials deputed on such missions had to have texts to read out from. In the two Separate Rock Edicts, instruction is expressly given that the edicts were to be read out on the four full-moon nights of each of the three seasons and on the nights of the *tisa* (*tiṣhya*) asterism, which were auspicious occasions, presumably, when people gathered. But the edicts were also to be read out in the intervals even if there was only a single person present. In Rock Edict III, Ashoka directs his officers, viz. *yutas*, *rajūkas* and *pādesikas*, to go forth once every five years for preaching the message of *dhaṁma*; in Rock Edict V (*Extract 2.3*), the *dhaṁma-mahāmātas*, their office created in Regnal Year 13 (*c*. 257 BC), are enjoined to preach *dhaṁma* as part of their duty. In Pillar Edict VII (*Extract 2.7*), of Regnal Year 27 (*c*. 243 BC), Ashoka requires his officials (*purisā*) and *rajūkas* to instruct the people in *dhaṁma*, a procedure conceived to be mainly oral, since it is treated as distinct from the recording of his edicts on stone. One should assume that such oral dissemination was expected to take place in the local spoken languages, but this matter is nowhere actually touched upon in the edicts.

Both oral and written means are likely to have been employed also by *dūtas* or envoys sent to such territories outside the Empire as the dominions of Antiochus and other Macedonian rulers, the south Indian principalities and Taṁbapaṁnī (Sri Lanka). These missions are mentioned in Rock Edict XIII (*Extract 1.4*), but their despatch is also implied in Rock Edict II (*Extract 2.2*), so that these must have been despatched in or before Regnal Year 12 (*c*. 258 BC) and so were possibly another manifestation of the early enthusiasm for *dhaṁma* propagation. No references to such missions occur in the Pillar Edicts of Regnal Years 26 and 27 (*c*. 244–243 BC). Now, with inscriptions of Ashoka in Greek and Aramaic being found in Afghanistan, it is possible to suppose that his envoys to Hellenistic West Asia and beyond were armed with missives in both these languages. While Ashoka's despatch of missions to Sri Lanka had lasting effect and entered Sri Lanka's later annals as a major event of its past, his envoys to the Hellenistic states have gone unmentioned in Greek texts, in contrast to the surviving reference to Bindusāra's envoys to Antiochus I.

The *dhaṁma* propagated by Ashoka primarily concerned individual conduct. But the king himself, with all his authority, was also an individual; and it is a significant aspect of Ashoka's effort in the cause of *dhaṁma* that he held himself as much bound by it as his subjects. In Rock Edict VI (*Extract 2.5*), he declares that, unlike former rulers who did not care to concern themselves with state affairs (*aṭhakaṁma*) when enjoying their hours of pleasure, he had decreed that he could be reached any time in any place for work concerning the people's welfare. As for compassion for animals, he confesses in Rock Edict I that "many hundred thousands of animals" (surely, an exaggeration) used to be daily slaughtered for food in his kitchen; and he claims that he had brought the number down to two peacocks and one deer a day, and promises that their slaughter too would stop.

Beyond his own personal commitment to the kind of conduct required by *dhaṁma*, Ashoka touches on the measures that the state had to take in order to put into effect the message of compassion that *dhaṁma* enjoined. Of great interest here is the material form that he gave to what, in his Rock Edict VI, he calls the "welfare of all people" (*savalokahita*). In our *Extracts 2.2* and *2.7 [B]*, we give translations of his Rock Edict II (*c.* 258 BC) and a passage from Pillar Edict VII (*c.* 243 BC), where these material measures of **public welfare** are specified. These measures essentially consisted of medical assistance and provision of relief and comfort for people and cattle on the roads.

Medical assistance itself was conceived to be of two kinds. First, treatment (*chikisā*) was to be provided to both human beings and cattle. One can suppose that physicians and cattle experts (primitive veterinarians) were employed at various places for this purpose. Second, medicinal herbs (*osadhāni*), for human beings and for cattle, were to be supplied, and also planted, wherever they were not found. So also were roots and fruits, medically deemed beneficial, to be provided. The provision of such assistance to various localities might have done much for diffusing the medical and pharmacological knowledge that (with all its limitations) had been assembled by the time.

On the roads (*maga*), shade was sought to be provided by the planting of trees, especially the banyan tree. Mango-groves were also planted. Wells were dug to furnish water for human beings and cattle, and the distance at which they were spaced is said to be half a *kosa* (modern Hindi *kos*). The exact distance that half a *kosa* then represented is not known, but is hardly likely to have been more than two or three kilometres. Resting places (*niṁsidhiyā*) were established, possibly at day-journey distances. These were probably shaded platforms, rather than inns or serais. Another traditional object of meritorious work also makes its appearance: the *āpānāni* or drinking-water stations, where, as in recent times, water in pots used to be kept for being given to the thirsty, especially in summer. Ashoka claims that water was here provided for cattle as well.

We do not know the scale on which these measures were undertaken; yet, that these were envisioned as a duty of the state is an important fact. In Pillar Edict VII, Ashoka seems to suggest obliquely that earlier rulers too had undertaken similar works for the "happiness" of their subjects, and so in effect disclaims any innovation or originality here on his own part. He distinguishes his own effort by its motive: drawing people towards *dhaṁma*. For that very reason, too, we may expect that his own investment of resources in this effort was probably much larger than that of any of his predecessors.

Another kind of public works was represented by irrigation tanks. Built under Chandragupta, the Sudarshana lake at Girnar ('Girinagara') in Saurashtra (Gujarat) was provided with sluices or outlets (*praṇālī*) in its dam under Ashoka. These details come to us from Rudradāman's Junagarh rock inscription of AD 150. The sluices were meant presumably to release water for irrigation.

A major element of administration is **dispensation of justice**. While Ashoka says that all his subjects were his children (Separate Rock Edicts), he also recognized that "it is easy, indeed, to commit sin" (Rock Edict V: see *Extract 2.3*). If the sin consisted of violation of *dhaṁma*, it naturally involved offences against other persons. Ashoka understood that this must then call for punishment. In his Pillar Edict IV (*Extract 2.6*), he demands of his *rajūkas* that they should exercise equity (*samatā*) in both their judgements and awards of punishment. Up till now, a passage in this edict was interpreted to mean that upon capital punishment being given, a respite of three days was to be provided before the carrying out of the sentence, so as to enable the *rajūkas*, as judges, to be approached again, or to ensure that the person had time to make final meditations, undertake fast and give alms. K.R. Norman has suggested an entirely different interpretation, which we follow in our *Extract 2.6*. He shows that the crucial word *vadha* means not execution but beating. In Separate Rock Edict I, it is expressly mentioned that a person could be subjected to imprisonment and physical harm (*palikilesa*), and the latter could be the same as beating. The word *yota*, rendered 'respite' by others, Norman relates to Sanskrit *yautaka*, or gift, hence subsistence allowance. The sense, as he establishes it, is that after the physical punishment was given, a three-day maintenance was provided. This passage, then, shows that Ashoka was concerned about redeeming offenders after they had received their punishment, though it may be quite an exaggeration to describe it as "a system of after-prison care".

It may be noted that though this passage from Pillar Edict IV might not refer to capital punishment, Ashoka nowhere speaks of having abolished it. Indeed, in Rock Edict XIII (*Extract 1.4*), he appeals to the forest people not to so behave that they might have to be killed (*haṁñeyasu*).

But his own desire is made clear in Rock Edict XIII and Separate Rock Edict II, where he promises to pardon all whom he can pardon. In line with this policy of compassion, he elsewhere proclaims his wish to lighten punishments and release as many from prison as possible. In Rock Edict V he puts among the duties of the newly created *dhaṁma-mahāmātas*, the work of "caring for fettered prisoners, releasing them from fetters [and] setting them free", for such reasons as having dependants and children, or having been the victims of incantations (!) (*katābhikāra*), or being old (see *Extract 2.3*). In Pillar Edict V, Ashoka claims that by his Regnal Year 26 (*c*. 244 BC), he had ordered general acts of release of prisoners as many as twenty-five times.

The principle of compassion for living beings led to Ashoka's adopting a number of measures to prevent or restrict the **slaughter of animals** and their subjection to cruel acts. Some of these measures, as we shall see, were bound to affect adversely the livelihood and beliefs and rituals of certain classes of people. In Rock Edict I, probably of Regnal Year 12 (*c*. 258 BC), Ashoka refers to his earlier measure of reducing the daily slaughter of a huge number of animals in the palace kitchen to just that of three animals. The Kandahar bilingual edict of Regnal Year 10 (*c*. 260 BC) refers to this measure, and its Greek version specifically mentions that the king's huntsmen and fishermen thereafter abstained from their calling.

The second step came, possibly in *c.* 258 BC, with the decree (Rock Edict I) that no sacrificial offering of an animal for slaughter was henceforth to be made "here", presumably the capital, Pāṭaliputra. No festive gathering (*samāja*), in which such rites apparently took place, was to be held, though other gatherings were permitted. It is difficult to escape the impression that what Ashoka was forbidding was the grand Vedic sacrifices accompanied by the slaughter of large numbers of animals, which had been denounced so strongly by the Buddha, as quoted in the canonical texts.

A mutilated slab inscription found at Deotek, southeast of Nagpur (Maharashtra), seems to contain orders of a governor or commandant (*sāmi*) to officials (*amachā*) at Chikambari (Deotek) to prevent capture and slaughter (of animals), any further details being lost. The date 14 (being presumably Ashoka's Regnal Year, and so = *c.* 256 BC) is preserved. This broken text may be set by the side of the two roadside Aramaic inscriptions found in Laghman (Afghanistan), where it is stated that in Regnal Year 16 (*c.* 254 BC) Ashoka threw out of the prosperous ranks of the populace those who lived by hunting and fishing. These inscriptions help provide the context for the warning tones that Ashoka had adopted towards the people of the forests (*aṭavi*) in his Rock Edict XIII, issued a little earlier: since the forest tribes subsisted mainly by hunting, they, by their very means of livelihood, deserved censure.

In his Pillar Edict V, of Regnal Year 26 (*c.* 244 BC), Ashoka set out certain restrictions on the killing of animals. Here, an obvious distinction is made between domesticated animals slaughtered for food in rural and urban communities, and those that might have been caught for food or for their skin by the lowlier, 'gathering' communities of the forests. The former are plainly in Ashoka's mind when he decrees that no quadruped should be killed unless it "enters into consumption (*paṭibhogaṁ*) or is eaten". Among those whose killing was thus permitted, it was laid down that the females of goat, sheep and pig, when with young or in milk, were not to be slaughtered, nor their young until six months old. Curiously, there is no mention of any ban laid on the slaughter of ox and buffalo, unless it is assumed that these are covered by the ban on killing animals that are not eaten.

Acts that imposed suffering of some sort on domestic animals were also put under restraint. Cocks were not to be caponed at all, and on certain specific days, bulls, and males of goat, sheep and pig, were not to be castrated. Nor, on certain days, were horses and bullocks to be branded. These measures obviously applied to the settled communities.

The animals whose slaughter is absolutely prohibited are carefully listed, and the detailed examination of the list by Norman reveals that they consist of talking birds and three species of the pigeon/dove family; a number of water birds, including a species of bat; some aquatic animals; and some reptiles. The reason they are listed here seems only to be that these were consumed and eaten among forest tribes, though not among settled communities. Otherwise, the prohibition would have been a meaningless act. While the catching of fish was not generally prohibited, certain days were specified when they were not to be caught and sold. And, in the "elephant forests", no animals of any kind (including, presumably, wild ones such as deer and peacocks that were eaten earlier by Ashoka himself) were to be killed.

Another sentence reflects the effort to fetter the forest tribes further: "The forest should not be burnt without purpose or for causing harm (to animals)." Such a measure seems designed to prevent the practice of forest-burning to smoke out animals sought for their meat or skin; it could also have been directed against the slash-and-burn ('jhum') practices of the forest's primitive agriculturists.

In order to carry out the *dhaṁma* project on which he had embarked, Ashoka had necessarily to carry out a considerable amount of **administrative reform**. In his edicts he tries visibly to breathe a humanitarian spirit into Mauryan administration. As noted above (2.2), he acknowledged (Rock Edict IV and Separate Edict II) that he owed a debt to the people, which he had to discharge by working for their happiness. In Separate Rock Edict I, he reminded his officials that they, on their part, were similarly placed in such debt to him, which required that they carry out his orders. This vision of a contractual relationship, by which the good of the people would be secured, was then supplemented by a sentimental one. In the two Separate Rock Edicts, he claims that all men were his children, obliging him to strive for their welfare just as for his own children. Of such general statements one has necessarily to be wary, but Ashoka's air of modesty and lack of vain-glory infuse an element of sincerity into his statements which too one finds hard to disregard.

Whether Ashoka was able to transmit the same spirit to his hard-headed bureaucrats is quite another matter. He himself thought, as Rock Edict V (*Extract 2.3*) tells us, that he needed to create, for the promotion of *dhaṁma*, a new cadre of officials, called *dhaṁma-mahāmātas*. This was done in Regnal Year 13 (*c.* 257 BC), the same edict says, and it goes on to specify the major duties assigned to these officials. The description of their work here is supplemented by references in Rock Edict XII (*Extract 2.4*) and Pillar Edict VII (*Extract 2.7*). As we would expect, their primary duty was to spread the message of *dhaṁma* among all classes of people and all religious sects throughout the Empire, including communities on its borders. This they presumably did chiefly by oral means. They were also to engage in humanitarian work, such as looking after the poor, the aged, etc., and caring for prisoners and getting them released. They were asked particularly to promote amity and mutual knowledge among all sects, and Pillar Edict VII expressly mentions their being assigned to the Buddhist *Saṁgha*, the Brahmans, Ājīvikas and Jains, to look after their needs. Much of this work required resources, and so the *dhaṁma-mahāmātas* were made the dispensers of imperial alms. Their posting in the establishments of queens, princes and princesses, mentioned in Rock Edict V, is explained by Pillar Edict VII, where it is stated that these officials also dispensed the charities or gifts (*dāna*) of the queens, royal female establishments, etc., "here [at Pāṭaliputra] and in the provinces". The Queen's Pillar Edict (Allahabad) does us some service by specifying what forms some of the charities of the imperial family took, viz. "mango-groves, retreats (*ārāma*), almshouses, etc."

It can be seen from the above enumeration of the *dhaṁma-mahāmātas*' duties that they hardly took over any functions of the established bureaucracy (for which see Chapter 1.6 above). This latter class of officials, therefore, also needed to be asked to turn a new leaf, put up the rock and pillar inscriptions, go on tour to propagate *dhaṁma*, introduce equity and clemency in the administration of justice, etc. They were all pressed, with what degree of success we today just cannot judge, to join in the pursuit of *dhaṁmavijaya*, 'the *dhaṁma* conquest'.

In Rock Edict XIII (*Extract 1.4*), *dhaṁmavijaya* is counterposed to simple *vijaya* or territorial conquest, or to conquest by arms. This brings us to a consideration of the place **the army** occupied in Ashoka's scheme of things. It is characteristic of Ashoka's use of the term *dhaṁma* in a sense different from what it meant in the Brahmanical tradition, that his *dhaṁmavijaya* has nothing in common with the act of the 'righteous conqueror' (*dharmavijayī*), as described in the *Arthashāstra*, XII.1.11, who, upon victory, is satisfied with the submission of the defeated opponent without seizing the land and goods of the latter. Ashoka's *dhaṁmavijaya*, on the other hand, means victory or success in the moral world. Yet, clearly, the principle of *dhaṁmavijaya* had its implications for imperial policy, which Ashoka spells out in Rock Edict XIII. There should be no new territorial conquest, he says; conquest by arms should be abjured by his descendants. Yet, with an element of realism, he does not make the ban absolute. Should his successors still decide to undertake a new conquest by arms, let it be achieved, he urges, "with mildness and light punishments". These are hardly the words of a ruler who was leaving for his successors no army to pursue their political ambitions. The singling out of the *aṁta-mahāmātas*, the officials on the borders, for the last words of exhortation in Pillar Edict I, by itself shows that Ashoka retained special concern for the control of the border territories. There is no sanction for so reading the last sentence of this edict as to imply that Ashoka wanted the officials to protect the borders by means of *dhaṁma* alone.

Rock Edict XIII makes it clear that it was not also Ashoka's intention to weaken the grasp of imperial power within the Empire. He wished to pardon all who could be pardoned, and wished that the apparently defiant people of the forest were informed of his remorse over the slaughter in Kalinga. But, at the same time, they were also to be told of his "might" (*pabhāva*) so that they might not be slain. In Separate Rock Edict II, practically similar sentiments are expressed towards the unsubdued border-people (*aṁta-avijita*). Military power was thus retained as a means in reserve if the policy of pacification by persuasion failed. We may recall that in a very late edict, the Schism Edict (Sarnath version), Ashoka refers to *koṭavis̲h̲aya*, 'districts-with-forts'; and this, again, suggests that forts were maintained to keep various territories under subjection.

The relatively recent evidence of Ashoka's Greek and Aramaic inscriptions has shown that Ashoka remained militarily powerful enough to keep control over a very large part of Afghanistan. The Aramaic Kandahar bazaar inscription corresponds to a portion of Pillar Edict VII, and so attests to Ashoka's control in the area continuing till at least down to his Regnal Year 27 (*c*. 243 BC). A Brāhmī boulder-slab from Buner carrying a portion of Pillar Edict VI is similarly evidence of Ashoka's writ running in the northern part of the North Western Frontier Province until at least Regnal Year 26 (*c*. 244 BC). Control over such difficult and distant areas could not have been exercised without the continued presence of Mauryan armed power.

It is just possible, though, that a retreat occurred in the Deccan. This is because no Ashokan inscription has been found south of the Narmada after the series of the Fourteen Rock Edicts, the two Separate Edicts and the Deotek inscription, which means that there is no certain proof of Mauryan control surviving in the area after *c*. 256 BC. Yet, the fragmentary Amaravati pillar inscription, if it carries an edict of Ashoka, would make it unlikely for Mauryan power to have retreated from coastal Andhra before *c*. 250 BC, which is the earliest date we have for any Brāhmī pillar inscription of Ashoka.

The belief among many historians that Ashoka's personal dedication to *dhaṁma* led to a neglect of the military power and so hastened the decay of the Empire is thus, at best, speculative, and is certainly not provable on the evidence we have.

According to the Purāṇas (with all the texts in agreement – *Extract 1.1*), Ashoka died after a reign of thirty-six years, that is, in *c*. 234 BC. The Sri Lankan Buddhist chronicles *Dīpavaṁsa* and *Mahāvaṁsa* give him a reign of thirty-seven years, and if they have their dates set in the current years, as the *Mahāvaṁsa* passage (XX.1–6) definitely implies, the Christian-era year of Ashoka's death would remain the same, *c*. 234 BC.

It is time now for considering the extent of **Ashoka's achievement**. Ashoka's own assessment in Pillar Edict II (*c*. 244 BC) is both general and generous, as he speaks of the great favours he had rendered to both human beings and animals. But, surely, the short edict is a declaration of satisfaction with what had been achieved, rather than a display of "megalomania" or "growing self-adulation". That the latter is too harsh a judgment is shown by Pillar Edict VII (*Extract 2.7*), the longest, but also, keeping in view its logical scheme, probably the best framed of Ashoka's edicts. Issued in Regnal Year 27 (*c.* 243 BC), Ashoka here tells us how he had issued edicts for the preaching of *dhaṁma*; carried out works of public welfare; looked after all the religious sects; arranged for distribution of alms and charities; and promoted *dhaṁma* by both regulation (*niyama*) and persuasion (*nijhati*). He acknowledges that regulations, such as the one prohibiting the killing of certain animals (which he expressly offers as an illustration), were of "small account", compared to persuasion. He was thus astute enough to realize that the larger ends he was aiming at could not be secured by simple administrative fiat. His vast effort to persuade, both by written word and word of mouth, could itself be deemed an enormous achievement, in so closely anticipating the methods adopted by propagators of modern causes.

How much did this effort succeed in altering the outlook of Ashoka's contemporaries? Ashoka is silent over what both the Sri Lankan and Mahāyānist traditions regard as his greatest achievement: the spread of Buddhism. We shall consider the question in Chapter 3.3. Here, it would be sufficient to anticipate the conclusion reached there, and to say that, from being just one of the barely tolerated non-Brahmanical sects, Buddhism under Ashoka became the religion chiefly patronized (see how the Buddhist *Saṁgha* is placed first, above the Brahmans and the rest, in Pillar Edict VII: *Extract 2.7*). For the next six hundred years or so, the gifts it received from rulers and the common people (as recorded in inscriptions), and the monuments it built, are evidence of the dominant status it now acquired. Ashoka's patronage undoubtedly played the role of a catalyst in this religious revolution.

While the ascendancy of Buddhism can be established from historical evidence, the social and cultural impact of Ashoka's *dhaṁma* is less easy to determine. He sidesteps the issue of caste and shows himself particularly solicitous towards the lower classes, including "slaves and servants" (see 2.2 above). At the same time, his orders are directed against the practices of the forest peoples, whose number at the time must have been proportionately quite large. It is, however, legitimate to argue that, in general, Ashokan ethics represented a counter-current to the evolving regime of the caste system (for which see Chapter 3.2 below). Such an orientation accords well with the elements of universality in Ashoka's approach, characteristically brought out by his friendly references to the Yonas (Greeks) within his Empire, and to Yona rulers outside. He did not open India to Iranian and Greek influences, for Achaemenid intrusions and Alexander's invasion had forced the opening earlier; but he certainly greatly enlarged the opening. This is reflected also in the art that he patronized (below, Chapter 3.5), a sphere in which he is so important because it is with him that the history of Indian art really begins. Ashoka's achievements were, then, really much greater than he himself sets out for us in his Pillar Edict VII. He remains, without any need for qualification, one of the towering figures of Indian history.

2.4 Ashoka's Successors and the End of the Mauryan Empire

Our knowledge of Ashoka's family as gleaned from his edicts is naturally limited. In Chapter 1.6 we have seen how the edicts indicate that *kumāras* or princes were posted at Ujjain, Taxila and Tosali (Orissa), and an *ayaputa* ('the lord's son') at Suvaṁṇagiri (south India). Only one, *kumāra* Saṁva, is named (Pangaruria inscription). But the relationships of these princes with Ashoka remain unknown, and all these references belong to the Regnal Years 10–13, or *c.* 260–257 BC. In his Rock Edicts VI (*Extract 2.5*) and XIII (*Extract 1.4*), he refers to his "sons and grandsons" as his future successors; but in Rock Edict V (*Extract 2.3*) proclaiming his appointment of *dhaṁma-mahāmātas* in Regnal Year 13 (*c.* 257 BC), he mentions their posting to only his own female establishments (*orodhana*) and those of his brothers, sisters and other relatives. Presumably, by this year his sons were still too young to have married and so to have their separate households. In his Pillar Edict VII (*Extract 2.7*), issued in Regnal Year 27 (*c.* 243 BC), he speaks of the gifts of "my queens (*devi*), of all my female establishments", and those of his "sons (*dāraka*) as well as those of princes born of queens (*devikumāra*)". His brothers and sisters are no longer mentioned, and had, perhaps, by now suffered in importance. On the other hand, clearly enough, his queens and his sons had come to have their establishments separate from his own *orodhana*, which was home presumably to his lesser consorts and other women of his household.

A confirmation of this situation comes from the so-called "Queen's Edict". To judge from its position on the Allahabad Pillar, it was probably inscribed there after the engraving of Pillar Edicts I–VI, issued in Regnal Year 26 (*c.* 244 BC). This edict refers to the gifts of "the Second Queen (*dutiya devi*) Kāluvākī (Kāruvākī), mother of Tīvala (Tīvara)", made by her in the form of mango-groves, retreats, almshouses, etc., which Ashoka desired, at her request, to be so recognized by "the *mahāmātas* everywhere". It is doubtful if anything greatly political is to be read into this edict. Kāluvākī is styled as the Second Queen, and so must have been lower in status to the First Queen, whose name remains unknown to us. There are no grounds at all for seeing in Kāruvākī the ambitious and vengeful Tissarakkhā, Ashoka's young, premier queen of later days, portrayed for us in the Buddhist tradition.

This brings us again to the problem of the amount of credence to be given to the traditional Buddhist accounts, late in time and often full of fable and fantasy. Of Tissarakkhā (Ti<u>sh</u>yarak<u>sh</u>itā), it can at least be said that she is mentioned in both the Sri Lankan *Mahāvaṁsa*, XII.3–6 (though not in the earlier *Dīpavaṁsa*) and the Mahāyānist *Divyāvadāna*; so the lore about her and her animosity to the sacred Bo-tree had early origins. The tale of her enmity to Ashoka's son, Kunāla, is confined to the *Divyāvadāna*, but Kunāla appears in all the Purāṇic lists as Ashoka's son and immediate successor; and he too is, therefore, likely to be a historical figure. He might even have been the viceroy of Taxila during his father's lifetime, as the *Divyāvadāna* alleges. Some credence may also be given to the statements in the same work that Ashoka's excessive gifts to the Buddhist order tended to empty the treasury. The ministers, we are told, at last appealed to the crown-prince, Saṁpadi or Saṁpati, son of Kunāla, who forbade further inroads on the treasury. Ashoka was thus left powerless in his last days, though he continued to be acknowledged as sovereign till his death (*c.* 234 BC). Saṁprati is remembered as a ruler of Ujjain and as a great patron of Jainism in Jain tradition (recorded by Hemachandra, twelfth century). In 'Version A' of the Purāṇic lists (our *Extract 1.1*), he is listed among the successors of Ashoka, though not as a son of Kunāla but as a son of Dasharatha, apparently a great-grandson of Ashoka.

Dasharatha brings us back to firmer history, because he has left for us from his year of accession short inscriptions in three caves of the Nagarjuni hills in south Bihar, dedicated to the use of the Ājīvikas. He is there rather modestly styled "Dashalatha Devānaṁpiya". The reign periods assigned to the various Mauryan rulers in Version A of the Purāṇic lists far exceed the total period assigned by both versions to the Mauryan dynasty, so we cannot really fix the date of Dasharatha's accession, though that event must have occurred well before *c*. 211 BC (the date if we simply deduct the reign periods of Ashoka's successors preceding Dasharatha from the year of Ashoka's death, *c*. 234 BC). The language and script of Dasharatha's inscriptions also suggest a close proximity in time to Ashoka.

The divergences in the lists of Ashoka's successors given in the two sets of Purāṇic texts and the *Divyāvadāna* may be explained by the emergence of rival Mauryan princes in different regions, leading to the existence of parallel lines of Mauryan rulers. The Purāṇic Version A apparently traces the main or Magadha line, since it contains the name of Dasharatha, and his cave inscriptions establish the existence of his rule in Magadha.

The northwest seems to have broken away after Ashoka's death. The *Rājataraṅgiṇī*, the celebrated history of Kashmir composed by Kalhaṇa around the mid-twelfth century AD, tells us (I.101–152) that Ashoka, a votary of Buddhism, who "reigned over the earth", was succeeded by his son Jalauka, who turned out to be a very powerful ruler of Kashmir, and a devotee of Lord Shiva. If true, and had Kashmir really been previously within the Mauryan Empire, this suggests the secession of that province under a Mauryan prince. But the tradition is late, and Jalauka is not otherwise heard of.

Other evidence of the secession of the northwest comes from Greek sources and is stronger. When, in his Rock Edicts II and XIII, Ashoka spoke of the Seleucid ruler Antiochus II (261–247 BC), he regarded him as a neighbour. But, about 255 BC, the Macedonians or Greeks in Bactria (north Afghanistan) established their independence under Diodotus. Further west, Parthia (northern Iran) marked its independence by instituting the Parthian era of 248–247 BC. The latter event decisively blocked the access of the Seleucids to parts bordering upon Mauryan possessions in Afghanistan. The Greek geographer

Eratosthenes visited eastern Iran and northwestern India at about this time or a little later, but there is nothing about the political situation of the region in such passages of his text as have come down to us through the works of later writers. We learn otherwise that an attempt of Seleucus II (247–226 BC) to recover Parthia towards the close of his reign proved abortive. However, his successor, Antiochus III ('the Great') (223–187 BC), undertook a determined campaign to restore Seleucid authority in the east. In *c.* 210–209 BC, he forced the Parthian ruler Arsaces to accept the position of a vassal; and then, marching through Aria (western Afghanistan), in a two-year-long war (208–206 BC), he similarly compelled the Bactrian king Euthydemus to accept a subordinate position. Now, *c.* 206 BC, he turned towards India.

In a fragment of the universal history by a near-contemporary Greek historian, Polybius (XI.34), we are told that Antiochus crossed the Hindukush ('Caucasus') Mountains and, presumably, near Kabul, "renewed his friendship with Sophagasenus, the king of the Indians". No ruler of the name Subhāgasena (the presumed Sanskrit form of the name) occurs on any of the traditional lists of Mauryan rulers; and we must conclude that northwestern India had by now passed into the hands of either a parallel line of Mauryan princes or an independent dynasty. According to Polybius, Antiochus received many elephants from Sophagasenus so as to have 150 altogether (he had obtained some from Euthydemus). He also obtained an unspecified amount of treasure. Antiochus then marched through Arachosia (Kandahar), crossed the Erymanthus (Helmand) river and passed through Drangene (Zarang = Seistan), on his way to Iran (*c.* 205 BC). His passage through Arachosia suggests that Kandahar (the site of Ashokan inscriptions) was now reclaimed by the Seleucids.

Since northwestern India was no longer a part of the Empire, these events on its erstwhile borders were probably no longer of any concern to the Mauryan court at Pāṭaliputra. The Purāṇic lists agree in having the same names (with minor variants) for the last three Mauryan rulers, who are assigned the same reign periods (see *Extract 1.1*). The last ruler, Brihadratha, after a reign of seven years, is said to have been overthrown by his commander (*senānī*), Pu<u>sh</u>yamitra, the founder of the Shuṅga dynasty. Since the Purāṇic accounts also agree that the Mauryas ruled for 137 years, this event can be placed in *c.* 185 BC.

It is natural to seek the **causes** for the rapid splintering and, then, the end of the Mauryan Empire within fifty years of Ashoka's death. We must recognize that our knowledge of these fifty years is so meagre that even speculation has its limits. A fairly common tendency has been to put the blame on Ashoka's neglect of military power under the influence of his pacifist principles. We have seen above (2.3) that there is no tangible evidence of such neglect; and so far as we can judge, Ashoka maintained intact the northwestern frontiers (militarily the most vulnerable area) till late in his reign.

Another, and equally nebulous, is the suggestion that a strong Brahmanical reaction set in against Ashoka's pro-Buddhist policies, and swept away the Mauryan Empire. There is, however, no proof that Brahmans were persecuted or ill-treated by Ashoka. In his last major Pillar Edict VII (Regnal Year 27: *c.* 243 BC), he continues to speak of gifts to Brahmans along with the *samanas*. In any case, none of Ashoka's successors has left any edicts like his (except for Dasharatha's three cave-gift inscriptions), so that none seems to have been concerned to continue his *dhaṁma* project. There should have been left little grounds, accordingly, for any Brahman resentment. Moreover, had a Brahmanical 'restoration' taken place, say, under the Shuṅgas, who overthrew the Mauryas, we would have expected some word of approval for them in the Purāṇas; but such approval is entirely lacking. The Buddhist *Divyāvadāna* even holds Pu<u>sh</u>yamitra ('Pu<u>sh</u>pamitra') to be of the royal Mauryan line itself, though it does attribute to him some hostility towards Buddhism. We may remember that the *stūpa* complex at Bharhut (Satna district, Madhya Pradesh) was mainly built under "the sovereignty of the Shuṅgas". Nor did the regime that succeeded the Mauryas in coastal Andhra do anything to obstruct the enlargement of the Amaravati *stūpa* complex. Indeed, as far as physical remains are concerned, those of Buddhism continued easily to dominate over those of its rivals in post-Mauryan times, throughout most of India.

A more likely factor might have been rivalries in the imperial family, even if we disregard the Kunāla story in the *Divyāvadāna*. Ashoka's own edicts show princes (*kumāra*, *ayaputa*) serving as viceroys and governors. In Pillar Edict VII, we also get evidence of their having separate establishments and adequate resources to make gifts on their own. Such a situation could manifestly lead to individual princes obtaining power in particular regions and extending their influence through patronage; this, in turn, would prepare the ground for rival claims to the throne and an ultimate division of the Empire. Such conflicts could also have been brought about by the fact that the Mauryan bureaucracy had diverse ethnic and linguistic elements in it. We have seen, in Chapter 1.6, that there must have been a fairly large group of officials from the northwest, alongside the old Magadhan nobility. Tensions between such groups could grow once the imperial crown became the object of ambition of rival princes, or imperial authority became weaker for any other reason.

The process of disruption must also have been greatly aided by the factor of distance. Mauryan armies might have overcome this factor in the initial stages by superiority in arms and techniques of war, especially their use of cavalry and massed chariots, and possibly, also, of infantry formations and siege-engineering learnt from the Macedonians and Greeks (see Chapter 1.6). Such superiority would disappear once different segments of Mauryan armies themselves faced each other; or once local potentates too began to organize their armies on the same lines and attempted, on this basis, to break their bonds of vassalage. In such conditions, sufficient military superiority would no longer be available to the imperial authorities to outweigh the difficulties posed by distance.

Other factors could, in time, have reinforced local acceptance of secessions. An empire depends for the maintenance of its possession of distant provinces on its control of the routes, communications and transport. Generally, empires have, therefore, been good for trade. But the central power within a large empire tends to lack flexibility in accommodating its fiscal system to local features. Within a generation or two of their passing away, the Mauryas were remembered by the grammarian Patañjali (*Mahābhāṣhya*, V.3.99) (*c.* 150 BC) for "their greed for gold (or money, *hiraṇya*)". This might be a reflection on the severity of the tax burden they had imposed, though the context (sale of images of gods) does not necessarily imply this. Regional rulers might succeed better in obtaining a larger surplus through adjusting to local circumstances and so without causing as much distress. This could again be a reason why, during the later days of the Mauryan Empire, the sense of allegiance to a distant ruler might come under increasing strain, and local attempts at secession might win increasing acceptance.

The personal abilities of Mauryan rulers could also have had a role to play in their failure adequately to meet problems of the kind we have discussed above. But though this factor cannot be discounted, we must admit that we know almost nothing for certain about Ashoka's successors, and so any judgement on them as individuals must remain suspended.

2.5 South India and Sri Lanka

South India may be said to enter recorded history no earlier than the closing years of the fourth century BC, when Megasthenes wrote his account of India. Arrian (*Indica*, VIII) quotes him as saying that the divine hero Herakles (Hercules) had a daughter in India called Pandaia, whom he placed as queen over a strong kingdom, rich in its yield of sea-pearls. These pearls, added Megasthenes, were so much prized in India that these were worth three times their weight in refined gold. Here we have obviously the earliest reference to the Pāṇḍiya (Pāṇḍya) kingdom (with its later capital, Madurai), on whose coasts the Tuticorin pearl fisheries are located.

The next references to this kingdom and other south Indian principalities come from Ashokan inscriptions. In Rock Edict II, Ashoka speaks of his extending his medical assistance beyond his borders, among "the Choḍas, Paṁḍiyas, Satiyaputas, Keralaputas and Taṁbapaṁnī", the last being Sri Lanka. In Rock Edict XIII, he mentions his despatch of envoys to preach *dhaṁma* to the neighbouring kingdoms, among which he includes "Choḍas and Paṁḍiyas, as far as Taṁbapaṁnī". One may infer from this that the Choḍas (Cholas) and Paṁdiyas (Pāṇḍiyas) formed the two major independent kingdoms of south India, while the Satiyaputas and Keralaputas were of lesser importance, not thought deserving of mention again. The traditional territory of the Choḍas ('Choḷa' in Tamil) lay in the Kaveri delta, centred on the later city of Thanjavur. Incidentally, the plurals employed in the territorial names do not necessarily indicate (as also in the case of 'Kalingas': see Chapter 1.5) that the names are those of "tribes". Territories were commonly designated by making plurals of their names; the analogous development in Iranic languages can be seen in territorial names such as Mukrān, Kirmān, Khurāsān, Īrān, etc., where the ending

-*ān* denotes a plural. The use of the ending *-puto* ('sons') tacked on to 'Satiya' and 'Kerala' may, on the other hand, suggest dynastic states, the initial parts of the names representing those of supposed ancestors of the ruling families. The title *Satiyaputo* has, in fact, been found in a Tamil Brāhmī inscription of the first century AD at Jambai (Viluppuram district, Tamil Nadu), which not only helps to locate the region of the Satiyaputas (for long subject to speculation), but also confirms the identification of Satiyaputa with classical Tamil 'Atiyamāṇ'. Similarly, the Ashokan 'Keralaputa' survived in Tamil 'Chēramāṇ', the Cheras being originally located not in Kerala but in the Coimbatore district of Tamil Nadu (see *Map 2.5*).

Ashokan inscriptions are found at many places in Karnataka and southern Andhra, but all situated above the line of 14 degree of latitude North, that is, well to the north of Bangalore. Besides these inscriptions, there has been found at Amaravati, in coastal Andhra, a slab probably cut out of an Ashokan pillar (see 2.1 above). A number of other inscriptions are also found at Amaravati written in Prākrit with characters of Ashokan Brāhmī. These have, therefore, been assigned to the late Mauryan period or early second century BC. They are all associated with a Buddhist *stūpa*. Not far from here is Bhattiprolu, the site of Buddhist casket inscriptions, again, in Prākrit. In the Ashokan Brāhmī used here, the inherent vowel *-a* in consonants is eliminated. In this one can surely discern the influence of early Tamil or Dravidian orthography.

Logically, Bhattiprolu stands midway to the script of the earliest inscriptions found in Tamil Nadu. These, known as the 'Tamil Brāhmī' inscriptions, were deciphered and their meanings established after it was recognized that: (a) the Brāhmī consonants in Tamil Nadu have no inherent vowel *-a* assigned to them, just as at Bhattiprolu; (b) additional letters or characters have been provided to represent Tamil consonants *ḻ*, *ḷ*, *ṉ* and *ṟ*; and (c) though influenced by Ashokan Prākrit ('Dialect B'), the language is basically Tamil. The proximity to Ashokan Brāhmī makes it possible to assign the earliest set of the Tamil Brāhmī inscriptions to late Mauryan times and the second century BC. Tamil, thus, is the earliest Indian language, next only to Prākrit, to be represented in inscriptions.

The earliest set of Tamil Brāhmī inscriptions on rocks assign-

MAP 2.5 South India and Sri Lanka, *c.* 300–100 BC

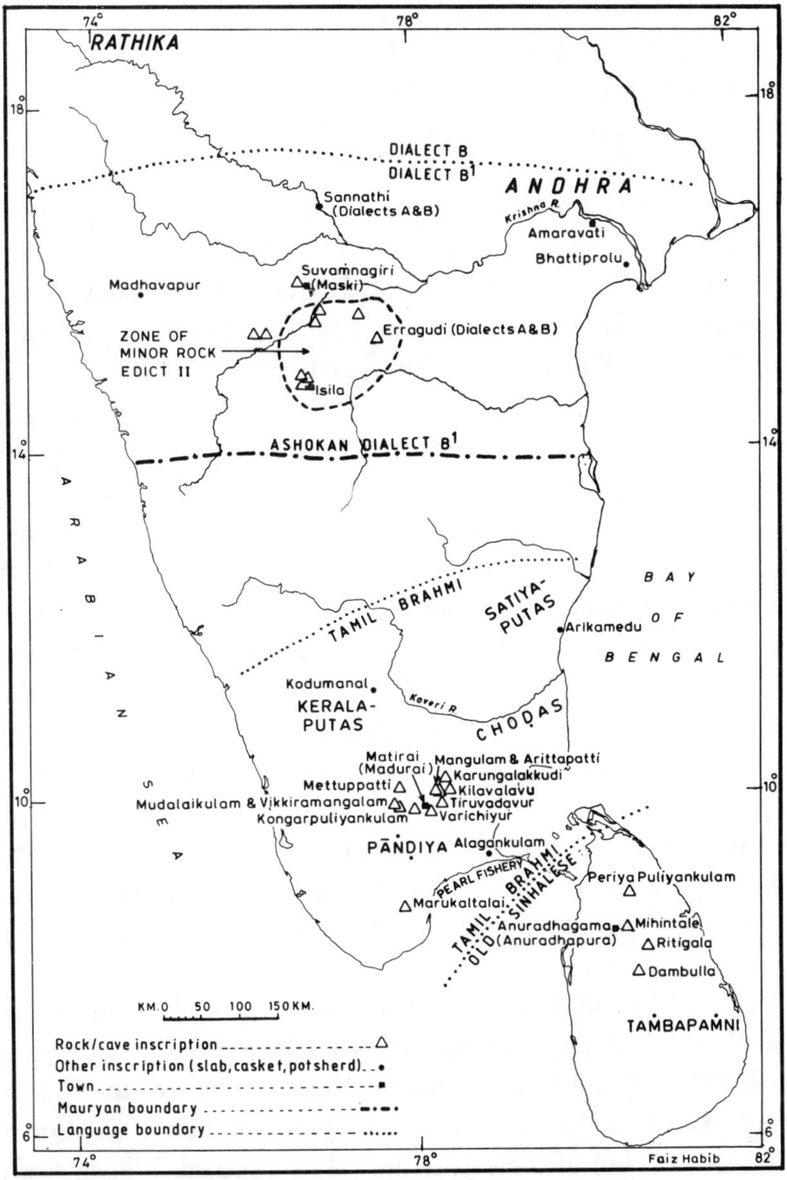

able to late Mauryan or immediately post-Mauryan times are concentrated in Madurai district, with only two sites outside of it: one just on its northern border, and the other much to the south, on the Tambaparni river not far from Tirunelveli. All the inscriptions are thus located in the traditional Pāṇḍiya (Tamil: Pāṇṭiya) country. On the other hand, potsherds bearing Tamil Brāhmī writing, dated to second century BC, have been found at sites much wider afield, viz. at Arikamedu (Pondicherry), Kodumanal (Erode district) and Alagankulam (near Ramesvaram).

The rock inscriptions generally commemorate donations, and are mainly concerned with caves and hermitages of Jain recluses. The favourable reception given to Jainism in the Pāṇḍiya kingdom offers an interesting parallel to the reception given to Buddhism in Sri Lanka, which we shall consider below. It may, however, be argued that the very name 'Paṁḍiya' (in Ashokan inscriptions) and the name of the kingdom's capital 'Matirai' (modern Madurai), recall the Pāṇḍavas and Mathura of the *Mahābhārata* lore, and imply an earlier influx of Brahmanical influence in the area. The Tamil Brāhmī inscriptions give us a limited amount of information on other matters as well. Neṭuñchaḻiyan could well be the name of a Pāṇḍiyan ruler that they have preserved. There is a reference to a "superintendent of pearls" (*kāḻitika*), which reminds us of the importance of the Tuticorin pearl fishery for the Pāṇḍiyan state and economy. The same official was also the head of a merchant-guild (*nikama*). The profession of 'mason' appears as a family style. Among the few place-names, 'Matirai' (Madurai) occurs more than once: it could already have been a town and the capital of the Pāṇḍiya kingdom. Of agricultural produce, the sole mention is that of rice, through a reference to a gift of a hundred measures of paddy (*nel*). An inscription refers to a village (*ūr*) collectively building a "large tank" (*pēr-ayam*), but whether for irrigation or for use by Jain recluses is not clear. The material is not sufficient to establish whether the caste system in any form had been planted in the Pāṇḍiyan kingdom by this time.

The traditional history of **Sri Lanka**, as embedded in the chronicles *Dīpavaṁsa* and *Mahāvaṁsa*, gives the pride of place to the arrival of Buddhism in the island through the assistance of the Indian emperor Ashoka in the third century BC. There is also in this tradition a myth-shrouded account of the earlier arrival of a prince, Vijaya, from an unlocated town Siṁhapura ('Lion's town') in north India. He, with his followers, founded a kingdom in the island about the time of the death of Gautama Buddha (early fifth century BC). This event has been held in modern times to explain the fact that the Sinhalese language of Sri Lanka is an Indo–Aryan language, although the traditional account also alleges that Vijaya, subsequent to his arrival, brought in a large number of women from the Pāṇḍiyan ('Pāṇḍu') kingdom with its capital at 'Madhura' (*Mahāvaṁsa*, VII.48–74) . Recent archaeological work at Anuradhapura ('Anurādhagāma', the traditional capital of the early Siṁhala kingdom) has unearthed evidence that tends to confirm an early Indo–Aryan presence in Sri Lanka. The evidence comes from early Brāhmī graffiti on potsherds from excavated strata assigned to *c*. 450–275 BC. The total amount of material is small, but the language has been definitely identified as Prākrit. Anuradhapura developed into a true town, presumably based on its position as the island's capital, the inhabited site reaching an area of nearly 70 hectares. Its prosperity, as also links to a large trade network, is indicated by finds of lapis lazuli imported from Afghanistan or Baluchistan, and of cornelian imported from Gujarat.

This evidence of writing and language raises interesting questions about Sri Lanka's cultural contacts with India. The Prākrit that prevailed in Sri Lanka, as revealed to us by inscriptions contemporaneous with late Ashokan years, does not seem to show much influence of Māgadhī, although it too has no compound consonants (e.g., *ksh*). But in omitting all long vowels and diphthongs (*ā*, *ai*, *au*, *ī*, *ū*), it has an unmistakable affinity with the Prākrit of northwestern India as carried by Ashoka's Kharoshṭhī inscriptions. The general avoidance of aspirated consonants (*bh*, *dh*, *gh*, etc., except *jh*) and the remarkable shift from *s* to *h*, are both features strongly indicative of Iranic influences. These facts suggest the possibility that: (a) the original Prākrit of Sri Lanka was derived from a northwestern Prākrit dialect; and (b) the Brāhmī script, as established in Sri Lanka in the fifth or fourth century BC, was created under the influence of Aramaic, the undifferentiated assimilation of short vowels in Aramaic being reflected in the assimilation of *-a* to every consonant sign in Brāhmī. As archaeological evidence now stands, with no trace of pre-Ashokan Brāhmī writing found anywhere except in Sri Lanka, the possibility cannot be excluded that Mauryan India received that script from Sri Lanka. The absence of long vowels in the two Mauryan-period Brāhmī inscriptions (outside the corpus of Ashokan edicts) at Piprahwa and Sohgaura assume an added significance, since this is a trait they share with Sri Lankan Brāhmī. Ashokan Brāhmī, then, can be seen essentially as the standardized form, based on the imported script but with certain additional characters and long-vowel signs incorporated in it soon afterwards (see below, Chapter 3.4).

It was probably in his Regnal Year 12 (*c*. 258 BC) that Ashoka sent a mission to 'Taṁbapaṁnī' (Sri Lanka) to preach his message of *dhaṁma* and carry medicinal assistance (Rock Edicts II and XIII: *Extracts 1.4* and *2.2*). According to the Sri Lankan tradition (*Dīpavaṁsa*, XI), the Sri Lankan ruler at that time should have been Muṭasiva, whose son Devānaṁpiya Tissa succeeded him in Ashoka's Regnal Year 17 (*c*. 253 BC). The title of *Devānaṁpiya* prefixed to Tissa's name already suggests the influence of the style of Mauryan royalty. Tissa, it is said, sent an embassy to Ashoka with presents, leading ultimately to the arrival in Sri Lanka of Ashoka's son Mahinda, a monk of high status. Later, Ashoka despatched certain relics of the Buddha and, then, a branch of the Bo-tree, escorted by his daughter, Saṁghamittā, a nun. Tissa's own conversion to Buddhism and his great ardour for it are described in great detail in the chronicles. The gift of a cave to the Buddhist *Saṁgha* by 'Devanapiya Maharajha Tisa' at Dambulla, and the gift of another cave by his son 'Devanapiya Tisa Abaya (?)' in Ritigala hills are recorded in characters so identical with Ashokan Brāhmī that the reigning king here must be the same as Devānaṁpiya Tissa of the chronicles. Upon his death after forty years of rule (*c*. 213 BC), his brother Uttiya is said to have reigned for ten years (*c*. 213–203 BC); and three donative inscriptions have survived from his reign. These attach the title 'Devanapiya' to him as well. Buddhism had by now secured firm patronage from royalty, which henceforth it rarely lost in Sri Lanka until colonial times.

TABLE 2.2 Chronology

	Ashoka's Regnal Year	*c.* BC
Ashoka's accession	–	270
Conquest of Kalinga (RE XIII)	8	262
Proceeds to Saṁbodhi (RE VIII); begins proclaiming *dhaṁma* (Kandahar bilingual); probable date of issue of Minor Rock Edicts	10	260
Sends missions to Antiochus II and other Greek rulers, and to south India and Sri Lanka (RE II and XIII) in or before	12	258
First set of Rock Edicts issued (RE III, IV and PE VI); gifts two caves to Ājīvikas in Barabar hills (cave inscriptions)	12	258
Appoints *dhaṁma-mahāmātas* (RE V)	13	257
Rock Edicts V–XIV, and Separate Rock Edicts I and II issued in or after	13	257
Enlarges Konākamana *stūpa* (Nigali Sagar PE); orders given against hunting (Deotek inscription)	14	256
'Expels' hunters and fishermen (Laghman Aramaic inscriptions)	16	254
Devānaṁpiya Tissa's accession as king of Sri Lanka (*Dīpavaṁsa*)	18	253
Excavation of third cave in Barabar hills (cave inscription)	19	251
Visits Luṁmini (Rummindei PE)	20	250
Pillar Edicts I–VI issued (PE I, IV–VI); 25 general amnesties of prisoners till this year (PE V)	26	244
Pillar Edict VII issued (PE VII)	27	243
Schism Edict and Queen's Edict, probably issued in or after	27	243
Ashoka dies (Purāṇas, *Mahāvaṁsa*)	36	234
Devānaṁpiya Tissa of Sri Lanka dies; succeeded by Uttiya (*Mahāvaṁsa*)		213
Dasharatha, Mauryan ruler: accession (Purāṇas), before		211
Antiochus III's expedition into Indian borderlands (Polybius)		206–205
Overthrow of Brihadratha, last Mauryan ruler, by Pu<u>sh</u>yamitra, founder of the Shuṅga dynasty (Purāṇas)		185

Abbreviations: PE = Pillar Edict(s); RE = Rock Edict(s).
Note: Ashoka is to be presumed, where subject is omitted.

EXTRACTS

Extract 2.1
The *Dhaṁma* Formulary

[A] Rock Edict XI (in or after Regnal Year 13)

King Devānaṁpiya Piyadasi declares thus: There is no such gift [as good] as the gift of *dhaṁma*, or friendship in *dhaṁma* or sharing in *dhaṁma* or kinship through *dhaṁma*. This [*dhaṁma*] comprises the following: decorous behaviour towards slaves and servants; [holding as] good, obedience to mother and father; [holding as] good, liberality (*dāna*) to friends, associates, and relatives, to Brahmans and *samanas*; [and holding as] good, non-killing of living beings. Concerning this, let a father, son, brother, husband, associate or friend, or even a neighbour, tell [one]: 'This is good, this should be done.' If one acts thus, this world is gained, and in the next, endless merit accrues by this gift of *dhaṁma*.

[B] Statement of Principles in Aramaic

(Kandahar Greek/Aramaic Bilingual Inscription: Aramaic Version)

Ten years having elapsed [since his anointment] our lord king Priyadarshi, the king (*malik*), became the institutor of truth (*qshyt*). Since then evil has diminished among all men; and he has caused adversity to disappear; and upon all earth there is peace and joy. Furthermore, there is this about food: For our lord, the king, few (animals) are killed, and, seeing this, all men have ceased [to kill animals], and such as catch living beings have been forbidden to do so. Similarly, those who were unrestrained [in their conduct] have ceased to be unrestrained. And [there prevails] obedience to one's mother and father and to elders (or, old people), as destiny has prescribed for everyone. And there is to be no Judgement [in the next world] for all men that are pious. This [piety] has been of benefit to all men and will continue to be beneficial.

(Translation based on renderings by G. Garbin/B.N. Mukherjee, A. Dupont-Sommer/J. Filiozat and J. Harmatta.)

Note: See also *Extract 2.7*, paragraph *[E]*.

Extract 2.2
Measures of Public Welfare

Rock Edict II (in or before Regnal Year 12)

Everywhere in the dominions of king Devānaṁpiya Piyadasi, and among neighbours such as the Choḍas [Cholas], Paṁḍiyas, Satiyaputas, Keralaputas, and Taṁbapaṁnī, the Greek king Aṁtiyoka [Antiochus], by name, and those who are the neighbouring kings of this Aṁtiyoka – everywhere, king Devānaṁpiya Piyadasi has had arrangements made for two kinds of medical treatment (*chikisā*): medical treatment for human beings and medical treatment for cattle (*pasu*). Medicinal herbs (*osadhāni*), good for human beings and good for cattle, have been caused to be supplied and planted wherever they are not found. Similarly, [medicinal] roots and fruits, have been caused to be supplied and planted wherever they are not found. On the roads (*maga*), trees have been caused to be planted and wells (*udupānāni*, var. *kūpa*) have been caused to be dug for the comfort of cattle and human beings.

Note: See also *Extract 2.7,* paragraph *[B].*

Extract 2.3
Appointment of *Dhaṁma-Mahāmātas*

Rock Edict V (Regnal Year 13)

King Devānaṁpiya Piyadasi declares thus: Doing good deeds (*kayāna*) is difficult. He who begins doing good deeds does something difficult. I have done many good deeds. If my sons or grandsons or my descendants coming after them, to the end of time, will follow this [conduct of mine] in the same manner, they will do well. But he who will neglect a part [of a good deed] will commit wrong. It is easy, indeed, to commit sin (*pāpa*). Throughout the long past, there were no *dhaṁma-mahāmātas*, by name. But, anointed thirteen years, I appointed *dhaṁma-mahāmātas.* Among all [religious] sects (*pāsaṁḍa*) they are occupied in the establishment of *dhaṁma* and the growth of *dhaṁma*, and for the welfare and happiness [var. happiness here] of those faithful to *dhaṁma*, among the Yonas, Kaṁbojas, Gaṁdhāras and Raṭhikas-Pitinikas, and other western borderers (*aparaṁta*). Among servants (*bhaṭa*) and masters (*aya*), the Brahmans and the wealthy (*ibhiya*), the poor and the aged, they are occupied for the welfare and happiness [var. happiness here] of those faithful to *dhaṁma*, releasing them from fetters. That is, they are occupied in caring for fettered prisoners, releasing them from fetters, [and] setting them free for the reason that such a one has dependants and children, or is victim of incantation or is old.

They are occupied everywhere among those faithful to *dhaṁma*, here [var. at Pāṭaliputa] and in outlying towns (*nagara*), in all my female establishments and those of my brothers and sisters and other relatives. The *dhaṁma-mahāmātas* are occupied in this dedication to *dhaṁma*, the establishment of *dhaṁma* and alms-giving, throughout my dominions [var. the earth]. For this end has this *dhaṁma*-edict (*dhaṁmalipi*) been written, that, [this] enduring for a long time, my children may act accordingly.

Note: In *bhaṭamayesu*, *aya* is taken to represent Sanskrit *ārya*, as in *ayaputa* in the Brahmagiri group texts of Minor Rock Edict I. In *baṁbhanibhiyesu*, the second part *ibhiya* is taken to mean the lowliest by D.D. Kosambi (*Indo–Iranian Journal*, VI, pp. 181–84), but *ibhya* in Sanskrit means wealthy, and *ibhiya* seems to be its Prākrit form.

Extract 2.4
Religious Coexistence

Rock Edict XII (in or after Regnal Year 13)

King Devānaṁpiya Piyadasi honours recluses (*pavajita*) and householders (*gahatha*) of all (religious) sects (*pāsaṁḍa*), with gifts and various means of honouring. The Devānaṁpiya, however, does not think of making gifts and honouring so much as that there may be growth of knowledge (*sāravaḍhi*) in all sects. The growth of knowledge is of many kinds. But its root is this, viz. restraint in speech, so that there may be no honouring [alone] of one's own sect and blaming of other sects, without reason, and it may be [always] moderate [even] when made on this or that [point], with reason. Thus other sects must [also] be honoured in every way. He who so acts secures the growth of his own sect and also benefits other sects. By doing otherwise one hurts one's own sect and injures other sects. He who honours his own sect and blames other sects, out of respect for one's own sect, and with a view to promoting one's own sect, in thus acting harms exceedingly his own sect. Therefore amity (*samavāya*) alone is excellent; and they should hear and follow each other's *dhaṁma* (doctrine). The Devānaṁpiya so desires that all sects should be rich in heard-knowledge (*bahusruta*), that is, well-informed, and be possessed of propitious beliefs. And those who are affiliated to different [sects] need to be told: The Devānaṁpiya does not think of making gifts and honouring so much as that there may be growth of knowledge in all sects. Many are occupied for this purpose: the *dhaṁma-mahāmātas*, the *mahāmātas* superintending women (*ithidhiyakha-mahāmāta*), overseers of public places ('cow-pens') (*vachabhūmika*) and other sets of officials. Such is the fruit of this that the growth of one's sect occurs as well as glory to *dhaṁma*.

Note: See also *Extract 2.7,* paragraph *[C].*

Extract 2.5
Ashoka and Conduct of Government

Rock Edict VI (in or after Regnal Year 13)

King Devānaṁpiya Piyadasi declares thus: For long past, formerly, it did not happen that all the time there should be work on affairs [of state] (*aṭhakaṁma*) and receiving of reports (*paṭivedana*). But I have done the following: All the time, whether I am at a meal, in the female apartments, in private chamber, in a public place (lit. 'cow-pen'), in the palanquin, in the garden, everywhere the reporters (*paṭivedaka*) should report to me about the affairs (*aṭha*) of the people (*jana*). Everywhere I attend to the people's affairs. When I give any oral orders regarding donation or instructions to be obeyed or when urgent matters are entrusted to the *mahāmātas*, [and] should, then, there be a dispute about it or deliberation arise in the *parisā* (council) [thereon], it should be immediately reported to me anywhere [I may be], at all times. Thus I have ordered. I am never satisfied with my exertion over the despatch of state business. I regard it as necessary for the welfare of all people (*savalokahita*). However, its root is exertion over the despatch of state business. Never is anything more important than the welfare of all people. Any exertion that I make is to discharge my debt to all living beings so that they obtain happiness here and gain heaven in the next world. It is for this purpose that this *dhaṁma*-edict (*dhaṁmalipi*) has been written so that this may endure for a long time and that my sons and grandsons and great-grandsons may exert themselves for the welfare of all people, for this is difficult [to achieve] without the utmost exertion.

Extract 2.6
Administration, Judgement and Punishment

Pillar Edict IV (Regnal Year 26)

King Devānaṁpiya Piyadasi declares thus: Anointed twenty-six years I had this *dhaṁma*-edict written. My *rajūkas* have been appointed over many hundred thousand living beings, among the people. Hence accusation (lit. complaint) and punishment has been left to them, so that the *rajūkas*, in tranquillity and without fear, may perform their important work and may confer gain and happiness on the people of the *janapadas* by treating them kindly. They will know of their joys and sorrows, they will exhort the people of the *janapadas* to be loyal to *dhaṁma*, so that they may gain here as well as in the hereafter. The *rajūkas* will be eager to serve me. My officials (*purisā*) who know of my wishes, they will obey them [too]. And these [officials] will exhort the *rajūkas* so that they are able to please me. Just as a child is made over to a clever nurse (*dhāti*), (with the thought) that 'the clever nurse will be able, in tranquillity, to bring up my child well', so my *rajūkas* have been appointed to bring gain and happiness to [the people of] the *janapadas*. That the *rajūkas* may, in tranquillity, without fear, and peaceably perform their important work, I have left the [work of] accusation (lit. complaint) and punishment to them. So it is to be desired that there be equity in judgement (*viyohāra-samatā*) and equity in award of punishment (*daṁḍasamatā*). And up to now [this has been] my [own] practice: To those persons who having been imprisoned, have completed their punishments, [or] have received their beatings (*patavadhānaṁ*), an allowance is given by me for three days [thereafter]. Their relatives are to make them meditate on a refuge for saving their [further] life. Being made to think, indeed, of death as the end, they will either make a gift connected with the other [world] or undertake a fast. My desire is that in the limited time [in this world] they may attain the other [world]. There is thus increase, among the people, of various ways of *dhaṁma*-conduct, self-control and alms-giving.

Note: The above translation takes into account K.R. Norman's emendations of previous interpretations.

Extract 2.7
A Proclamation of Achievement

Pillar Edict VII (Regnal Year 27)

[A] King Devānaṁpiya Piyadasi declares thus: For a long time past, kings had this wish, that somehow people may grow with growth in *dhaṁma*; but people did not grow proportionately with growth in *dhaṁma*. On this king Devānaṁpiya Piyadasi declares thus: The following occurred to me: For a long time past, kings had this wish, that somehow people may grow proportionately with growth in *dhaṁma*; yet people did not grow proportionately with growth in *dhaṁma*. How, then, could people be made to so conform? How could people grow proportionately with growth in *dhaṁma*?

How could I raise some [of them] with growth in *dhaṁma*? On this king Devānaṁpiya Piyadasi declares thus: The following occurred to me: I will cause *dhaṁma* proclamations to be preached, and instructions on *dhaṁma* decreed. Having heard these, the people obeying [them] will strongly grow with growth in *dhaṁma*. Hence for this purpose I have had *dhaṁma* proclamations preached and various instructions on *dhaṁma* decreed, so that the officials (*purisā*), who are set over many people, will instruct them in detail. The *rajūkas*, who are set over many hundred thousands of persons, even they are ordered thus and thus to instruct people in *dhaṁma*. Devānaṁpiya Piyadasi declared thus: Considering this matter, I have set up *dhaṁma*-pillars, appointed *dhaṁma-mahāmātas* and issued *dhaṁma* proclamations.

[B] King Devānaṁpiya Piyadasi declares thus: On the roads banyan trees were caused to be planted by me in order that they provide shade to cattle and men; and mango (*aṁbā*) groves were caused to be planted. At every half *kosa* wells were caused to be dug by me, and resting places (*niṁsidhiyā*) were caused to be established. Numerous drinking-water stations (*āpānāṇi*) were caused to be established by me at different places for the comfort of cattle and human beings. This comfort is [however] a small matter. By various means leading to happiness, have former kings and I made people happy. But this has been done by me with the intent [especially] that they should conform to the requirements of *dhaṁma*.

[C] Devānaṁpiya Piyadasi declares thus: My *dhaṁma-mahāmātas* are occupied with various beneficial affairs, viz. of recluses and householders. They are also occupied with all [religious] sects, that is, I have caused them to be occupied with the affairs of the *Saṁgha* [Buddhist order]; similarly, I have caused them to be occupied with the Brahmans [and] Ājīvikas; so too I have caused them to be occupied with the Nigaṁṭhas [Jains]. With various sects I have caused them to be occupied. Thus, according to different needs of each, the *mahāmātas* are differently [engaged]. [Indeed,] my *dhaṁma-mahāmātas* are engaged with these as well as other sects.

[D] King Devānaṁpiya Piyadasi declares thus: For this and other [business], many high officials are occupied with the distribution of gifts of mine, of the queens (*devi*), and of all my female establishements, in various ways among the different deserving recipients they are informed about, here [at Pāṭaliputra] and in the provinces (*disā*). I have also caused them to be occupied with the distribution of the gifts of my sons (*dāraka*), as well as those of princes born of queens (*devikumāra*) for deeds for *dhaṁma* and

conformity with *dhaṁma*. This, indeed, is a deed for *dhaṁma* and conformity with *dhaṁma*, that compassion, liberality, truthfulness, purity, mildness, and goodness should thus increase in the world.

[E] King Devānaṁpiya Piyadasi declares thus: Whatever good deeds have been done by me, the world has followed and conformed to it. Thereby have grown and will grow [the practices of] obedience to mother and father, obedience to elders (*guru*), rendering reverence to the aged, decorous behaviour towards Brahmans and *samanas*, the poor and the wretched, and even (*āva*) slaves and servants.

[F] King Devānaṁpiya Piyadasi declares thus: Among human beings this growth with the growth of *dhaṁma* has been accomplished by these two means: *dhaṁma* regulations (*niyama*) and persuasion (*nijhati*). Of these the *dhaṁma* regulations are of small account, persuasion much greater. *Dhaṁma* regulations are such as the one that such and such animals are not to be killed. There are many other *dhaṁma* regulations that have been issued by me. But by persuasion more human beings attain growth with the growth of *dhaṁma*, ceasing to cause harm to creatures and abstaining from slaughter of living things.

[G] Now, for this purpose this [edict] has been caused [to be written] that it may endure so long as my sons and great-grandsons [reign] and the moon and the sun [remain], so that [people] may conform to it. By thus conforming to it, there will be gain here and in the next [world]. Anointed twenty-seven years, this *dhaṁma*-edict has by me been caused to be written. About this, the Devānaṁpiya declares: This *dhaṁma*-edict shall be engraved wherever there is a stone-pillar or a stone slab, so that it may long endure.

Note 2.1
Epigraphy

As the word itself directly suggests, **Epigraphy** is concerned with the study of epigraphs or inscriptions. An *inscription* literally means an inscribed text, but in ordinary usage the texts so designated are those engraved on hard surface, such as that of stone, metal, brick, baked clay, pottery and wood. Such material survives long (except for wood), but necessarily carries only a limited amount of writing. The word 'inscription' is not generally applied to writing on soft material such as papyrus, palm-leaf, processed skin (parchment), cloth and paper, which can contain longer texts, books and volumes within smaller space, but, except under certain conditions of climate and soil, have shorter periods of survival. By convention, methods that have been developed to study this kind of writing are assigned not to Epigraphy, but to the realm of History proper, or to what is called archival research. The written material that has survived from ancient India in its original form consists almost entirely of writing on stone and metal, and so belongs properly to the field of Epigraphy.

Inscriptions have some sub-classes. *Graffiti* (plural of *graffito*, Italian for 'scratched') are scrawls or pieces of writing on walls, generally of an informal or casual kind. *Legends* are inscriptions put on coins, medals or seals. In the study of the legends on coins, which often give the names of issuing rulers, the area of Epigraphy coincides with that of *Numismatics*, which is the science that studies coins.

Epigraphy consists of a number of branches. The primary one is **Palaeography**, or the study of ancient scripts or modes of writing. As we have seen in *Indus Civilization, Note 2.1*, one can logically classify all writing as (a) ideographic (including pictographic), (b) syllabic, or (c) alphabetic. Ideally, an *alphabet* should be strictly phonetic, each consonant and vowel being represented by one distinct character or letter. But there are in practice no such perfect alphabets, the Brāhmī script being no exception. In Brāhmī, vowels suffixed to consonants are shown by certain forms of extensions of the characters. Yet, each character standing for a consonant without such vowel sign contains an inherent short vowel, *-a*, suffixed to it. Strictly, therefore, except for its initial vowel letters, the Brāhmī (as also its descendant Devanagari) may be held to be a syllabic script. But, at the same time, wherever a mark for a suffixed vowel other than *a* (viz. *ā, i, ī, u, ū*, etc.) was put on a character, the latter lost its syllabic character and represented just a consonant, the vowel being supplied by the mark. In view of this, the Brāhmī script may yet be treated as belonging to the category of alphabets.

Palaeography is broadly concerned with two tasks: first, *decipherment*; second, the study of evolution of scripts. In case of phonetic scripts, whether syllabic or alphabetic, the work of decipherment, in turn, involves two stages: (a) establishing the phonetic value of each character or letter, confronting such complexities as we have just discussed in the case of Brāhmī; and (b) establishing the meaning of the text once it has been read. In practice, the two stages are intertwined, the phonetic values of characters assigned being tested and often corrected by reference to probable words drawn from a language in which the text is likely to have been written. Of this, the story of the decipherment of Ashokan Brāhmī offers a good illustration. By modern times the script had been absolutely forgotten. Some early Brāhmī characters were recognized in 1836 by C. Lassen from the name of an Indo–Greek ruler Agathocles, given in both Greek and Brāhmī legends on a coin of his. Next year came the decisive break, with early Sanchi inscriptions being deciphered by James Prinsep (1799–1840), who had begun his studies of Ashokan inscriptions in 1834. Noting that two characters, the second with a dot, occurred repeatedly at the end of short, presumably donative inscriptions, he read the characters as *dānaṁ* (the dot taken, as in later Indian scripts, for the *anusvāra* sign), the word meaning 'gift' in Prākrit. With his earlier isolation of diacritical signs and tentative identifications of early Brāhmī characters such as *sa*, Prinsep now "became possessed of the whole alphabet", with which he successfully read the Ashokan edicts on the Delhi–Topra pillar, and then the Rock Edicts. By 1839, he had not only identified the Ashoka of the Buddhist tradition with the author of the edicts, but also largely correctly identified the Macedonian rulers named in Rock Edict XIII.

The edicts of Ashoka, once deciphered, played a pivotal role in the decipherment of Kharoshṭhī, the other contemporary script. Only a few Kharoshṭhī characters were known from bilingual Indo–Greek coins, with Prinsep again as the pioneer. But in 1846, Edwin Norris, by comparing the Brāhmī copies of the Rock Edicts of Ashoka with those inscribed at Shahbazgarhi in Kharoshṭhī, recovered practically the entire Kharoshṭhī alphabet.

If Ashoka had not issued his Rock Edicts in many copies, Kharoshṭhī might, indeed, have taken a very long time over its decipherment, since it has had no linear descendants known to us, except perhaps the one in which "the third" inscription at Dasht-i Nawur (in Afghanistan) of early Kushan times was written, and which has recently been deciphered by J. Harmatta. The case has been quite otherwise with Ashokan Brāhmī. All the fifteen Indian scripts, in which the value of the Indian currency note is given on its back, are descendents of Ashokan Brāhmī, except for Urdu and Kashmiri, which are written in the Arabic script. One can see how divergent the scripts appear, from Tamil to Devanagari (for Hindi), and, therefore, one may imagine how, over a long time, changes must have occurred in the parent script in each region, until this diversity of form has been achieved. (See *Table 2.3* for a comparison of Ashokan Brāhmī with modern Devanagari characters.) Without in any way modifying our appreciation of Prinsep's achievement, it can be legitimately argued that, unlike Kharoshṭhī, early Brāhmī would have been deciphered in the natural course as epigraphists worked back stage by stage from its varied contemporary descendants to the ancestral Brāhmī. Prinsep's work, however, not only greatly hastened the discovery, but also quickened decipherments of intermediary scripts by enabling his successors to work from two ends, namely, the parent script and its recent variant forms.

Palaeography studies such *evolution of forms* of characters in various scripts, this being, as we have mentioned above, its second major task. The study is important in itself, but it has also other advantages. As Palaeography discriminates between successive stages of a script's evolution, it can assign each style of a script to a particular period, by referring to dates that may be contained in inscriptions written in that style. Even when such a period cannot be established within very narrow limits, Palaeography can tell us which forms are primitive and so earlier, and which are 'evolved' and so later. We can establish, let us say, that Khāravela's Hathigumpha inscription in Orissa is later than Ashokan inscriptions, of which the period is well established. We can, therefore, say with some confidence that Khāravela cannot have been reigning before 200 BC, and possibly not even before 100 BC. Palaeography is thus an important tool for reconstructing ancient Indian chronology: it establishes the

Table 2.3

Roman	*Ashokan Brāhmī*	*Devanagari*	*Roman*	*Ashokan Brāhmī*	*Devanagari*
a	𑀅	अ	ma	𑀫	म
ba	𑀩	ब	na	𑀦	न
bha	𑀪	भ	ṇa	𑀡	ण
cha	𑀘	च	ña	𑀜	ञ
chha	𑀙	छ	o	𑀑	ओ
da	𑀤	द	pa	𑀧	प
dha	𑀥	ध	pha	𑀨	फ
ḍa	𑀟	ड	ra	𑀭	र
ḍha	𑀠	ढ	sa	𑀲	स
e	𑀏	ए	sha	𑀰	श
ga	𑀕	ग	sha	𑀱	ष
gha	𑀖	घ	ta	𑀢	त
ha	𑀳	ह	tha	𑀣	थ
i	𑀇	इ	ṭa	𑀝	ट
ja	𑀚	ज	ṭha	𑀞	ठ
jha	𑀛	झ	u	𑀉	उ
ka	𑀓	क	va	𑀯	व
kha	𑀔	ख	ya	𑀬	य
la	𑀮	ल			

By way of illustration, some of the forms the Brāhmī consonantal characters assumed to indicate changes of suffixed vowels are shown in the case of *da* below:

𑀤 *da* 𑀤𑀸 *dā* 𑀤𑁂 *de* 𑀤𑀺 *di* 𑀤𑀻 *dī* 𑀤𑁄 *do* 𑀤𑀼 *du*

sequence of styles of writing, and, then, the approximate period of each style by reference to dated inscriptions.

An allied but distinct field within Epigraphy is the study of the *linguistic and literary* aspects of the contents of the inscriptions. Beginning from Ashoka's time, inscriptions become a major source for our knowledge of Indian languages. Ashokan inscriptions tell us not only about the vocabulary and grammar of Ashokan Prākrit, but, by indicating its dialectal variations, they give us strong hints about certain features of the spoken or substrate languages in different regions at the time. The gradual increase in the popularity of Sanskrit in literary writing can be traced by recording its occurrences in inscriptions from Rudradāman's Junagarh inscription of AD 150 to Samudragupta's Allahabad inscription of the fourth century. Quotations from or imitations of verses or styles of well-known authors found in inscriptions can give us a bottom-line for the period the original authors lived in.

Inscriptions are also important in other ways. Our knowledge of Ashoka would have been quite wrong and inaccurate had Epigraphy not supplied us with a decipherment of Ashoka's inscriptions. And the Imperial Guptas, without inscriptions, would have remained a closed book to us. From the late fourth century AD onwards *prashastis* or eulogies of the reigning kings and their predecessors, included as a matter of form in royal inscriptions, become our major source of knowledge for dynastic histories. We can also derive information about agrarian relations, administrative organization, guilds, artisans, etc., from the various kinds of inscriptions we encounter. The place-names that inscriptions often contain and their original sites themselves are of primary importance in studying historical geography. The references to deities, etc., within the inscriptions, and the religious denominations receiving gifts recorded in them, can help us to establish the status of different religious sects in particular epochs. Inscriptions also help us to date such events in the history of mathematics as the use of decimal positioning of digits and of zero, from the way the numerals (or symbols for numbers) are written in them.

Epigraphy is thus practically the mistress in our study of ancient Indian history, from the third century BC to the twelfth century AD, a span of some fourteen hundred years.

Note 2.2
Bibliographical Note

On Ashoka much has been written. V.A. Smith's *Asoka* (third edition, Oxford, 1920; many reprints), is now partly obsolete but still readable. Scholarly works on Ashoka by D.R. Bhandarkar (1925; third edition, Calcutta, 1955) and Radhakumud Mookerji (London, 1928; third edition, Delhi, 1962) were followed by B.M. Barua, *Asoka and his Inscriptions*, Vol. I (second edition, Calcutta, 1955) and *Inscriptions of Asoka*, Vol. II (Calcutta, 1943), and Romila Thapar, *Aśoka and the Decline of the Mauryas* (Oxford, 1963; revised edition, New Delhi, 1997, with an Afterword). All these works contain translations of Ashokan edicts.

Ashoka

The standard edition and translation of Ashokan inscriptions is still E. Hultzsch, *Inscriptions of Aśoka*, Vol. I, in the *Corpus Inscriptionum Indicarum* series of the Archaeological Survey of India (London, 1925; Indian reprints available). Inscriptions discovered since this publication are edited and translated in D.C. Sircar, *Aśokan Studies* (Calcutta, 1979; reprint, 2000). The Aramaic and Greek inscriptions of Ashoka have been edited, with translations and commentary, by B.N. Mukherjee, *Studies in the Aramaic Edicts of Asoka* (Calcutta, 1984). For more recently discovered inscriptions, see *Indian Historical Review*, XIV (1990), pp. 36–42 (Sannathi inscription, edited by K.V. Ramesh); *South Asian Studies*, IV (1988), pp. 99–102 (Buner rock fragment, edited by K.R. Norman, but probably a forgery); and *Epigraphia Indica*, XLIII (1), 2011–12 (copy of Minor Rock Edict I at Basaha, Bhabua district, Bihar). Alfred C. Woolner, *Asoka: Text and Glossary* (Calcutta, 1924; reprint, Delhi, 1993), remains a handy work of reference. Another useful volume is Radhagovinda Basak, *Aśokan Inscriptions* (Calcutta, 1959), with texts (synoptical) and translations of the edicts. On the sites of Ashokan inscriptions, there is a detailed survey by Harry Falk, *Aśokan Sites and Artefacts: A Source-Book with Bibliography*, Mainz, 2006.

The *Mahāvaṁsa*, containing the most extensive account of Ashoka in the Sri Lankan tradition, is best available in the translation by Wilhelm Geiger (London, 1912; Indian reprints, 1986, 1993). P.H.L. Eggermont, in his *Chronology of the Reign of Asoka Moriya* (Leiden, 1956), offers a close scrutiny of the Buddhist traditions of both Sri Lanka and the Mahāyānist denominations; but the reasoning is often strained.

On the Tamil Brāhmī inscriptions, the definitive work is by Iravatham Mahadevan, *Early Tamil Epigraphy: From the Earliest Times to the Sixth Century AD* (Chennai, 2003). Early Brāhmī inscriptions of Sri Lanka are recorded, with transliterated texts and translations, in S. Paranavitana, *Inscriptions of Ceylon* (Colombo, 1970). The results of recent archaeological work in Sri Lanka are discussed in F.R. Allchin, *The Archaeology of Historic South Asia* (Cambridge, 1995), Chapter 9 by R.A.E. Coningham and Allchin.

On Epigraphy, one can recommend without hesitation Richard Salomon, *Indian Epigraphy: A Guide to the Study of the Inscriptions in Sanskrit, Prakrit and the Other Indo-Aryan Languages* (New Delhi, 1998). It has fairly full references to earlier work.

3
Economy, Society and Culture

3.1 Economy

It should be logical to begin our survey of the economy of Mauryan times with the way the land was occupied. A very large part of it was then undoubtedly covered by **forest**. This being so, it is not surprising that the people of the forest (*aṭavi*) should find special mention in Ashoka's Rock Edict XIII as a source of defiance to imperial authority. The major product of forests that was in demand in settled society was obviously timber, used as building material and as the main component of carts, chariots, ploughs and other tools. Megasthenes, as quoted by Strabo, speaks of the long wall of Pāṭaliputra being made of wood. Even if we discount the length given to the wall, we would still have to concede that much timber must have been used here (see Chapter 1.6 and below). Much of the wooden architecture (and carving) of the time obviously served as the model for depictions of buildings in later stone sculpture (second century BC onwards) at Bharhut and Sanchi; this too suggests extensive use of timber in the buildings of the time.

The *Arthashāstra* (II.17.5–8) also reminds us that the forests provided bamboo and reeds, employed in making baskets, and serving as flexible (as well as hard) materials for tools and weapons; forests also contained wild plants that yielded fibre for making woven covering and ropes. Unfortunately, the individual plants named cannot be identified. The *Arthashāstra* (II.17.12–13) also lists among forest produce medicinal plants, and skins and body parts of numerous wild animals, the latter having some use in decoration or for satisfying some superstition. Ivory was included under the category of 'teeth' of certain wild animals, the elephant being one of them.

Elephants, the source of ivory, were themselves a major

economic product of the forests. Though domesticated, the true breeding grounds of elephants lay in the forests, from where they were caught and tamed to be used in battle and courtly display (Megasthenes: Strabo, XV.1.41–43; and Arrian, *Indica*, XIII; *Arthashāstra*, II.32.1–7). The elephant forest (*nāgavana*, Pillar Edict V; *Arthashāstra*, II.2.7, 10; in *Arthashāstra*, II.1.19, II.2.6 and II.31.1, it is also called *hastivana*) probably denoted not only a forest where elephants could be captured in large numbers, but also one where such capture was a royal monopoly. Strange as the idea may seem to us today, elephants were an important item of 'national wealth' at the time. Even if Pliny's figure of 9,000 elephants for Chandragupta's army is exaggerated, the more reliable number of 500 elephants secured from him by Seleucus, to be used later at the decisive battle of Ipsus (301 BC), still gives us some measure of the number of elephants trained for use in warfare alone. If ordinary elephants under domestication were many times this number, we can imagine how large the number of wild elephants themselves was, and how extensive must have been the forests where the beasts had their habitat.

At the same time, the area of the forests was being gradually reduced. In his Pillar Edict V, Ashoka forbids the burning of the forests without purpose or in order to destroy animals. The edict seems to target the practice of slash-and-burn cultivation, as well as of hunters burning down forests to smoke out wild animals. Under both practices, a process of forest clearance would continuously take place. That roads already ran through large stretches of deforested country is shown by the need to plant banyan and other trees along them so as to provide shade to "cattle and men" (Rock Edict II; Pillar Edict VII: *Extracts 2.2* and *2.7 [B]*).

There is nothing in the Ashokan edicts about giving encouragement to clear the land and expand the area of **cultivation**. But one can see that for enhancing fiscal resources, if not for any other reason, such encouragement was dictated by the state's own self-interest. The policy that the *Arthashāstra* (II.1.1–18) commends in this respect could well have been that of the Mauryan state. The king, the text says, should increase settlement in a *janapada* or province (the term also occurs in Ashokan edicts) by getting people from outside, particularly "Shūdra peasants (*karshakas*)", to settle in villages formed of 100 to 500 families. They were to be granted loans in "grain, cattle and money"; but their rights over the land were for life only, and conditional upon their continuing to cultivate it. Such a policy had social implications, since it set the peasants against the forest people, whose territory would have been progressively reduced to spaces left between village clearings (as suggested in *Arthashāstra*, II.1.6).

The *Arthashāstra* (II.24.3) provides no particulars of cultivating tools (*karshaṇayantra*), but the mention of bullocks alongside of them makes it clear that ox-drawn ploughs are being thought of. The need of smiths and carpenters (*karmāra–kuṭṭaka*) to support the work of cultivation reminds us that the tools were mainly of wood with some iron in them, and so had to be made or repaired by these two artisans. The increasing use of iron in agricultural tools is also evidenced by the archaeological record. From the Mauryan-period levels at the township of Atranjikhera (western Uttar Pradesh) comes an iron share fixed to the wooden frame of the plough; and so also iron sickles (*Fig. 3.1*).

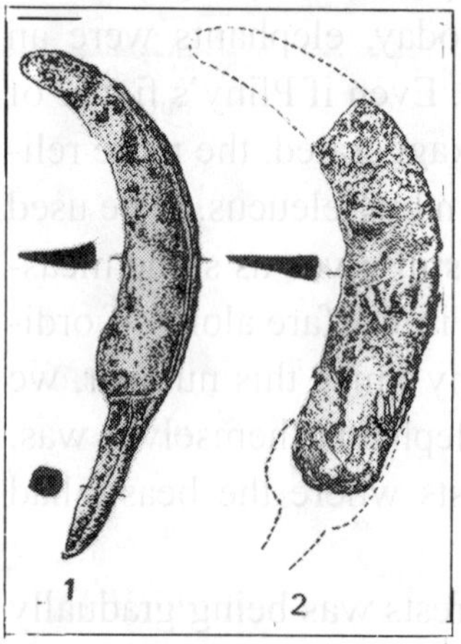

FIG. 3.1 Iron sickles from Atranjikhera, NBP phase. (After R.C. Gaur)

In respect of water-lifting devices, a passage in the *Arthashāstra*, II.24.18, is of considerable interest. Arranging these devices according to the expenses incurred on them (and setting a lower tax rate for the more expensive), it assumes the one moved by "the hand" to be the most expensive. This must be the hand-pulled water-bucket that is drawn up out of a well by oxen by rope over a pulley-wheel, a device presumably also known in earlier times (see *The Vedic Age*, 1.3). The next device, "moved by the shoulder", can only be the noria, an early form of *araghaṭa*, which literally means a wheel "with pots tied to its spokes", and which probably appears in an early Buddhist text, *Chullavagga Nikāya* (*c.* 350 BC) as *chakkavaṭṭaka* (turning wheel). Pear-like pots, suitable for such a wheel, have been found in large numbers at the Mauryan-period Bhir Mound at Taxila. Without gearing and the chain of pots, the noria could have been worked only on ponds, or streams, with the wheel turned by the pressure of human shoulders (see *Fig. 3.2*

Fig. 3.2 Late form of noria, Mandor frieze, twelfth century. Note that the pots have been transferred from tops of rimless spokes to the wooden rim, but there is no pot-garland (*mālā*) discernible (though known in India from the sixth century AD).
(After T. Schioler, checked with photo-reproductions)

with explanation). The third, and least expensive, was the device that let water into channels (*srotoyantra*), which was presumably the wooden scoop worked by the operator's feet.

Canals and tanks are left out in this passage of the *Arthashāstra*, though elsewhere there is a general recommendation (II.1.20–22) that the state should build, or help build, a dam (*setu-bandha*), which ought to have involved at least small canals or channels led out from the dammed lake through sluices. Strabo (XV.1.50), drawing apparently on Megasthenes, speaks of Indian officials who "inspect the sluices by which water is let out from the main canals into their branches, so that everyone may have an equal supply of it". It is perhaps an unfair aspersion on Strabo to suppose that he has inserted this sentence purely on the basis of his own knowledge of Egypt, without any authority from Megasthenes. In any case, Rudradāman's Junagarh inscription of AD 150, with its description of the construction of the Sudarshana lake in Saurashtra under Chandragupta Maurya and then its improvement under Ashoka, suggests that irrigation works, with canals led out of dammed tanks, were in fact being constructed by state officials in Mauryan times. It is another matter that the total area served by such works might not have been very large.

As for the crops, we have two short lists. One comes from Eratosthenes, *c.* 230 BC, who speaks of the two seasonal harvests and lists the following crops under each (Strabo, XV.1.13):

Crops of the rainy season ('kharif')	*Winter crops ('rabi')*
Flax	Wheat
Millet (Ragi?)	Barley
Sesamum	Pulse
Rice	Other edible crops
Bosmorum ('Bajra'?)	

'Bosmorum' is obviously the 'bosmoran' of Onesicritus (see Chapter 1.1). Elsewhere, as cited by Strabo (XV.1.20), Eratosthenes also mentions large sweet reeds, or sugarcane. The *Arthashāstra* (II.24.12–14) too gives a list, which is longer and practically includes all the crops Eratosthenes has listed. It arranges them, however, according to the order of precedence in sowing in either of the two seasons, three such stages being determined. Its statements are summarized in Table 3.1.

Looking at these two lists, one finds that a considerable balance in food crops had been achieved, with the three main cereals (rice, wheat, barley) supplemented by millets and pulses. The cultivation of the 'urad' pulse (*Phaseolus mungo*) is also reported from the Mauryan-period (NBP) strata of Atranjikhera. In each season (*kharif* and *rabi*), such food crops could now be raised as were most suited to that season, without endangering food availability. It is not clear whether the practice of rice transplantation had been introduced. There seems to be no suggestion of it in the *Arthashāstra*, but Strabo (XV.1.18), writing before AD 23, quotes an earlier writer, Megillus, as saying that in India rice "requires irrigation and transplantation". If rice transplantation was thus being practised in the first century BC, one cannot be definite in excluding its presence from Mauryan India.

The *Arthashāstra*, II.24.20–21, says, justly, that sugarcane cultivation involved much expense and risk. However, profits too could be considerable, since, by Mauryan times, varieties of sugar had begun to be manufactured. The making of *guḍa* (*gur*, 'concrete' sugar) is mentioned in Pāṇini (*c.* 350 BC) (IV.4.103) and it gets mention, along with *khaṇḍa* (candied sugar) and *sharkarā* (hard-grained sugar), in the *Arthashāstra* (II.15.14). A statement attributed to Megasthenes about sweet stones being dug up is considered to refer to sugar-candy that used to be laid in the ground in the final stage of its production. Indeed,

TABLE 3.1 List of Crops (*Arthashāstra*, II.24.12–14)

	Harvest in which now usually gathered
Early Sowing	
Rice (*shāli-vrīhi*)	*kharif*
'Kodo' millet (*kodrava*)	*kharif*
Sesamum (*til*)	*kharif/rabi*
'Kaun' ('Italian') millet (*priyaṅgu*)	*kharif*
Udāraka (unidentified)	–
'Varagu' or cheena (common millet) (*varaka*)	*rabi/kharif*
Middle Sowing	
'Mung' pulse (*mudga*)	*kharif*
'Urad' pulse (*māsha*)	*kharif*
'Sanwan' (poor man's millet) (*shaiṁbya*)	*kharif*
Late Sowing	
Safflower (*kusumbha*)	*rabi/kharif*
Lentils (*masūra*)	*kharif/rabi*
Horse-grain (*kulattha*)	*rabi/kharif*
Barley (*yava*)	*rabi*
Wheat (*godhūma*)	*rabi*
Kalāya (unidentified)	–
Linseed or Flax (*atasi*)	*kharif*
Mustard (*sarshapa*)	*rabi*
Add (II.24.21–22)	
Sugarcane (*ikshu*)	*kharif*
Long pepper (*pippalī*)	*rabi*

Note: See also *Arthashāstra*, II.15.25–30.

India seems to have primacy over all other countries in developing sugar products.

The position of cotton is more complex. It is not recognized as an agricultural crop by either Eratosthenes or, more importantly, by the *Arthashāstra*, and apparently escapes mention by Pāṇini, who does mention linseed and hemp. We have seen (Chapter 1.1) that Alexander's admiral Nearchus described cotton as being gathered from trees and, therefore, from the perennial plant and not the small bush that forms the annual crop. Even so, a statement from Aristotle's successor Theophrastus (*c.* 300 BC), drawn doubtless from accounts of Alexander's companions, shows that while cotton was gathered in India from a perennial tree resembling a dog-rose, the plants were "arranged in rows", like vines. This meant that the process of domestication of cotton was, in any case, far advanced, and through selection the annual strains could now be developed in the next few centuries. The cultivation of indigo, the blue dye, seems to have been introduced, since, while Pāṇini (IV.1.42) has a reference to *nīla* for cloth dyed with indigo, Kātyāyana (*c.* 250 BC), in his gloss on Pāṇini (IV.2.2), treats *nīlī* (indigo) as a plant.

Horticulture seems to have been well-established. Ashoka speaks of his planting medicinal plants, roots and fruits where these were not to be obtained (Rock Edict II). He refers also to his planting mango-groves (*aṁbāvaḍikā*) (Pillar Edict VII); and in the Queen's Edict (Allahabad Pillar), these appear as an important item of gifts the 'second queen' had made. The *Arthashāstra* (II.24.22) has a reference to the cultivation of grapes (*mridvika*), but apparently not to the mango, for which the Ashokan inscriptions seem to offer very early, firmly dated evidence.

With the progress of agriculture, the share of food supply contributed by it increased continuously. Kosambi has pointed out how the cultivation of pulses (including peas, grams and beans) provided the proteins that correspondingly reduced the need for meat consumption. Yet, agriculture was far more affected by the vagaries of the monsoons than the pristine natural forests with their own capacities for local water retention. The frequency and scale of famines was, therefore, bound to increase as the dependence on agriculture grew. The first enlightenment the people expected to get every year from their 'philosophers', Megasthenes tells us (Diodorus: *Extract 3.1*), was about whether a drought would or would not ensue. It was a long severe famine, Jain tradition says, that persuaded Chandragupta Maurya to abdicate and take to the life of a recluse.

Agriculture now engaged the labour of a large proportion of the population which Megasthenes assigns to the second of the seven castes – that of the *geōragoi*, or peasants, who are said to be "far more numerous than the others" (see *Extract 3.1*). In the *Arthashāstra* (II.1.2) it is prescribed, as we have seen, that the land should be settled with Shūdra *karshakas* (peasants), the most appropriate equivalent of the *geōragoi*. They were tax-payers (*karada*); and they were obliged to till the land, for, if they did not do so, it would be taken away from them (II.1.8–10). If such peasants were not available, village servants (*grāmabhritaka*) and tradesmen (*vaidehaka*) could be allowed to cultivate the land. The peasants had their own "seed-grain and cattle" (*dhānyapashu*); if they did not possess them, loans were to be given in kind or money, to be returned on easy terms (II.1.18).

Other passages in the *Arthashāstra* give us a glimpse of a different mode of organization. We read of ploughing by slaves (*dāsa*), labourers (*karmakara*) and persons forced to undertake labour to pay off fines, when the plough, implements and bullocks were provided by the superintendent of agriculture (*sītādhyaksha*). To such slaves and labourers, food proportionate to the number of their dependants, together with a small monthly wage (1¼ *paṇas*), was to be provided (II.24.28). An alternative arrangement is also prescribed (II.24.16), where land was cultivated by peasants for half the produce (*ardha-sītikāḥ*), but sharecroppers "supplying their own labour only" (*sva-vīryopajīvinaḥ*) were allowed only a fourth or fifth share of the crop.

The kinds of arrangements described in the preceding paragraph prevailed in the king's estates, for which the *Arthashāstra* appears to give no specific designation, the term *sītā* (despite Kosambi's adoption of it in this sense) meaning no more than agriculture or agricultural produce. We may further assume that the practices the *Arthashāstra* describes here were modelled after those followed in the estates of princes, high officials and local potentates. Indeed, many estates of the latter type could, with political changes, have been subsumed in the royal estates. At the same time, other estates were created by royal grants, such as those the *Arthashāstra*, II.1.7, mentions, being tax-free lands given to Brahmans (*brahmadeya*), bureaucrats and territorial officials, and others. The gifts of the emperor and the royal family that Ashokan edicts refer to probably included such lands, although the only specific form of land-grant mentioned there (the Queen's Edict) is that of mango-groves.

The royal power to make a tax-free grant out of any land

implied the capacity to create landed property, since, given this relief, the grantees could make a profit for themselves by bringing waste land under cultivation in the same manner as in the royal estates. The king's right to impose a heavy tax (and so claim a large share of the surplus) could have itself made him appear as the owner of all land. The statement to this effect made by Megasthenes, and duly copied by Diodorus (*Extract 3.1*) and Strabo, need occasion us no surprise. That no such claim is made on behalf of the ruler in either the *Arthashāstra* or any other Indian texts, is doubtless attributable to the fact that their authors were necessarily aware of the petty rights to property in ordinary land that always survived so long as there was any share of the surplus left that royal taxation did not or could not annex to itself. There must also have existed limitations to royal power in dealing with old property-holders or tax-paying peasants, who could not be treated as mere tenants-at-will. A strikingly similar case would arise in the seventeenth century, when European travellers almost unanimously asserted that the Mughal emperor was the owner of all land in his dominions, a claim that is wholly absent from the Indian texts of that century.

The relationship between agriculture and the **pastoral economy** can be seen to be mutually complementary. When cultivation was formed of clearings surrounded by forests, a large area became available within, and on the fringes of, the forest for pasturing cattle and sheep. As agriculture and commerce expanded, the relative importance of the pastoral sector within the economy necessarily declined, but even in late Vedic times wealth would be counted in numbers of cattle (*The Vedic Age*, 1.1 and 2.1). Megasthenes describes, as the third of his seven castes, that of cattle-herders and shepherds, who had to live outside towns and villages in tents (see *Extract 3.1*). Strabo (XV.1.41) adds that these people sold draught cattle to peasants and hunted wild animals; and Arrian (*Indica*, XI), that they paid their tax to the king in cattle. The *Arthashāstra*, II.29.1–4, speaks of large herds of cattle (including buffaloes) under the charge of the cattle superintendent (*go'dhyaksha*), a hundred animals being entrusted to one herdsman (*gopāla*). The large herds necessitated the animals being branded with ownership marks (*Arthashāstra*, II.29.9–11), a fact confirmed by Ashoka's Pillar Edict V and by Eratosthenes (Arrian, *Anabasis*, V.3). While the cattle herds provided draught animals and milk products, their meat retained some importance. Megasthenes and other Greek writers are silent about cattle slaughter, but the *Arthashāstra*, II.29.8, refers to buffaloes marked for slaughter. Ashoka's Pillar Edict V clearly implies that goats, sheep and pigs were slaughtered and eaten. The fact, mentioned in the same edict, that, along with the male of goat and sheep, that of pig was also castrated, presumably at an early age to improve (supposedly?) the flavour of meat, shows that pigs were now fully domesticated.

Ashoka's Pillar Edict V is also good evidence for domestication of poultry. Except for the *Vājasaneyi Saṁhitā* of the *Yajurveda*, which has a reference to the call of the cock (*kukkuṭa*), where the fowl could still be a wild one, the reference in this edict to the caponing or castration of the cock means that it could not be a wild bird, and poultry was at least being reared for the purpose of meat, if not eggs. The ultimate luxury in meat, let us remember from Rock Edict I, yet came from peacocks and deer, both semi-wild animals, at best.

In considering **non-agricultural production**, one may begin with **pottery**, which engaged, perhaps, the largest number of craftsmen after agriculture and pastoral pursuits. The characteristic pottery of the Mauryan times, from Taxila in western Punjab to Sisupalgarh in Orissa and Ujjain in Malwa, is the Northern Black Polished (NBP) Ware. It involves a technological change of some note, since the fusion of its alkaline slip requires firing at high temperatures. Its beginnings are traceable to the fifth century BC, but it reached its greatest extent during Mauryan times and, by then, practically displaced at its sites the survivals of earlier wares, such as Painted Grey Ware and Black and Red Ware (for both of which, see *The Vedic Age*, 3.1). It is difficult to resist the conclusion, from its extensive spread, that a considerable amount of technique diffusion, accompanied doubtless by artisans' migrations on some scale, must have taken place before and during the period of the Mauryan Empire.

On **minerals** other than metals, our information from Mauryan times is quite limited. We have seen (Chapter 1.1) that salt was extracted out of rocks in the Salt Range in northwest Punjab. The abundance of cornelian and agate beads found in the Bhir Mound, Taxila, suggests that these semi-precious stones were being mined at their

MAP 3.1 Economy

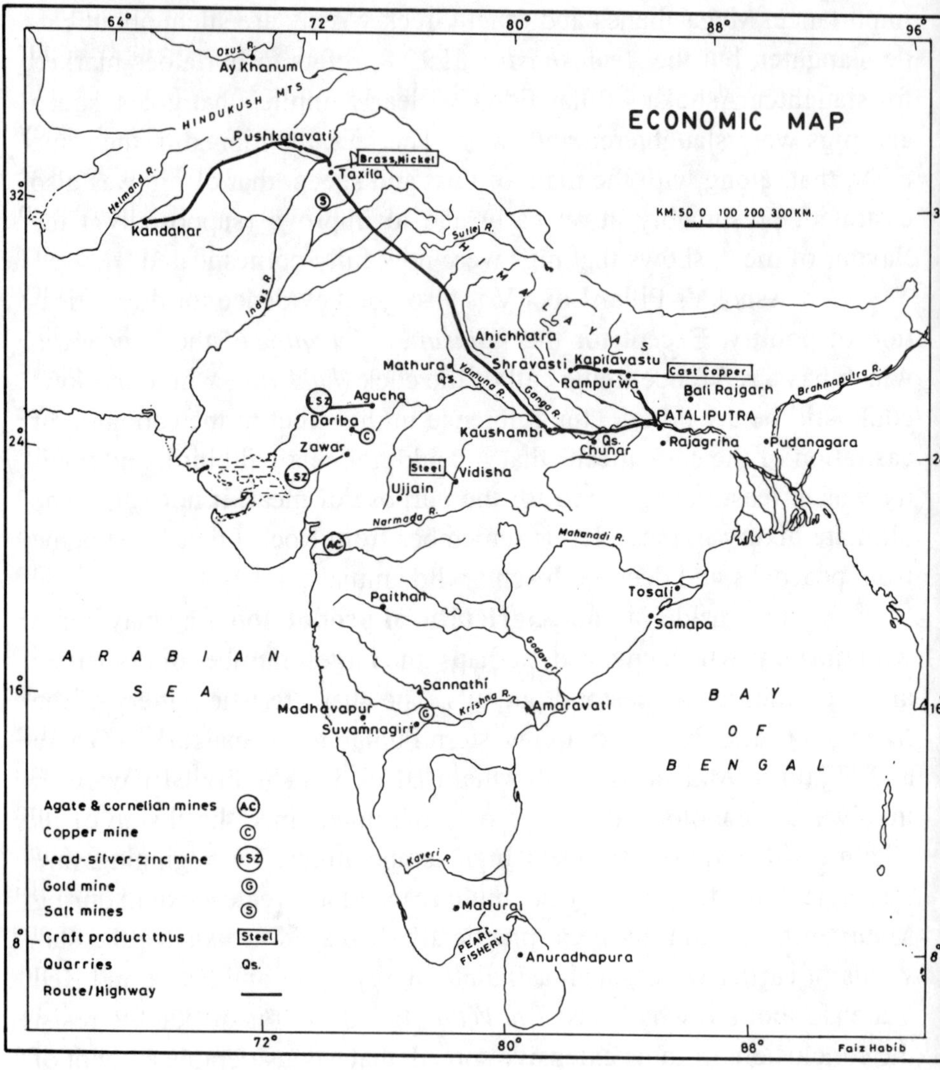

well-known sites in Rajpipla, southern Gujarat. We may mention here a sea product as well: pearls that were gathered in the Tuticorin fisheries off the coast of the Pāṇḍiyan kingdom (see Chapter 2.5).

There is good evidence for progress in the mining and use of **metals**. It is likely that the name of the viceregal seat in the Deccan, Suvaṁṇagiri, 'Gold-city', was due to the proximity of gold mines in its neighbourhood. A possible site of it could, therefore, be Maski (in Karnataka), which has traces of old gold workings nearby. Explorations in the Aravalli mines of Zawar, Agucha and Dariba (all in Udaipur district, Rajasthan) have revealed shafts, with timber supports for galleries, that had reached a depth of 100 metres by Mauryan times. They have been described as being "among the most sophisticated and extensive known from antiquity", in a British Museum report. The carbon dates for the early phase of mining give a period from the fifth century BC onwards, with a concentration of the dates within the third century BC. In Mauryan times silver and lead were mined at Zawar and Agucha, and copper at Dariba. Zinc was not yet isolated, but some was probably obtained through reduction. Activity in these mines seems to have ceased in the first century BC, not to revive until the thirteenth century AD.

It has been held that the *Arthashāstra*, II.13–14, shows knowledge of both cementation and cupellation for obtaining purity in gold and silver. This portion in the text, as much else besides, may have been added or enlarged in post-Mauryan times, but there is much to suggest from the excavations in the Aravalli mines that both methods might well have been practised in Mauryan times. At Taxila (Bhir Mound), in strata dated to the third–second century BC, there was found a brass vase, composed of copper (55 per cent), zinc (34 per cent) and lead (3 per cent). This is the earliest specimen of brass found in India. The high presence of zinc and lead suggests links with the Aravalli mines, where, after the separation of silver, by cementation, the remainder must have often contained a high proportion of zinc with lead. This could now be alloyed with copper in order to produce brass. Mining appears to have collapsed in the Aravallis once silver ceased to be the coinage metal in the first century BC, so that, along with its extraction, the supply of natural zinc and lead alloys also ceased. Brass manufacture, therefore, appears to have disappeared thereafter almost for a millennium. There was a shorter phase still of a copper–nickel alloy, which first appears in Mauryan times. An antimony rod and a bangle from the Bhir Mound (third–second century BC) had a nickel content of 9 per cent and 19 per cent, respectively. In some Bactrian rulers' coins of the second century BC, the nickel content rises to over 20 per cent. But the use of this alloy ends there. Where the nickel was obtained from remains a mystery, the suggested source in Yunnan, China, being surely far too distant.

An ability to cast large pieces of copper was attained by Ashoka's time. At Rampurwa (Champaran district, Bihar), a "massive" copper bolt of cast copper joined the capital of the Ashokan pillar to its shaft. The cast piece was 72.33 centimetres in length, while the circumference in the middle was 33.66 centimetres and at each end 27.31 centimetres. Nearchus (Strabo, XV.1.67) reported that Indians delighted in casting vessels, but these were breakable like pottery. This is borne out by material from the Bhir Mound (Taxila), where bronze with a high tin alloy was cast, but is "exceptionally brittle". In other cases, lead was also added to aid casting. The hollow-cast method (*cire perdue*) was not apparently known to Mauryan craftsmen.

The metal most used was, of course, iron. India is fortunate in possessing good iron ores close to the surface. Abundant charcoal could be obtained from the extensive forests of the time to enable the ores to be smelted and reduced to iron of high purity. At the Bhir Mound (Taxila), despite much loss through corrosion, iron artefacts greatly outnumber those of copper. These show considerable variety in shapes suited to various uses as bowl, spoon and saucer, spear-head, arrow-head and goad; and, especially, in such tools as axe, adze, chisel, knife, tongs, anvil, nail and hoe. (See *Fig. 3.3* for the Bhir Mound tools.) Sockets were now the normal way for fitting the main iron tool to wooden handles.

It is probable that Mauryan India also produced steel. The Greek traveller Ktesias (fifth century BC) is reported to have received two Indian steel swords from the Achaemenean court. The first actual surviving example of steel within India comes from the iron strips placed at the base of the Heliodorus column at Besnagar (near Sanchi), set up about 101 BC. The iron has 0.7 per cent carbon, the strips being apparently taken from a broken sword. This carries us fairly close to Mauryan times.

In considering the state of **textile crafts**, we must bear in mind the fact that since cotton had not yet become an annual crop, its production was limited and it was by no means the sole source of clothing. The *Arthashāstra* (II.23.2) lists many fibres out of which yarn might be spun: wool (*ūrṇa*), bark-fibres (*avalka*), cotton (*kārpāsa*),

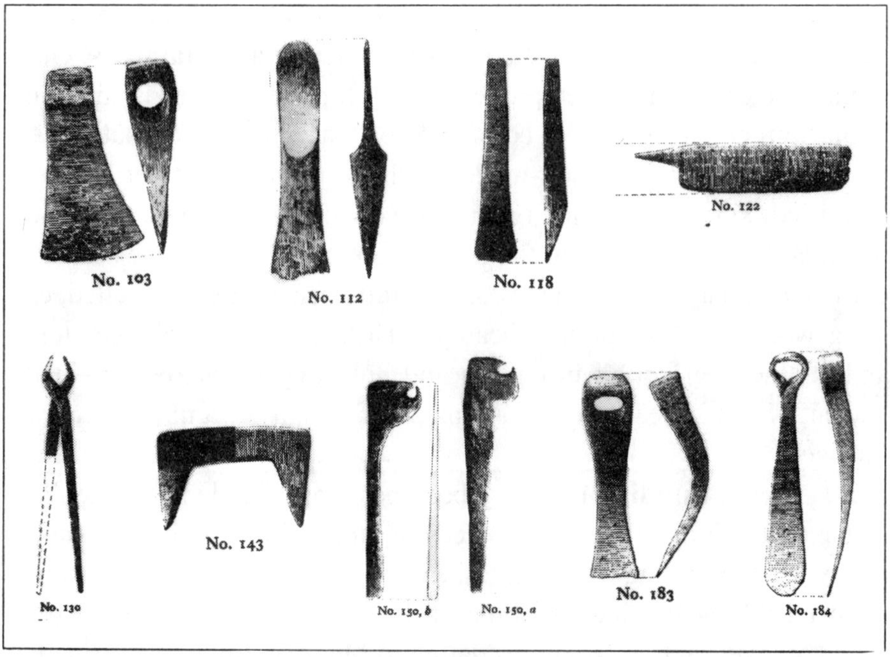

FIG. 3.3 Iron tools from Taxila: axe (no. 103); adze (no. 112); chisel (no. 118), knife (no. 122); tongs (no. 130); anvil (no. 143); nails (nos. 150*a* and *b*); hoes (nos. 183 and 184); Bhir Mound, Stratum II (except no. 112, which is from the lower Stratum III). (Reprod. J. Marshall)

silk-cotton (*tūla*), hemp (*shaṇa*) and flax (*kshauma*). Further on (II.23.8), in addition to flax and cotton yarn, it refers to *dukūla* (muslin?), silk (*krimitāna*) and deer-hair (*rānkava*), from which cloth could be woven. The silk intended here is presumably the semi-wild 'tasar', collected widely in Indian forest zones in pre-colonial times. Cotton cloth alone, however, has been found as wrapping material for punch-marked coins at Bairat and Rairh (both in eastern Rajasthan), and this may suggest that, by the end of Mauryan times, limited as the ordinary Indian's clothing might have been, much of it was being woven out of cotton.

The *Arthashāstra*, II.23.2, 11, makes it clear that spinning was exclusively the work of women, especially women bereft of support: widows, disabled women, virgins, homeless women, women having to pay fines, courtesans' mothers, old women slaves of the king, and unwanted women slaves (*devadāsī*) of temples. In the case of weaving (II.23.8), it seems implied that it was men who undertook this work.

A set of crafts, for which the best evidence comes from the Bhir Mound, Taxila, produced articles for **personal ornaments**. Glass seems to have been here employed mainly for bangles, beads and seals, in blue, green, black and red colours. Shell was also used as material for bangles and beads; a "shell-worker's shop" fronting a street has been identified, since it contained many pieces of cut shell and mother-of-pearl. But it was in carving the beads of semi-precious stones, notably cornelian and agate, that the Mauryan craftsmen at Taxila excelled, creating works of "exceptional beauty". They employed "choice stone" and attained perfection in cutting and polishing, "unsurpassed in the ancient world". Beads were also made of amethyst, amber, coral and faience.

The **building industry** becomes more visible in archaeology as baked bricks and large cut pieces of stone join mud-bricks, rubble and wood as building material. Baked bricks, reappearing after a gap of almost 1,500 years since the time of the Indus Civilization, have been found at levels and in structures dating to Mauryan times at Kaushāmbī and Bhita (Allahabad district) and Ahichhatra (Bareilly district, Uttar Pradesh: 1963–65 excavations). In Taxila (Bhir Mound) wooden pillars were raised to support the roofs (of wood and straw?). But at Pāṭaliputra a great hall has been excavated with traces of 84 polished sandstone pillars, each some 9.6 metres in length, the visible height being nearly 7 metres. Then there are the free-standing pillars erected at various places in the Gangetic basin, and some outside of it. As works of art, these are discussed in Chapter 3.5 below. What strikes us is the extent of labour that must have been required to cut the stone from the quarries of Chunar and Mathura, and to take it in such enormous slabs to spots up to some hundred kilometres away. We know what devices had to be employed by Firoz Tughluq in the fourteenth century AD to bring two such pillars to Delhi, using capstan and rope, and cart and boat (*Fig. 3.4*). It is, indeed, possible that the use of capstan was known to Ashokan engineers, for they or their precursors could well have learnt of it from reports of Alexander's ballistic machines, or from their encounters with such Greek and Macedonian officials as took service with the Mauryas.

Fortifications of towns should also have required much use of labour and other resources. If the Pāṭaliputra defence walls were as long

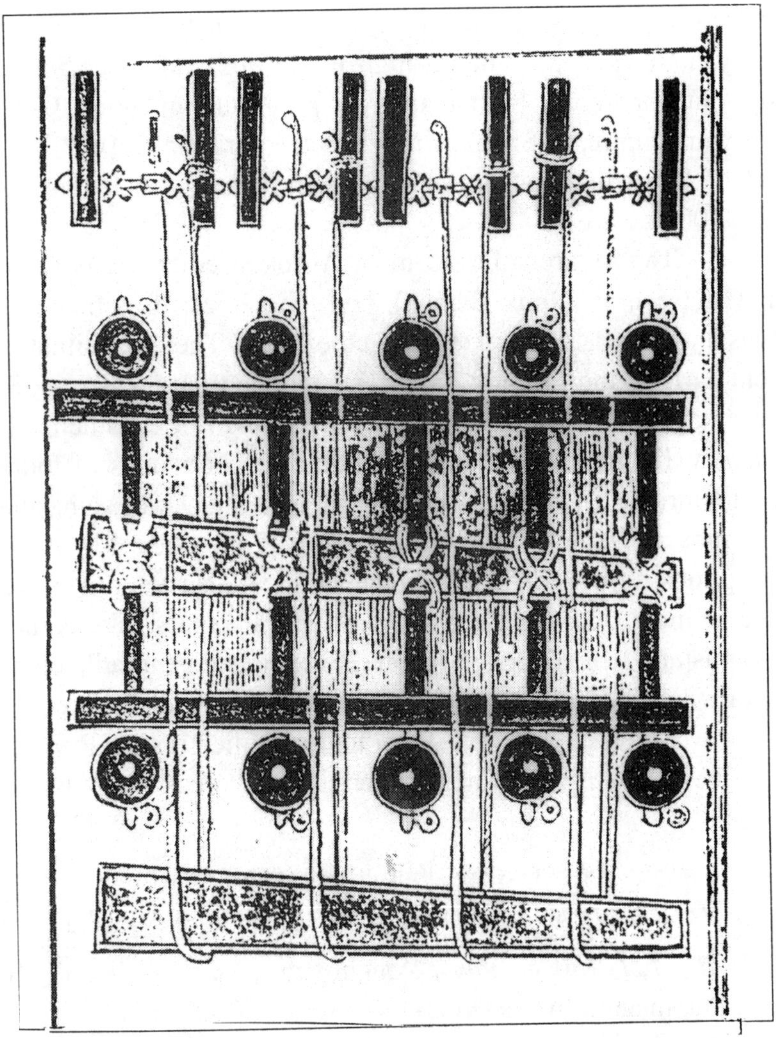

FIG. 3.4 Ashokan pillar hauled by means of rope and capstan from ground on to a ten-wheel cart. Diagram in *Sīrat-i Firozshāhī* MS. (Courtesy: Khuda Bakhsh Oriental Public Library, Patna.) There are ten other diagrams in the same manuscript, illustrating its account of transport of the pillar from Topra to Delhi, fourteenth century.

as Megasthenes said they were, and if they were all built of wood, as archaeology partly confirms (see Chapter 1.6 above), then certainly very large quantities of timber must have been needed for the initial construction and subsequent maintenance. Kaushāmbī offers a different kind of fortification with massive rammed mud ramparts and revetments datable to the Mauryan period. Tosali (Sisupalgarh, Orissa), similarly, had massive mud ramparts laid out behind a moat in late Mauryan times. Ujjain had a high mud-brick wall over 5 kilometres long, but apparently built mainly in pre-Mauryan times. Outside the Mauryan Empire, in Sri Lanka, within the period *c.* 350–200 BC, at the town of Anuradhapura were built earthen ramparts enclosing an area of about 100 hectares.

Towns are referred to in Ashokan edicts as *nagara* (Rock Edict V, Separate Rock Edict I), and the names of as many as seven towns, besides Pāṭaliputra, occur in the edicts. These are situated in different parts of the Empire: Taxila, Ujjain, Kaushāmbī, Tosali, Samāpā, Suvaṁṇagiri and Isila (see Chapter 1.6 above). Megasthenes (Arrian, *Indica*, VIII) mentions Methora (Mathura). The names of four others, Saviti (Shrāvastī), Varanashi (Varanasi), Puḍanagara (Mahasthan) and Chikambari (Deotek), are furnished to us by other Mauryan-period inscriptions (see *Map 1.2*). Archaeological excavations have taken place at most of these twelve places and at others, like Kandahar in Afghanistan, Ahichhatra in Uttar Pradesh and Anuradhapura in Sri Lanka, where Mauryan-period remains have been discovered.

Based largely on archaeological indications, F.R. Allchin has made the following estimates of the inhabited areas of Mauryan-period towns:

Grade I, above 240 hectares: Pāṭaliputra (estimated area: 340 hectares)

Grade II, 181–240 hectares: Rājagriha, Kaushāmbī, Vidisha (Besnagar)

Grade III, 121–180 hectares: Ahichhatra, Shrāvastī, Tosali (Sisupalgarh), Puḍanagara (Mahasthan)

Grade IV, 61–120 hectares: Ujjain, Samāpā (Jaugada), Paithan, Anuradhapura (Sri Lanka)

Grade V, 31–60 hectares: Kandahar, Taxila, Balirajgarh (in Bihar), Sannathi, Madhavpur (in Karnataka), Dhanyakataka (Amaravati)

Grade VI, 16–30 hectares: Kapilavastu (in northeastern Uttar Pradesh), Pushkalavati (Charsadda, North Western Frontier Province).

If we try to turn these area figures into population estimates at the same ratio of inhabitants to built-up land that we used for the Indus Culture towns (*Indus Civilization*, 2.4), that is, about 400 persons to a hectare, Pāṭaliputra, the largest town in the Empire, should have contained nearly 140,000 inhabitants, while Kapilavastu in the lowest 'grade' should have had a population of 6,000 to 12,000. The urban portion of the population, spread over towns of differing sizes, must thus have been considerable, though there is hardly enough data to even speculate on the ratio the urban inhabitants bore to the whole population.

Towns needed to be fed and supplied with raw materials by drawing on agriculture, grasslands and forests. This formed the basis of one sector of commerce. The towns themselves were centres of crafts, whose products not only met the demand generated within the towns, but also fulfilled some rural needs (as in the case of iron for agricultural implements or weapons); and towns might produce also for distant markets. All this made the towns centres of much commercial activity. In Taxila's Bhir Mound, chambers in rows facing the street have been plausibly identified as shops.

As for long-distance trade, the *Arthashāstra*, II.11, provides information on regions from where precious articles were obtained. In part, this chapter of the text seems to be of a post-Mauryan date, with its references to Sri Lanka as Pārasamudra, and to Alexandrian coral, 'Nepāla' wool and 'Chīna' silk (see *Note 1.2*). But, as we have seen, Megasthenes tells us that pearls from the Pāṇḍiyan kingdom in south India were in demand throughout India; and from archaeological finds we learn that cornelian and agate from south Gujarat and sea-shells from the Arabian Sea coast were taken to Taxila to be turned into beads.

Long-distance trade was carried on both over water and on roads. According to Megasthenes, as quoted by Strabo (XV.1.11) and Arrian (*Indica*, III), one could undertake a voyage from Pāṭaliputra to the sea (the Bay of Bengal) over the Ganga, the waterway having a length of 600 stadia (or 1,110 kilometres), an apparent overstatement. To the west, the capital is said to have been connected by a royal road with the Empire's western frontier, the road having a length of about 1,000 stadia (or 1,850 kilometres). In the Gangetic plains, the course of this road may well be marked by the line of Ashokan pillars (inscribed and uninscribed) set up, east to west, at Prahladpur, Sarnath, Allahabad, Kaushāmbī, Sankisa, Meerut and Topra (the last two, in later times, removed to Delhi). In Afghanistan, the Laghman road inscriptions in Aramaic attest to the presence of this highway (*kārapathi*, army road).

Another line of pillars marks another road – possibly a Buddhist pilgrim road – leading northwards from Pāṭaliputra through Kolhua (near Vaishali), Lauriya Araraj, Lauriya Nandangarh, Rampurwa, Rummindei and Nigali Sagar, and terminating at Shrāvastī. (See *Maps 2.1–2.3* for the sites of the pillars.) It is possible that many Ashokan rock inscriptions were put by the roadside, but it may be too speculative to draw the lines of major Mauryan roads on the basis of spots that are so distant from each other.

It is most unlikely that the highways were, in much of their length, anything more than strips of land cleared of jungle, thicket and bush, only roughly levelled but well marked by cart-ruts. There is no evidence from excavations in the Bhir Mound that the surface of any road even within the city was paved, except in small patches. Ashoka's Rock Edict II and Pillar Edict VII (*Extracts 2.2* and *2.7 [B]*) show that rows of trees, especially banyan trees, would be planted along the highways, and at short distances there would be wells to provide water. Rest-places (possibly, sheds) are also mentioned, presumably established at longer distances. It was probably these facilities, along with some provision of security, rather than a stable smooth surface, that were regarded as the necessary adjuncts of an ideal road. What amount of traffic these roads actually carried is, however, a closed book to us.

One can legitimately presume that the cattle for which Ashoka wished to provide water to drink were mainly pack-oxen and oxen drawing carts and chariots. Camels could also have been so used, but the camel sculptured in the Ashokan pillar-capital at Udayagiri is still of the Bactrian species with the double hump. This hairy beast could not have worked well in the hot Indian plains, where the single-humped dromedary would serve far better. But the latter had apparently not yet reached India. The cart-wheel as sculptured in Ashokan capitals (as at Sarnath, *Fig. 3.11*) is a fairly sophisticated one, with twenty-four to twenty-eight spokes radiating from the hub, and giving some indication of 'dishing' or sloping of the spokes. Pottery toy-carts from Atranjikhera also show similar wheels. Attached to chariots, these would have provided speedier and smoother travel along the rutted surfaces that the chariots had to pass over. Dishing was known in contemporary China, but was not employed in Europe until the fifteenth century AD.

In Chapter 1.6 we have touched on the use of money for the

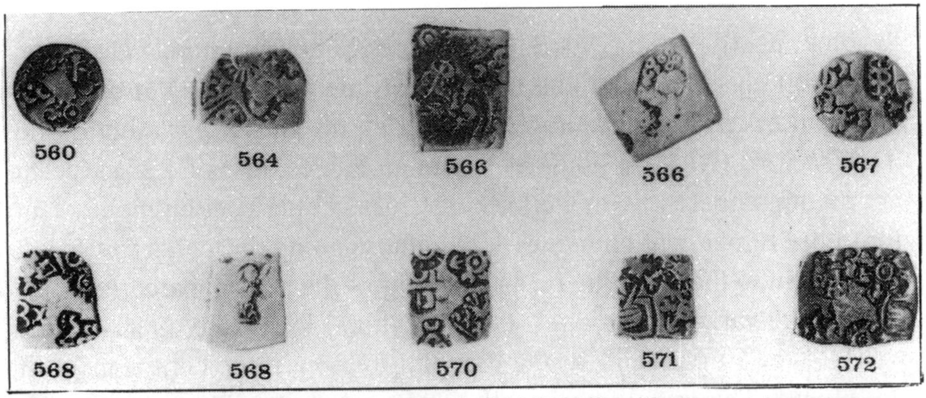

Fig. 3.5 Mauryan punch-marked coins of 'Series VIb'. (Classification, catalogue nos. and reprod., P.L. Gupta and T.R. Hardaker)

payment of taxes, and the minting of silver **punch-marked coins** to serve as money (*Fig. 3.5*). These coins also served commerce, and it is probable that their circulation led to the rise of a class of money-changers, who tested and verified the coins, and put their marks ('bankers' marks') on them. Whether these 'bankers' engaged in money-lending, based on their reserves of coins, is not known. During the Mauryan times official post-mintage marks tend to replace these private marks; and it is possible that the Mauryan Empire established a better scrutiny of its own mint issues. On the other hand, a major phase of debasement now ensued, with the content of copper raised to about a quarter, while the weight of individual coins was retained at 3.3 to 3.5 grams. Since the surviving hoards show a large amount of increase in coinage under the Mauryas, it is obvious that the Mauryan treasury sought to make a profit, through debasement, while meeting the increasing demand for coined money. But such debasement was ultimately bound to drive down the market worth of the coin and so bring the phase of extra profit to a close. The *Arthashāstra* (II.12.26) provides for punishment to private minters so as to remove competition with state mints; but counterfeit coins from the Mauryan period have come down to us. Like their modern successors, the counterfeiters sometimes took recourse to the most recent technology. Thus, a counterfeit coin assigned to the times of Ashoka is really a piece of copper coated with silver – the earliest known application of this technique in India.

The wider use of coinage must have helped to expand the network of credit. We have no definite evidence of bills of exchange. On the other hand, Pāṇini (IV.4.31) introduces us to usury pure and simple, when he treats as 'mean' the charging of interest (*kusīda*) of one on a principal of ten (*dashaikadasha*, '10:11'), presumably per month. The *Arthashāstra* (III.11.1) holds as lawful an interest rate of 1.25 per cent per month, apparently on well-secured loans, 5 per cent on money lent for trade, 10 per cent on money lent to those going through a forest and 20 per cent to those setting on a sea voyage – the risks apparently determining the variations in rates. On agricultural loans, the interest is set (III.11.4) at 50 per cent for the cropping season, to be compounded if not repaid. This would practically amount to what Pāṇini had considered to be a usurious rate.

3.2 Society

From our accounts of the Mauryan administration (Chapter 1.6) and the economy of the time (3.1), it should be clear that a strong imperial **ruling class** had established itself, with a claim to a very large part of the economic surplus. In two portions of the *Arthashāstra*, there are indications of two kinds of groups out of which this class could have originated. One is designated *paurajānapada*, literally, '(people) of towns and provinces' (II.14.1). The account of it that our text gives makes it clear that by this designation not ordinary people but influential and wealthy persons of the administered or settled country are meant, from whom offices could be filled and on whom other favours might be conferred (or punishments inflicted). We may remember (see Chapter 1.6 above) that the term *janapada* occurs in Ashokan edicts, where it carries the sense of province or territory, so that the term *paurajānapada*, found in Khāravela's Hathigumpha inscription (1st century BC) and in Rudradāman's Junagarh inscription of AD 150, could still be of Mauryan vintage. The second group is described in the *Arthashāstra* (XI.1) under the term *saṁgha*, rendered as 'corporation' or 'oligarchy', but here standing rather for clan or tribe. The *saṁghas* are put in two categories: (1) Kāmbojas, etc., living by wealth and as warriors, and (2) Lichchhivis, etc., claiming to be ruling clans. The names of clans listed in each group suggest an early date for at least this portion of the text (see *Note 1.2*). The *Arthashāstra* holds that such clans enjoyed intrinsic unity, but the king is advised to strive to undermine this unity, win over some of the clan leaders to himself, and isolate, neutralize or destroy the others.

What little information we get about individuals belonging to the Mauryan bureaucracy appears to confirm our supposition that it comprised elements both from the gentry of the settled zones and the professional and ruling clans. Tradition uniformly alleges that Chāṇakya or Kauṭilya, a Brahman, was the principal minister of Chandragupta Maurya; and in Rudradāman's Junagarh inscription, the same emperor's governor of Saurashtra is called 'the *Vaiṣhya* Pu<u>sh</u>yagupta', his caste suggesting that he came from the urban or mercantile classes (*paurajānapada*). His successor under Ashoka, the Hellenized Iranian Tushāsp, presumably came from Kāmboja, the region of the first among the warrior clans (*saṁgha*) listed in the *Arthashāstra*. There is other evidence too for the influx of northwestern elements in Mauryan officialdom, which we have already presented in Chapter 1.6.

This ruling class, itself composed of diverse elements, stood over a society in which the three basic institutions of the **caste system**, namely, hierarchy fixed by birth, fixed hereditary occupations and endogamy (see *The Vedic Age, Note 2.1*), had by now taken strong roots. Megasthenes, in his account of the Indian castes, preserved in the works of Diodorus (*Extract 3.1*), Strabo (XV.1.39–41, 46–49) and Arrian (*Indica*, XI–XII), recognizes the hierarchical structure of the caste system when he holds the 'philosophers' to form the caste deemed to stand highest in eminence. He insists, too, that no one could change the calling assigned to him by his caste or marry outside of it. Once these features were assigned to the seven divisions that he goes on to describe, it does not surely matter what word in Greek was used for them originally by Megasthenes – whether *merē* or *gene*, or both: the meaning here could be nothing else but caste.

This difficulty to find an adequate term for caste did not only exist for the Greeks, however; it also existed for Indians. The *Arthashāstra* follows throughout the system of the conventional division of Aryan society into the four *varṇas* (Brahmans, K<u>sh</u>atriyas, Vaishyas and Shūdras), ascribing to them the different status and functions indicated in the Dharmasūtras of earlier times and in the *Manusmriti* (second century AD). In the *Arthashāstra* (I.3.4–8: *Extract 3.2*), the different sets of duties (*dharma*) assigned to each *varṇa* – with Shūdras made submissive to the first three 'twice-born' *varṇas*, headed by Brahmans –

are concisely set out. In the same sub-chapter (I.3.9), members of all the *varṇas* are instructed to follow endogamy.

Yet, it is clear that the caste system extended much beyond the four *varṇas*, there being several castes that could not be fitted into any of the *varṇas*. These communities, termed *antarāla* ('intermediate'), of which the text names fourteen, are supposed to have arisen out of intermarriages between men and women of different *varṇas* as well as between members of different such communities (*Arthashāstra* III.7.20–34). Some of these communities are placed above the Shūdras but others below them, even at par with the Chaṇḍālas. But each of them was yet a separate caste, since each was required to pursue endogamy as well as to engage in the hereditary occupation assigned to it (III.7.36). The term *jāti*, which would subsequently become the recognized term for these castes, carries in Pāṇini (V.4.9) a rather vague sense of community or class; and is in the *Arthashāstra* also a term of varied import. In *Arthashāstra* III.7.40 and III.10.45, it means no more than a local community, placed alongside region, clan (*saṁgha*), village and family whose customs are to be followed; and in I.12.21, there is a reference to different *jātis*, that is, races or communities, of *mlechchhas*, or foreigners.

We can see from the case of the 'intermediate' communities that the caste system was now imposing its own institutions on these communities though they were outside the recognized *varṇas*. Caste institutions were similarly embracing the outcastes as well. The general word for such outcastes in the *Arthashāstra*, as in late Vedic texts, is Chaṇḍāla. It is remarkable that in the *Arthashāstra*'s list of castes arising out of intermarriages, a union with a Chaṇḍāla man or woman is not even countenanced as possible. There could, in other words, be no lower position than that of a Chaṇḍāla, as we are reminded, again, in III.7.36, where it is stated that all the 'intermediate' castes could pursue the duties of the Shūdras, but not of Chaṇḍālas. The Chaṇḍālas could not live within the towns, but only in the proximity of cremation grounds (II.4.23). There is direct evidence of 'untouchability' also in the stated fact that a well used by Chaṇḍālas could not be used by others (I.14.10), and in the heavy fine imposed on a Chaṇḍāla who happened to touch an Ārya woman (III.20.16). The Chaṇḍālas might be the lowliest of the outcastes, but there were other communities that could still be grouped with them, such, for example, as the Vāgurika (trappers), Shabara, Pulinda and Araṇyacharā (forest people), entrusted with watch-and-ward duty (II.1.6). Like Chaṇḍāla, the name Shvapāka seems to cover all the outcastes (IV.13.34–35), a Shvapāka being adjudged worthy of death if he had relations with an Ārya woman. In the *Manusmriti* too (X.51–56) the Chaṇḍālas and Shvapākas are put at par in practically every disability that could be thought of.

If, then, the four *varṇas* did not alone constitute caste society, and there were the 'intermediate' castes as well as the outcastes, it should not surprise us that Megasthenes should have exceeded the conventional figure of four when he set his own number of the major castes at seven. It is obvious that he followed a broadly occupational basis for his classification. It is easy thus to see that his first caste, "philosophers", and the fifth, "military", correspond to the *varṇas* of Brahmans and Kṣhatriyas, respectively. But, in fact, *samanas* (who were also 'philosophers') could have come from any caste; and the *Arthashāstra* (IX.2.24) recognizes that Vaishyas and Shūdras could also serve effectively as soldiers, and not just the Kṣhatriyas.

In the case of Vaishyas and Shūdras, the lines of theoretical status were drawn very sharply but the occupational lines were blurred. Being once the successors to the *vish*, the mass, the Vaishyas were still theoretically assigned the pursuit of "agriculture, cattle-rearing and trade" (*Arthashāstra*, I.3.7); and chariot-makers (*rathakāras*) were conceded the status of Vaishya because of their work (*karman*). But, in fact, the status of the Vaishyas was being denied to most peasants, as is indicated by the prescription that new lands should be cultivated by Shūdra peasants (*karṣhaka*). Composed in about the second century AD, the *Manusmriti* (X.80, 84) held trade to be the commendable occupation for a Vaishya, and condemned agriculture, though keeping this profession permissible for the Vaishyas. It may, therefore, seem that Megasthenes's fourth caste, of artisans and traders, corresponded to the Vaishyas, and his second and most numerous caste, that of peasants, to the Shūdras. Almost by a process of elimination, the third caste, of nomadic cowherds and shepherds and huntsmen, should correspond to the Chaṇḍālas. As we have just seen, the *Arthashāstra* (II.1.6) itself puts trappers and forest people at par with the Chaṇḍālas, while elsewhere (III.4.22), the cowherds (*gopāla*) are grouped with fishermen, fowlers, vintners, etc., to whom the *varṇa* rules for women did not apply. Thus, there was enough justification to put all these groups into a single lowly caste.

As for the remaining two 'castes' of Megasthenes, the sixth and seventh, of superintendents and councillors, respectively, we have here surely a reflection of the importance of the bureaucracy in the Mauryan Empire, whose members, as we have seen at the beginning of this sub-chapter, came from diverse groups and, by their occupations, could not be fitted into any particualr *varṇa*. This mixture may have spawned 'intermediate' castes of some status, such as the Ambaṣhṭhas, who supposedly arose out of the legitimate union of a Brahman with a Vaishya woman (*Arthashāstra* III.7.21).

The complexities of the caste system might make the four-*varṇa* scheme seem as much of a theoretical exercise as Megasthenes's seven castes. But the institutions of caste, hierarchy, endogamy, and occupational fixity, were not unreal; and for those in the lower ranks and the outcastes, the system was oppressive in the extreme. In the *Arthashāstra*, as in the Dharmashāstra texts generally, there is no concept of equality before the law, and punishments for civil offences often vary according to the *varṇa* of the offender, those of the higher *varṇas* getting off more lightly, as a rule, while for the Shūdras, these are as often brutally severe. Moreover, if status was fixed for all time, then harsh non-economic compulsions could be employed with impunity against those who stood tied to a low station by birth: thus Chaṇḍālas and others, deprived of any possibility of turning into Shūdra peasants, could be reserved for field labour or other servile work. Similarly, fixity of occupation meant that low-caste labourers were bound to accept whatever wages or recompense was offered to them, for they could take to no other calling. If products and services were thus cheapened, it would be the ruling class and the highest ranks of society who would derive the main benefit out of these caste restrictions, and not just the Brahmans, however great be the eminence that was claimed for them.

The lack of social mobility implicit in caste is brought home to us in a passage in the *Majjhima Nikāya*, 93, apparently composed in Mauryan times but put into the mouth of Gautama Buddha. Here the Buddha tells a Brahman listener that, "in Yona–Kaṁboja (the Graeco–Iranian borderland of the Mauryan Empire) and adjacent regions (*jānapada*), there are only two *varṇas* ('*vaṇṇā*'): masters (*ayya*) and slaves (*dāsa*). One who has been a master may become a slave, and one who has been a slave may become a master." Here the point is not only that among the Yonas, etc., society was divided into just two classes, but that a change of status was possible, with the free becoming slaves, and the slaves becoming free persons. The situation is obviously described to offer a contrast to India, where one was tied down to one's *varṇa* for one's whole life.

There could be a further possible meaning one can read into this statement, viz. that while the division in the Yona or Hellenistic society was between masters and slaves, the Indian social divisions, based on the fixed *varṇas*, were of a different kind, and **slavery** was not as important here as among the Greeks. Megasthenes asserts, in fact, that there was no slavery in India (Diodorus, II.39; Strabo, XV.1.54; Arrian, *Indica*, X). Arrian adds, perhaps on his own, that the Indians were like the Lakedaimonians (people of Sparta), who had no slaves but had helots or peasants bound to the land, though Indians did not even have helots. These statements are, however, clearly wrong. The only justification for Megasthenes's assertion can be that he had possibly heard the legal dictum invoked in the *Arthashāstra* (III.13.4) that "no Ārya can be reduced to slavery (*dāsabhāva*)", it being indicated in the preceding clauses that the term Ārya here covers the Shūdras as well and not only the three 'twice-born' *varṇas*. Yet, even if we believe that this legal principle was meticulously followed in practice, there were, as we have just seen, a sufficient number of people outside the four *varṇas*, such as the Chaṇḍālas, forest people, etc., from amongst whom a fairly adequate supply of slaves could be continuously procured. Ashoka's edicts (Rock Edicts IX, XI, XIII; Pillar Edict VII) mention *dāsas* or slaves, along with servants (*bhaṭaka*), as those who needed to be well-treated. Buddhist Pāli literature, some of which doubtless dating from Mauryan times, tells us of the harsh treatment the domestic slaves, particularly women, received at the hands of their masters and mistresses. It needs to be clarified that the protections the *Arthashāstra* offers in a sub-chapter on slaves (*dāsas*) and labourers (III.13) are practically entirely concerned with "Ārya" men and women, who might pledge themselves or their children to work under a master for certain periods. Leaving aside these clauses (III.13.5–19), one finds that a slave could be inherited, sold and gifted away, or might be born in a master's house as slave; and that both male and female slaves could be sold at the master's will, provided he rightfully owned them (III.13.20, 25). True, a slave could have some possessions of his own, because kinsmen could inherit his property (III.13.22). Yet there were no other rights that are mentioned, not even of proper provision of subsistence or freedom from physical assault. It is implied (III.13.23) that a female slave (*dāsī*) could be subject to her master's advances, and could win freedom only if she bore him a child. In a Mauryan-period cave inscription from Jogimara cave (Ramgarh hills), a man from Balanashi (Varanasi) declares his love for a *devadāsī*; and one thus strongly suspects that these female temple slaves were then, as in later times, used as courtesans. The *Arthashāstra* (II.23.2) has also a reference to *devadāsīs*, too old to serve in their profession and so compelled to spin yarn for livelihood. The treatment of slaves was, therefore, hardly humane, though it could, of course, have been still more brutal than it was. Although it is not mentioned anywhere, slaves, though not untouchable outcastes, were still, by definition, not Āryas, and, therefore, assigned to no *varṇa*.

Of the place of **women** in Mauryan society, a single picture can hardly be presented. In two sets of communities their role as equal partners in occupational activity was so extensive that the *Arthashāstra* (III.4.22) admits that restrictions on freedom of women could not apply to them. These were, first, the communities of "dancers and wandering minstrels", where men and women had to move and perform together; second, "fishermen, fowlers, cowherds, vintners and others", among whom women shared heavily in work. On women of the recognized *varṇas*, however, restrictions on movements were fairly severe, being enforceable by fines (III.4.1–23). Respectability obviously required women to be kept secluded in their homes (*anis̲h̲kāsinī*) (II.23.11; III.1.7). Yet, in order to get work, poorer women who spun yarn had to go out to fetch the fibre, give in the yarn and collect their wages. They were by no means treated with much consideration. If they did not turn in their work, their thumb and forefinger could be mutilated (II.23.14–15).

There were only two kinds of property (*strīdhana*) that women could lay claim to: means of subsistence (*vritti*) and ornaments (*Arthashāstra*, III.2.14). If there were sons, then daughters had no claims on inheritance from their father (III.5.1–2, 9–11) or even to the *strīdhana* left by their mother (III.2.36). The proclamation of male superiority is concentrated in the dictum that "wives (*strī*) are there for having sons" (III.2.42). In a late-Mauryan brick inscription from Mora (Mathura), the consort of a chief (*rājabhāryā*) mentions it as a particular point of honour that she had sons living (*jīvaputāya*).

Marriage is conceived in the *Arthashāstra* as a contractual transaction, where the bride's parents receive from the suitor, the bride-price (*shulka*), while the *strīdhana* ('wife's wealth') is for the bride (III.2.10–11, 15.14–15). This reminds us of the practice at Taxila, observed in Alexander's time, of poor people exposing their daughters for sale in the market-place as brides (Strabo, XV.16.2). There is though a suggestion in the *Arthashāstra* of payments received by the groom too (III.3.17–18). The notion of bride-sale is continued in case a wife's husband died, and she remarried: the remarriage had to have the sanction of her late husband's father, for, otherwise, she would have to return whatever she had received in her previous marriage (III.2. 19–30). Not only widow remarriage but a wife's fresh marriage after a husband's abandonment of her or disappearance is also permitted (III.4. 24–36). But, in such a case, a marriage with the dead husband's brother or next-of-kin is strongly prescribed (III.4.37–42). Even divorce is held possible in the *Arthashāstra* (III.3.15–19), if both parties loathed each other, and, on other occasions too, if what had been received was returned. On the other hand, polygamy was allowed, notably with the avowed object of getting sons (III.2.38–41). This may partly be the reason why, in the Queen's Edict, Ashoka's second queen has her son's name especially entered before her own. Since consummation was expected to take place when the wife was only twelve years old (*Arthashāstra*, III.3.1–2), it is obvious that women's health must have greatly suffered as a result.

3.3 Religion

In his edicts, Ashoka throughout refers to the religious classes as Brahmans and *samanas*. In Rock Edict XIII (*Extract 1.4*) he makes his meaning clearer: There is no region, he says, where there are no Brahmans and *samanas*, except the region of the Yonas; and, in any case, there is no place in any country where men are not attached to one *pāsaṁḍa* or another. Here, and in Rock Edicts VII and XII (*Extract 2.4*), the word *pāsaṁḍa* can only suit the context if it means a religious sect or denomination. In Edict VII (*Extract 2.7 [C]*), the same term expressly covers the Buddhist *Saṁgha*, Brahmans, Ājīvikas and Jains. Its use in this general, neutral sense contrasts with the meaning it has received in both Sanskrit and Prākrit. Of obscure etymology, *pāshaṇḍa* in Sanskrit means heresy, false doctrine or a follower thereof, so a Buddhist or Jain; also a pious hypocrite (Hindustani, *pākhanḍ*). The word does not occur in the Vedic literature, but is of frequent occurrence in the *Arthashāstra* (I.18.12; II.4.23). The *pāshaṇḍa-saṁgha* can be despoiled by a prince in need of money (I.18.9), *saṁgha* being the designation the Buddhists and Jains used for their orders. At another place (III.20.16), the Buddhists ('Shākya') and Ājīvakas (so spelt), along with other unspecified heretical (*vrishala*) mendicants, are deemed unfit to be fed at rituals. In the Pāli texts of the Buddhists, *pāsaṇḍa* retains its nature as a condemnatory word, being here applied to Brahmans and other non-Buddhists. That Ashoka should resort to this term to describe all religious sects was simply, perhaps, because no other word existed to supply this want. What his Rock Edict XII seeks to address, viz. the coexistence of contending religions, was apparently a novel situation for which language itself was unprepared. The situation was undoubtedly a long-range consequence of the religious revolution of the fifth century BC that had brought forth Buddhism and Jainism, to challenge the Brahmanical monopoly of the religious world. But it was the work of Ashoka to give recognition to the result, and, declaring the followers of all religions as *pāsaṁḍas*, to put them, at last, on the same plane.

Though challenged, the influence of **Brahmanism** was still probably the most widespread. It was quite natural that, by both internal evolution and the influence of the opposing religious movements, the ideas and practices of Brahmanism would also begin to be transformed. The one change, doubtless, was a decline of the Vedic ritual, notably the ritual of sacrifice, from the position it had occupied in the *Brāhmaṇas*. The *Arthashāstra* (I.9.9) asks that the king have as his most important minister a *purohita*, or Brahman priest, not only proficient in Vedic rites, but also in the omens and spells of the *Atharvaveda*. The greatest measure of impiety would be to ask such a *purohita* to officiate at a sacrifice (*yājana*) for a person not fit to offer it (presumably being of low caste). Rules for fees at the sacrifices are carefully laid down (III.14.28–36). Vedic deities like Indra, Varuṇa, Agni and others are also mentioned or invoked (I.15.55–57; IV.13.43; XIV.1.38; etc.). But Ashoka, in his Rock Edict I, prohibited the killing of animals as ritual offerings (*pajohitava*) and banned the gatherings (*samāja*) that were held for the purpose. The order shows not only that such animal sacrifices had continued till the time of the edict (*c.* 258 BC), but also that the popular support for the ritual had sufficiently weakened for it to be prohibited. Indeed, the concept of *ahiṁsā*, or non-injury to living beings, had by now so entered Brahmanical consciousness that the *Arthashāstra* (I.3.13) prescribes it as part of duty (*dharma*) for persons of all *varṇas*. By the second century AD, it would be so far accepted in such an orthodox text as the *Manusmriti* (X.84) as to enable it to condemn agriculture as a discredited occupation for higher *varṇas*, since the plough with its iron point injures the earth and kills its creatures.

In an interesting statement, the *Arthashāstra* (I.2.10) makes Sāṁkhya, Yoga and Lokāyata constitute philosophy (*ānvīkshikī*). No extant texts of the Sāṁkhya or Yoga schools can be dated to Mauryan times; and of Lokāyata no texts have at all survived. But as we saw in *The Vedic Age*, 2.5, the Sāṁkhya system can be traced to the theory of transmigration of souls and of *ātman* propounded in the Upanishads, and ideas based on this theory might have begun to be gathered together by Mauryan times in a largely atheistic tradition. Since Yoga, as a philosophical system, is an emanation of Sāṁkhya, with theism added and emphasis laid on control of the mind and body, its emergence should be subsequent in time to that of Sāṁkhya. Its reputed founder Patañjali, author of the *Yogasūtra*, cannot be identified with the grammarian Patañjali (second century BC), and his date is, therefore, also uncertain. Lokāyata is known to us only through its critics, as a doctrine of *asuras* (demons) believing in mere material pleasure and denying the truth of the Vedas. A passage in the *Maitrī Upanishad*, a late one but perhaps not of a post-Mauryan date, seems to refer to this doctrine as one taught by Brihaspati. It is strange, however, that the *Arthashāstra* should give Lokāyata such importance and treat it as an acceptable part of Brahmanical philosophy.

It is possible that the Mauryan period saw early glimmerings of *bhakti*, or devotion seeking the deity's grace. The most definite evidence for this comes from Heliodorus's column at Besnagar (Vidisha) near Sanchi, on which an inscription datable to *c*. 140 BC proclaims it as "the Garuḍa flagstaff for the great god Vāsudeva", the donor describing himself as "*bhāgavata* (devotee)". With this date as a firm bottom-line, we can look for earlier evidence. A reference to Vāsudeva and Arjuna as receiving reverence has, indeed, been traced back to Pāṇini (IV.3.98), *c*. 350 BC. In the *Arthashāstra* (XIV.3.44), the name Kri<u>sh</u>ṇa occurs, but put unimportantly among many spirits in a magic *mantra*. There is a reference, however, to a worshipper (*devatīya*) of Sankar<u>sh</u>aṇa (Kri<u>sh</u>ṇa's emanatory form). There is seemingly a firmer indication of the popularity of Vāsudeva in Megasthenes's account as quoted by Arrian (*Indica*, VIII). He speaks of an Indian god whom he identifies with Herakles, going on to say that this deity was held in special honour by the Sourasenoi (Sūrasenas), whose main cities were 'Methora' (Mathura) and 'Cleisobora' (?). The ascription of a daughter, 'Pandaia', to this Herakles suggests a double confusion between Kri<u>sh</u>ṇa's family and the Pāṇḍavas, and of the latter with the southern Pāṇḍiyas. Yet, whatever the degree of confusion, the influence of a strong Vāsudeva–Kri<u>sh</u>ṇa cult centred at Mathura is well attested.

The worship of Shiva must have continued from earlier times; yet, he is only put as one among the nine gods whose shrines are to be built in a city (*Arthashāstra*, II.4.17). Patañjali (V.3.99) does allege that the Mauryas sold away the images of Shiva, Skanda and Vishākha. Of the phallic aspect of the Shiva cult, there is little evidence yet, unless some uninscribed coins with the phallic symbol from Ujjain can be dated as early as the third or second century BC.

We noted (Chapter 1.1) that Alexander's historians do not mention the presence of temples in the northwest. The *Arthashāstra* (I.18.9) advises a needy prince to rob the wealth of temples (*deva*, lit. god), except such as were used by learned Brahmans; it speaks, too, of the temple-cattle (*devapashu*) (IV.13.20) and the temples' slave girls (*devadāsī*) (II.23.2). The temple itself is called *devagriha* (god's house') (II.36.28) and by other such names. Marshall identified a pillared hall in the Bhir Mound (Taxila) as a possible temple structure, since, in the debris of the building and nearby, were found numerous terracotta reliefs showing a male and female deity holding hands. The apsidal plan of a shrine, revealed by excavations at Besnagar near the Heliodorus column, apparently belongs to a period before the erection of the column (*c.* 140 BC) and so is probably of a Mauryan date.

It is likely that deities' images, if put in these temples, were made of wood, for no stone images of gods have been recovered, and wood, of course, would not be preserved over such a long time. The *Arthashāstra*'s reference (XIII.2.25) to the burning of a deity's image (*daivatapratimā*) in a shrine (*chaitya*) also implies the presence of a wooden representation.

A number of female figurines in terracotta found in Mauryan levels at several sites, such as Taxila, Ahichhatra, Sonkh, Kaushāmbī, Rajghat (Varanasi), Buxar and Patna, have been generally described as those of the "Mother Goddess" (*Fig. 3.6*). These were images probably kept in houses and huts to be worshipped or venerated, and possibly occupied a place in women's daily ritual: Ashoka, in Rock Edict IX, does complain that women performed "many varied, vulgar and useless rites (*maṁgala*)". The images themselves were probably representations of female spirits of the kind that the *Arthashāstra*, XIV.3.36, names for invocation in spells: Amilā, Kimilā, Vayuchārā, Prayogā, Phakkā, Vayuhvā, Vihālā and Dantakaṭakā. Their names do not otherwise occur in Brahmanical texts, but then the terracotta female figurines are also bereft of any identifying marks known to later iconography.

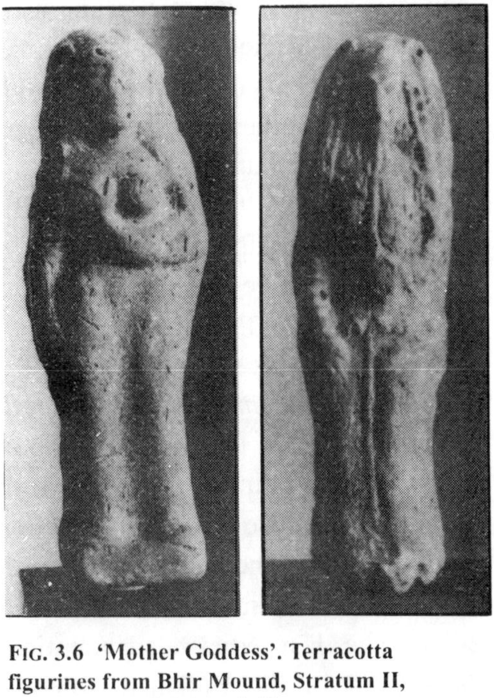

FIG. 3.6 'Mother Goddess'. Terracotta figurines from Bhir Mound, Stratum II, Taxila. (Reprod. J. Marshall)

Men, too, were affected by a superstitious addiction to rituals. Ashoka refers, in Rock Edict IX, to their performance of many rituals (*maṁgala*) during illness, on the marriage of a son or daughter, the birth of a child, or when setting forth on a journey. The addiction to rituals concealed a widespread fear of malevolent spirits and magic spells, and the need to counter them. There seems to have been a real terror felt at the possible appearance of *rākshasas* or demons (*Arthashāstra*, XIII.2.29–32). Evil spirits needed to be exorcised by resort to the *Atharvaveda* spells, or by means of magic and worship of trees with goat sacrifices and other offerings (IV.3.40–41). The *Arthashāstra* (IV.4.14–15, V.2.59–63) also shows how people's credulity could be preyed upon to make them perform peculiar or occult rites to gain some object. Omens of all kinds were to be looked for. Even the king was advised to have in his service fortune-tellers, soothsayers and astrologers (V.3.13). We may also recall Megasthenes's statement that people expected their 'philosophers' to tell them at the beginning of each year whether any misfortune was to ensue during it.

The Ashokan edicts mark the beginning of a period of some five hundred years during which **Buddhism** enjoyed a position in India well above the other religions, if we go by the records of donations and the monuments that survive.

Ashoka, remembered by Buddhists of all traditions for his patronage of Buddhism, provides us enough evidence about Buddhist beliefs and practices in his edicts for us to be sure that the religion was already present in the form we know it from the Pāli Canon (for which see below, 3.4). He repeats the established Buddhist formula of faith in the Buddha, *Dhaṁma* and *Saṁgha* (Bairat Rock Edict); and, if he does not directly refer to the Four Noble Truths, he does use the word *majhaṁ* (middle) in the sense of just or excellent (Separate Rock Edict I), recalling the use of this word in the fourth Truth about the 'Middle' Eight-fold Path. The *Saṁgha*, or Buddhist monastic order, is mentioned in Minor Rock Edict I, Bairat Rock Edict, Pillar Edict VII and Schism Edict. The last edict also mentions monks (*bhikkhu*) and nuns (*bhikkhuni*) of the Buddhist order by their traditional designations ('beggars'). It prescribes a change of robe (from yellow) to white for those expelled from the *Saṁgha*, a practice consistent with the Thera-vāda tradition. As in the latter, the word *upāsaka* too is used for the laity (not monks or nuns) in Minor Rock Edict I and the Schism Edict (Sar-nath). The Rummindei Edict (*Extract 3.3*) uses the name Luṁmini for the Buddha's birth-place, so also known from Buddhist tradition. In

Rock Edict VIII, Ashoka mentions *saṁbodhi*, the term for the sacred Bo-tree at Buddha Gaya in early Pāli texts. The Nigali Sagar Pillar Edict not only implies that the building of a *thuba* (*stūpa*) (relic chamber) was an established practice, but also confirms that the legend about Konākamana, one of the previous Buddhas, was already quite old. The Bairat Edict is of even greater significance since it shows that there was in circulation a collection of the Buddha's discourses, out of which Ashoka selected seven texts, with titles given. One must infer from this that the *Tipiṭaka* of the Pāli Canon was then known, in some form similar to what it has today.

We have already discussed, in Chapter 2.2, the relationship between Buddhism and Ashoka's *dhaṁma*. While it is true that Ashoka nowhere expressly traces his *dhaṁma* to Buddhism, he declares clearly his own devotion to Buddhism, and, in Pillar Edict VII, gives the Buddhist *Saṁgha* the pride of place among the recipients of his patronage. On the actual extent of his patronage, the edicts are silent, but the Buddhist traditions, both of the Theravāda and Mahāyāna, go to fantastic lengths in describing it: the *Dīpavaṁsa* and the *Ashokāvadāna*, both assert that Ashoka, after his conversion to Buddhism, built 84,000 Buddhist shrines (designated as *vihāras* or *stūpas* in the respective texts). While discounting these numbers, we can still not find it difficult to agree that the patronage was generous and so could bring about the results that the Sri Lankan tradition frankly describes: numerous "heretics", looking for easy income, donned the yellow robes and joined the *Saṁgha*; they then introduced their own practices and created much unruliness in the Buddhist order. When this led to disturbances, a vast assemblage of *bhikkhus* (monks) was convened at Pāṭaliputra, where the doctrines of the heretics were condemned, and they were expelled from the *Saṁgha*. The Schism Edict of Ashoka, which can be read in three versions on pillars at Sarnath (the most detailed), Allahabad and Sanchi, concerns precisely such a general expulsion of the monks and nuns who were causing a split (*bhākhati*) in the *Saṁgha*. Since the Schism Edicts are probably subsequent to Pillar Edicts I–VI and thus belong to Ashoka's late years, *c*. 243–234 BC, the expulsion seems to have occurred much later in Ashoka's reign than the Sri Lankan text *Mahāvaṁsa*'s chronology would allow.

The Sri Lankan tradition (*Mahāvaṁsa*, V, 268–281) also tells us that the assemblage that expelled the heretics acclaimed the *Vibhajja* ('logical') doctrine (the same as Theravāda) to be the correct one. Thereafter, under the monk Moggaliputta Tissa, the Third Council of Buddhism met at Pāṭaliputra. A thousand monks, labouring for nine months, made a compilation of the true *dhaṁma* on the basis of the *Tipiṭakas*, and refuted false doctrines. The Mahāyānist tradition does not acknowledge this Council; but the Council would seem to have been a natural outcome of the dispute with the heretics, which, as we have seen, is duly reflected in Ashoka's Schism Edict. It is also possible that the *Tipiṭaka* in its present form is a product of this Council, since such passages as the one containing a comment on the class division in Yona society are likely to have been inserted only after Alexander's invasion (see 3.2 above). On the other hand, had the *Tipiṭaka* been compiled after Ashoka, it is difficult to see how it could have escaped the insertion of references to Ashoka himself, or to Sri Lanka and such clans and tribes as came on the stage during and after Mauryan times. Only, perhaps, the language has been altered from the Prākrit of Ashoka's days to the later literary Pāli.

Certain steps were taken after the Council in pursuit of an ambitious project to make Buddhism a world religion. In or before his Regnal Year 12 (*c*. 258 BC), Ashoka sent a number of envoys to carry the message of *dhaṁma* abroad. But now, according to Sri Lankan tradition (*Dīpavaṁsa*, VIII.10; *Mahāvaṁsa*, XII.1–8), the leading Buddhist monk, Moggaliputta, decided to send missionaries to foreign countries. These missionaries included a Yona monk, Dhaṁmarakhita, sent to the western borderland (Aparāntaka); Mahārakhita, sent to the 'Yona' country; Majjhima, sent to Himavata (Himalayas); Soṇa and Uttara, sent to Suvaṇṇabhūmi (Southeast Asia); and Ashoka's son, Mahinda, sent to Sri Lanka. A cell near the Sanchi *Stūpa* 1 was found to contain a casket of relics (now lost), which an inscription in practically Ashokan characters declared to be those of Kosāpagota, "teacher (*achāriya*) of Hemavaṁta", and Majjhima and Hāritiputa. According to Sri Lankan accounts, Kassapagota had, indeed, accompanied Majjhima to Himavata, so that the mission to the Himalayas is possibly a historical fact. As we have seen (Chapter 2.5), epigraphic evidence also strongly supports the arrival of Buddhism in Sri Lanka during

Ashoka's time, since donations to the Buddhist *Saṁgha* began to be recorded in cave inscriptions on the island immediately thereafter.

For **Jainism**, the Mauryan period proved to be a time of both expansion and dissension. In Pillar Edict VII (*Extract 2.7 [C]*), Ashoka includes the Nigaṁṭhas among the sects receiving his patronage; and this designation (meaning 'without bonds, liberated') used to be especially applied to Jains. According to the tradition of the Shvetāmbara sect of the Jains, a grave famine had occurred in Magadha in Chandragupta Maurya's time, which led to migration of a number of Jain monks, led by Bhadrabāhu, to Karnāṭa (Karnataka). The Tamil Brāhmī cave inscriptions from the Pāṇḍiyan country around Madurai belonging to the late third century and the second century BC confirm the presence of Jainism in the south, since practically all donations recorded in the inscriptions are to Jain monastic establishments (see above, Chapter 2.5).

The same tradition tells us that this migration gravely affected the Jain monkhood in the north, where its head, Sthūlabhadra, concerned about preserving the memory of Lord Mahāvīra's teachings, convened a Council at Pāṭaliputra, which compiled the Jain Canon in twelve *aṅgas*. At the same time, the wearing of white garments by monks came into vogue. But the Jain monks who had migrated to the south, on their return, declined to accept the newly compiled Canon, nor did they agree to wear clothes. These orthodox dissidents came to be known as the Digambaras, while those who accepted the Pāṭaliputra Canon and the practice of robing obtained the name Shvetāmbara. It is true that this tradition is not accepted by the Digambaras, but at least part of it seems to have some historical basis.

Unlike Jainism, which continued to flourish subsequently and made important contributions to both Prākrit and Sanskrit literatures and to thought and art, the sect of the **Ājīvikas** enjoyed a much shorter span of life. The sect enters history along with Buddhism and Jainism, but our entire knowledge about it comes from its opponents, since no Ājīvika tradition or text has survived. From Buddhist and Jain reports about them, one infers that the Ājīvikas were recluses, who lived by begging, practised austerities (including nudity) and believed in non-injury to all living things. In the Mauryan times, they were undoubtedly a sect with considerable presence. We find them paired with the Buddhists in the *Arthashāstra* (III.20.16), but it is the Ashokan inscriptions that tell us much more about them.

Ashoka donated two caves in the Barabar hills near Gaya, south Bihar, to the Ājīvikas in Regnal Year 12 (*c.* 258 BC), and a third one in Regnal Year 19 (*c.* 251 BC), though, in the last case, the phrase *ājīvikehi* at the end of the donative inscription is omitted. In his Pillar Edict VII (*Extract 2.7 [C]*) of Regnal Year 27 (*c.* 243 BC), Ashoka mentions his patronage to the Ājīvikas, the reference to them preceding the one to the Jains. One of his successors, Dasharatha, in his year of accession, dedicated to the Ājīvikas three caves in the Nagarjuni hills in the same neighbourhood. These caves are important from the point of view of art and would be discussed below (see 3.5). The excavation, stone-cutting and polishing certainly needed considerable use of skill and labour; and this is also an indication of the status the Ājīvikas then enjoyed.

The cave inscriptions, however, also hint at the manner of their downfall. In four of the five inscriptions where the phrase *ājīvikehi* occurs, this has been wholly or partly defaced. Obviously, this was done by persons who could read and understand the original writing, and who nursed some respect for Ashoka or Dasharatha, so that they did not deface the entire inscriptions. These considerations point to the act having been carried out in late Mauryan times, when the Ājīvikas must simultaneously have been expelled from the caves. This was a setback to what, perhaps, was an already dying cause, since, after the Mauryan times, the Ājīvikas disappear from history, and when the name occurs again in much later times it is not at all certain if those it was being applied to had any real connection with the original Ājīvikas.

3.4 Writing, Languages, Learning, Literature

The arrival of **writing** marks an epochal advance in any society. Except for the Indus characters of the third millennium BC, there is no physical evidence of writing in India until the Ashokan edicts came to be inscribed on stone. No reference to writing has been traced in the Vedic texts and the *Brāhmaṇas*. The earliest literary evidence for writing is in Pāṇini, *As̲h̲tādhyāyī* (III.2.21), where the words *lipi* and *libi* ('script') occur, and though it is believed that Pāṇini wrote in *c.* 350 BC, there is no certainty about his date; and one might as well urge that, because of his reference to a script, as well as to *yavanānī* (see below), he should be put a hundred years later. Alternatively, as is more likely, he might have used the word *lipi* for the Aramaic script, which must have been known about 350 BC to people in Gandhāra, his native region. References to writing in early Pāli literature are also of little relevance, since it is generally accepted, on other grounds, that much of it was compiled long after the Buddha, in Mauryan times and later (see below). The Pāli Canon is itself believed to have been put into writing in Sri Lanka in late first century BC. The Greek evidence is largely against the presence of writing in India in the time of Alexander and Chandragupta. Strabo (XV.1.67) says that, while "other writers say that they (the Indians) make no use of written characters", only Alexander's admiral Nearchus reported that they wrote on closely woven cloth. Nearchus's statement could, like Pāṇini's, be treated as a reference to the use of the Aramaic script in the northwest. Strabo himself elsewhere (XV.1.53) quotes Megasthenes to the effect that Indians used only unwritten laws, for they were ignorant of writing and relied in all matters on memory. Since Megasthenes visited Pāṭaliputra and had greater knowledge of India than any other Greek source, this observation must be given much weight.

Those who hold that writing was known in India (other than in parts of the northwest) rest their case on two rather negative arguments. (1) A complex society such as the one at the time of the foundation of the Mauryan Empire could not have functioned without writing. (2) Since, in earlier times, the Indians wrote only on such perishable materials as palm-leaves, bark and cloth, the physical evidence of writing from pre-Mauryan times might not have survived. These are not unanswerable assertions. In the New World, fairly complex social and political structures, like those of the Aztec of Mexico and the Inca of Peru, existed without the use of writing. The Inca, for instance, had a system called 'quipu', which assisted memory by use of different kinds of strings and knots. In pre-Mauryan India, different kinds of marks and symbols have been found on potsherds and on punch-marked coins, which could have performed similar service. As for the second argument, one would naturally ask that if other marks could be put on pottery, why written characters should yet be absolutely absent from the pre-Mauryan archaeological record in India. In fact, as we have seen above in Chapter 2.5, Brāhmī characters have been found on potsherds at Anuradhapura, Sri Lanka, which have been confidently dated to the fourth century BC, if not earlier. Yet claims for a pre-Mauryan, or even early Mauryan date for pottery bearing Tamil-Brahmi characters from sites in Tamilnadu, have proved to be rather premature.

The question of the antiquity of writing in India is generally bound up with that of the origin of the Brāhmī script. Most of those who believe that writing existed in India in pre-Mauryan times tend to argue that the Brāhmī script evolved in northern India out of a process of internal development from marks and symbols. Some advocate even a connection with the Indus ideographs current over 1,500 years previously, where not the least similarity of form can be discerned. The best course seems to be to proceed from the known facts to the unknown. One fact that is fairly well established is the origin of the Kharoshṭhī script, employed to represent Ashokan Prākrit simultaneously with the Brāhmī. As shown by many scholars, notably G. Bühler, many characters of Kharoshṭhī have distinct resemblances to Aramaic characters bearing identical phonetic values; like Aramaic too, it runs from right to left; and it is first found in Gandhāra where Aramaic was simultaneously in use. Kharoshṭhī shares with Aramaic the difficulty in expressing vowels suffixed to consonants; and whereas Aramaic does not show such vowels at all but leaves them to be added by the reader, Kharoshṭhī makes each consonant by itself stand for a syllable, the short vowel '-*a*' being understood. The other short vowels are suffixed through diacritical extensions. This feature is shared by Brāhmī; but Ashokan Kharoshṭhī, like the Brāhmī of Sri Lanka and of some non-Ashokan inscriptions of northern India of the third century BC, also lacks long vowels. This raises the question whether early Brāhmī too drew on Aramaic, either with Kharoshṭhī as a model or in a parallel development. The evidence for Brāhmī in Sri Lanka in the fourth century BC suggests even the possibility of the script initially taking shape under northwestern Indian influences in Sri Lanka and then arriving from there in India in early third century BC (see Chapter 2.5). If the Sri Lankan evidence remains unshaken, it practically disposes of the possibility (recently suggested by H. Falk) that the Brāhmī was a deliberate creation of the time of Ashoka under the influence of Greek (and so written left to right) and Kharoshṭhī. But this much might yet be true, that Ashokan officials added marks for long vowels and characters for additional consonants such as 'sh', 'sh', 'ṇ' and 'ñ', and, perhaps, also standardized spellings to a considerable degree.

In whatever way the Brāhmī script arrived, early in Ashoka's reign or a little earlier, the art of writing would seem to have diffused rapidly. The interest Ashoka took in getting his edicts inscribed in places all over his Empire means that he expected that there would be some persons everywhere who could be able to read them aloud to others. He also distributed copies of his edicts written obviously on lighter materials. In the Sarnath pillar version of his Schism Edict, he specifically asks that one copy (*ikā lipī*) be kept at a place of assembly (*saṁsalana*) and another made available to the lay worshippers (*upāsaka*): this probably applied to every place where the Schism Edict was sent. In the scribe Chapaḍa, who put on stone the version of the Brahmagiri group of Minor Rock Edicts, we find a person who was versatile in writing both Brāhmī and Kharoshṭhī, in which he writes his professional title of 'scribe' (*lipikareṇa*). The Mahasthan slab inscription and Sohgaura plaque show how official business was now being conducted in writing. The Piprahwa soapstone vase inscription and the Bhattiprolu casket inscriptions offer, similarly, evidence of how writing was being put into use also in the Buddhist *Saṁgha*; and the Tamil Brāhmī inscriptions tell a similar story of its use among the Jain monks or those who made gifts to them. Perhaps, the best testimony to how far literacy had spread in society comes from the inscription in the Jogimara cave (Ramgarh hill), where Devadina, 'skilled in drawing pictures' (*lupadakha* = *rūpadiksha*) and a native of Varanasi, engraved a declaration of his love for Sutanuka, the *devadasi* (= *devadāsī*) (see *Fig. 3.7*). The inscription is in Ashokan Brāhmī, and the language is Ashokan Dialect A, which did not continue in use after Mauryan times. Writing had thus intruded into even the relations between a lowly artist and a slave-courtesan.

Such spread of the use of writing could not but have the most far-reaching consequences for various institutions of society. In the

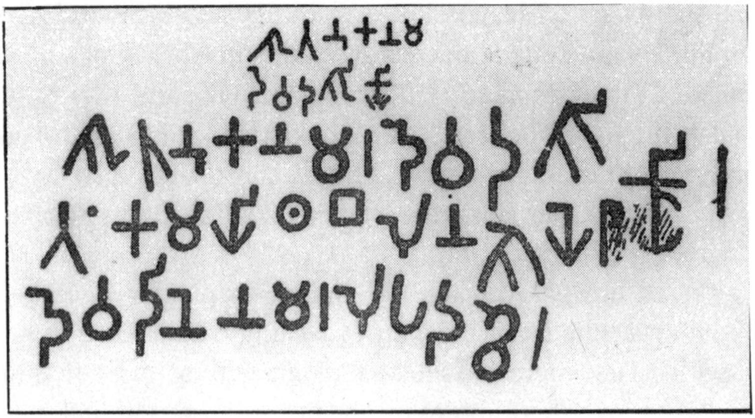

FIG. 3.7 Inscription, Jogimara cave, Ramgarh hill. (After A. Cunningham.) "Sutanuka, the *devadāsī*! Sutanuka, the *devadāsī*! – I, Devadina, artist, from Varanasi, love her." India's first romantic inscription?

administrative bureaucracy it might have begun to replace professional memorizers with scribes, and by simplifying the keeping of records and accounts, immediately improved the effectiveness of administration. For all religious sects, including the Brahmanical, writing offered an important means of preservation and transmission of the sacred texts, though the use of writing for this purpose took time. Secular compositions, in any case, were now likely to have a much better chance of survival than in earlier days, when preservation depended on memory and this was less readily available to texts without any claim to sanctity. Prose, difficult to memorize, could, with the aid of writing, be employed more confidently for learned or legal matters. Commerce too would have greatly benefited from written accounts and messages; and the path would be cleared for the use of letters of credit and bills of exchange – all possible once writing was in vogue, though all this is not positively attested for Mauryan times.

When we shift our attention from writing to the **languages** that obtained a written form, what strikes us immediately is the absence of **Sanskrit** from the inscriptions that are found in such large numbers from the third century BC onwards. Indeed, the first known Sanskrit inscription, that of Dhanadeva at Ayodhya, has been assigned on palaeographic grounds to as late as the beginning of the first century AD. Even a text to honour Lord Vāsudeva by a devotee (*bhāgavata*), as the one on Heliodorus's column at Besnagar (*c.* 140 BC) is in Prākrit, when, owing to the Brahmanical affiliation of the shrine, one should have expected the use of Sanskrit. One is led to suppose that, by Mauryan times, the knowledge of Sanskrit had become so restricted that inscriptions in Sanskrit, if set up, could be understood by only a very small number of persons. As against such a supposition, it has been pointed out that the grammarian Pāṇini, *c.* 350 BC, cites what he calls *Bhāshā* standing for Sanskrit as actually spoken; he himself sets rules for pronouncing words differently when calling from a distance and in natural conversation, and makes use of expressions derived from ordinary life. The presence of such expressions is also noticeable in the grammatical works of Kātyāyana (third century BC) and Patañjali (*c.* 150 BC). Indeed, Patañjali also does us some service by offering a possible solution to our problem. It was the *shishtas*, he says, who spoke correct Sanskrit in ordinary life, without needing to be tutored in it. And the *shishtas* were such disinterested (religiously inclined?) Brahmans as lived in Āryāvarta or northern India. In other words, it was a living language of speech among priestly Brahmans, though not of the mass outside their ranks. Outside their ranks, people would use incorrect forms, some of which, as Patañjali quotes them, are in fact Prākrit forms (for example, *kasi* for *krishi*); and for such people, we may add, inscriptions had to be written in Prākrit.

The bulk of the surviving inscriptions from Mauryan times, then, are in Prākrit, or what, in order to distinguish the language from later Prākrits, is called **Ashokan Prākrit**. It was now certainly the language of administration, and quite possibly the spoken tongue of the town and the market-place. Ashokan Prākrit, with a different grammar, shares the bulk of its vocabulary with Sanskrit, but with the forms of the words changed and combined consonants sharply reduced.

Ashokan Prākrit itself appears to us in four distinct dialects, which, for convenience, are indicated by us as Dialects A, B, C and D (see *Note 3.1* and *Map 3.2*). Of these, Dialects A and B are practically indistinguishable from each other, since the only point of distinction is that in Dialect A the consonant '*r*' is absent, with '*l*' serving for it in all words, whereas in Dialect B both '*l*' and '*r*' are used. Dialect A is the dialect used in all the Ashokan and other Mauryan-period inscriptions in the Gangetic basin and Orissa, and represents the official standard. It probably originated from the spoken language of Magadha, and is,

MAP 3.2 Languages and Ashokan Prākrit Dialects

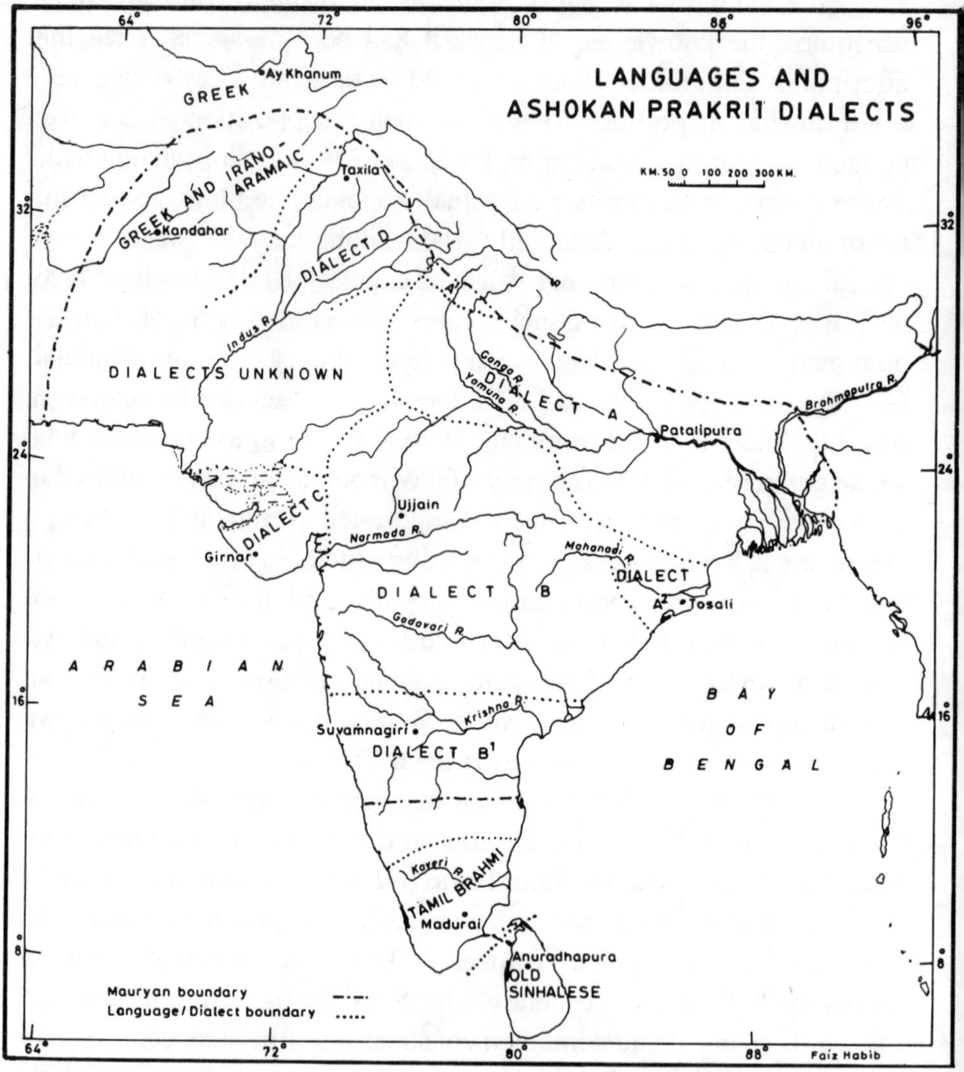

therefore, often called Māgadhī. Dialect B is found in central India and the southern parts of the Mauryan Empire. Dialect C, represented by the Girnar version of the Rock Edicts, has certain Sanskritizing tendencies. These latter are still more visible in Dialect D, represented by the two Kharoshṭhī inscriptions in the North Western Frontier Province, and therefore taken to be the earliest known form of Gāndhārī Prākrit.

To distinguish these dialects and establish the regions where they prevailed is not the same as to say that these were the spoken tongues of the ordinary people in those regions. Even Dialect A could not have been the spoken tongue of the different areas of the Gangetic basin, where most of the inscriptions in it are found. Had this been so, the shift of 'r' to 'l', which is such a marked feature of it, would have had a much longer life than it did: it is not at all attested in any inscription in the region after the end of the Mauryan Empire. The fact that, but for retaining 'r', Dialect B is identical with Dialect A, must lead to the conclusion that both dialects were used by the official class rather than by the ordinary people, since it is hardly likely that the same language, with two such closely similar dialects, could have been spoken over what comprises the bulk of the present Union of India. Rather, the retention of 'r' in Dialect B merely suggests that this was due to the influence of a form of Prākrit previously put to official use in the kingdom of Avanti (Malwa), but now replaced by Ashokan Prākrit. We can similarly see in the more divergent Dialects C and D, versions of Dialect A formed under the influence of the Prākrits previously used by the local elites, rather than the latter languages themselves. From what we know of Dialect D, we cannot even fully reconstruct the local Gāndhārī by which it has been influenced, partly because both the inscriptions carrying it retain the words of the original edicts issued in Dialect A, however much the spellings or forms of the words might be altered. When, however, the Shahbazgarhi inscription in Dialect D breaks with all the other inscriptions and uses the word *badaya* instead of *duvādasa* (and its variant forms) for the number 'twelve', we may be sure that people in Gandhāra used the ancestral form of Hindustani *bārā* rather than the longer word of official Prākrit. We can also infer from Dialect D that the grammar of Gāndhārī was different from that of Dialects A and B, and that compound consonants (closer in form to Sanskrit) were in far greater vogue in it than in the latter dialects. It is possible to argue that this greater affinity to Sanskrit might have been due to a strong local Sanskrit tradition of which Pāṇini, the great grammarian, had been a representative, and to Taxila, a greatly reputed centre of learning. It is also likely that Prākritisms were here thwarted by the influence of Iranic languages, where there was no tendency at all to do away with compound consonants.

Of such **Iranic** presence, Ashoka's own Aramaic inscriptions at Taxila and in Afghanistan are the best evidence. The Aramaic language is of Semetic origin, but, together with its script, it had spread as a general medium of inter-regional and official communication to a large area stretching from Syria to the eastern borders of the Achaemenid Empire. Those who wrote the Ashokan Aramaic inscriptions knew Aramaic grammar (which they largely followed) and used Aramaic vocabulary extensively (thus *mlk'*, or *malik*, for king). But they introduced such a large number of Iranic (mainly Avestan, but also Old Persian) words that one may even name the language they used as 'Irano–Aramaic'. J. Harmatta has found the Avestan element to be so predominant among the Iranic words used in these inscriptions that the languages or dialects spoken in Afghanistan at the time must be held to have been based on pure Avestan, with only some Old Persian intrusions from western Iran.

Another language that established itself in Afghanistan was **Greek**. Despite statements of Greek writers that there were Greek communities settled in the eastern parts of the Achaemenid Empire, there has been no archaeological evidence of the presence of the Greek language in India's borderlands before Alexander's conquest of the area. An early and quite forceful testimony to its presence comes from Ashokan edicts in Greek found at Kandahar. These are written in fine Greek script, and the dialect used is Koinē, the "common" form, current in practically the entire Hellenistic world. The Greek text containing translations of Rock Edicts XII and XIII is particularly interesting in that the translator of Rock Edict XII shows off his knowledge of Attic (the Athenian dialect), while that of Rock Edict XIII insists on pure Koinē. Both are erudite, and make use of their good knowledge of Greek literary and philosophical expressions.

Two southern languages make their appearance through inscriptions outside the Mauryan Empire (see Chapter 2.5 above). From the point of view of the linguistic history of India, it is an important fact that **Tamil**, already in the third century BC, was equipped with its own distinct grammar and vocabulary. Once properly deciphered, the Tamil–Brāhmī inscriptions are found to be in "Old Tamil, not materially different from the language of later Tamil inscriptions or even literary texts, in its basic phonological, morphological and syntactical features" (I. Mahadevan). This judgement is not affected by the fact that the Prākrit loan words in the Tamil–Brāhmī inscriptions amount to over a quarter of the vocabulary.

Cave inscriptions in Sri Lanka begin about the same time as Tamil Brāhmī, that is, from the latter half of the third century BC. **Old Sinhalese**, as the language of these inscriptions is called, can be classed as a Prākrit owing to such features as its Indo–Aryan vocabulary and an avoidance of compound consonants. But it has so many specific features of its own, including the absence of long vowels, a tendency to shift from '*s*' to '*h*' and a lack of aspirated consonants, that it must be deemed a distinct language in its own right.

Turning from languages to **learning**, the two fields in which progress is most visible are **grammar** and the science of polity. Pāṇini's *Ashtādhyāyī*, its eight books containing about 4,000 short *sūtras*, so composed as to be conveniently memorized, may be deemed to be the first such rigorous and extensive book on grammar in the world. He notably deals with the formation of words, the changes they are subject to under various rules and their correct pronunciation. The great authority he came to enjoy later for deciding what is correct or incorrect in Sanskrit composition led sometimes to the supposition that he sought to replace the confused but creative varieties of late Vedic Sanskrit with a new uniformity, partially with a vocabulary or forms of words of his own creation. But this was by no means his aim; and he seems to have been conscientious in determining what ought or ought not to be regarded as correct, from such information about usage as he himself had obtained or derived from his precursors. There seems to be an agreement among most scholars that Pāṇini lived in *c*. 350 BC and so before Mauryan times, but his reference (IV.1.49) to the form *yavanānī*, the feminine *yavana* (Ionian or Greek), suggests a date after Alexander's invasion, as does his mention (III.2.21) of the word *lipi*, script. But later interpolations are not impossible, and so the question must remain open.

Pāṇini's work was subjected to important re-examination by Kātyāyana. He was the author of *vārttikas*, or critical glosses, provided on as many as 1,245 *sūtras* of Pāṇini, and these Patañjali has preserved for us in his *Mahābhāshya* (*c*. 150 BC). He thus stands midway in time between Pāṇini and Patañjali, but sufficiently distant from Pāṇini for spoken Sanskrit to have undergone some change, especially in regional speech. His notice of the title *devānāṁpriya* makes a Mauryan (third century BC) date very likely for him. Kātyāyana is a restrained critic of Pāṇini, and only seeks to modify such rules or dictums as linguistic evidence did not, in his opinion, justify. This work Patañjali, more sympathetic to Pāṇini, continues and, in a sense, completes, while he also duly weighs Kātyāyana's criticisms.

Of the **science of polity**, the *Arthashāstra* is the major work we have to consider. The problem of its date has been discussed in *Note 1.2*, where it has been argued that while the *Arthashāstra* could have been given its final form as late as even *c.* AD 300, it undeniably contains material drawn from earlier versions or originally independent texts that go back to the third century BC, or still earlier. From such a compilation of materials extending over five or six centuries, it is doubtless hard to reconstruct what its shape exactly was in its earliest core existing in Mauryan times. But something can still be said about what it might have contained in its initial stage. In the Dharma-sūtras, which belong largely to the period 500–200 BC, the duties of the king, officials, taxes, military matters and justice are dealt with; and these, therefore, in some form, might already have been present in the earliest *Arthashāstra* text. But it is clear that the work must have had, from the beginning, an outlook different from that of the priestly jurists. This difference is neatly indicated in a dictum (I.7.6–7): "Worldly gain (*artha*) alone is supreme, so says Kauṭilya, for *artha* is the source of securing both the fulfilment of religious duty (*dharma*) and sensual pleasure (*kāma*)." Given this basic premise, the *Arthashāstra*'s endeavour is to show to a prince or king, the way to success in pursuing his ambitions in practically every worldly sphere. As the dictum quoted shows, worldly gain is not in contest with *dharma*, in so far as it embraces the maintenance of the established caste order (see *Extract 3.2*) and the Vedic ritual; rather, the result of worldly gain enables these to be the better protected. It is, however, recognized that in the process of securing worldly success, the ethics of *dharma* may have to be violated: this principle the *Arthashāstra* freely sanctions, as it coolly counsels deceit, plot, plunder and murder to secure one's aims. That is why *artha* is held to be supreme. Yet, the spirit of the *Artha-*

shāstra is not restricted merely to conspiracy and crime. It recommends moderation in policy, and a rigorous and systematic administration: an unagitated population – 'contented' would be too positive a word – is deemed best for a ruler aiming at security of position and wealth. By the time the work obtained its present form, it also aimed at being a comprehensive compendium of information that the ruler and his officials and judges might need, from agriculture and army organization to details of law. Some of this information too is demonstrably early, and may reasonably be assigned to Mauryan times. While claims of a place for the *Arthashāstra* by the side of great treatises on political philosophy seem rather excessive, there is no doubt that it represents an acute perception of the monarchical state, its inherent contradictions and requirements, and its proper place, for its own advantage, as the guardian of the established social order. This, surely, was achievement enough.

On **medicine**, early texts are lacking, but Patañjali (*c.* 150 BC) recognizes *vaidyaka* (medicine) as an established science. Nearchus reported (Arrian, *Indica*, XV), over 170 years earlier, that Alexander, told of Indian physicians' ability to cure snake-bite (!), had them collected to treat his troops; and then they also cured other diseases and pains. Ashoka's Rock Edict II (*c.* 258 BC) speaks of treatment (*chikisā*) for human beings and cattle, and also of the supply of medicinal herbs (*osadhāni*), roots and fruits, which he made arrangements for all over his dominions and abroad (*Extract 2.2*). The existence of at least a primitive veterinary science and pharmacology is implied here, besides the science of medicine.

In **mathematics**, important material is contained in the Shulbasūtra texts, which concern the construction of baked-brick fire altars for Vedic rites. These texts used to be assigned to earlier dates, the *Baudhāyana Shulbasūtra*, the oldest, for example, to the sixth century BC; but now that archaeology has failed to find the use of baked bricks before Mauryan times (see 3.1 above), it is probable that these texts with their concern for baked bricks of various forms should be assigned to the period *c.* 350–150 BC. In these texts there is much use of fractions in addition and multiplication, and of squares to determine the areas of surfaces. The measurements of the sides of the altar-pits led to an empirical discovery of geometric facts, very notably the Pythagorean theorem. This last is stated by Baudhāyana by specifying such whole numbers of units for the lengths of the two sides other than the hypotenuse ('diagonal') as can produce a square equal in area to the square of the hypotenuse also stated in a whole number: thus, sides 3 and 4 units in length are said to have squares together equal to the square of the hypotenuse [which shall be 5 units in length], etc., though the length within the square brackets is not actually specified. Interestingly, a Chinese work of the same time, the *Zhou Bi* (late fourth century BC), gives an almost identical exposition, making use of the same numbers, $3^2 + 4^2 = 5^2$. In both cases, the proof is to be obtained by actual measurement, rather than by any logical process independent of it, as in Euclidian geometry.

In **astronomy**, a small book of verse, the *Vedānga Jyotisha*, probably represents the state of knowledge or belief on astronomical and calenderical matters before 200 BC. Like the *Arthashāstra* (II.20.46–50, 66), it holds the solar year to be of 366 days and the lunar of 354, so that the solar year had to be adjusted to the lunar by an intercalary month every two-and-a half years. In both texts, the number of lunar stations (*nakshatras*) is put at twenty-seven. In his Separate Rock Edicts and Pillar Edict V, Ashoka shows that lunar months were in use and much attention was paid to the nightly lunar stations, the two treated as auspicious being specified by him as *tisā* (*tishya*) and *punāvasu* (*punarvasu*). The major advance under Ashoka, manifestly under the influence of the newly founded Seleucid era, was the successive numbering of each year. Ashoka's regnal years, in fact, represent the first known use of an era in India.

Owing to the immense difficulty in dating the various extant literary texts, it is difficult to present a satisfactory picture of **literature** in Mauryan times in either Sanskrit or Prākrit. As for **Sanskrit**, we assume that the final compilation of the great epic, the *Mahābhārata*, took place much later, though some of the compositions contained in it, from their archaic language, may be held to have originated in Mauryan times. While the composition of the *Rāmāyaṇa* was probably earlier than the final compilation of the *Mahābhārata*, the former (at least, that is to say, its Books II–VI) constitutes a unified work with none of the archaic materials of the *Mahābhārata*, and is also therefore presumably a work of post-Mauryan times.

Even if these two great epics entered Sanskrit literature later, there is good evidence that poetry in novel metres unknown to Vedic texts was now being produced. This evidence comes from Patañjali's *Mahābhāshya* (*c*. 150 BC), where even the limited number of verses that he quotes display a striking "richness and elaboration of metres", suggestive of a considerable development of poetry in the preceding Mauryan age. Indeed, the very advanced nature of the metres he bears testimony to has also been adduced as a reason for arguing a much later date for Patañjali than 150 BC. The verses (often fragmentary) quoted by Patañjali also show that heroic ballads or panegyrics, and romantic and erotic poetry as well as verses laden with pathos, were being produced.

In prose, the *sūtra* (short sentence) form seems still to have remained dominant. Here brevity was so much looked for that, according to Patañjali, a *sūtra* composer obtained as much joy from dispensing with a superfluous short vowel as from the birth of a son! But such brevity was often at the cost of clarity; and it is sometimes difficult today to reconstruct the intended meaning from some of the *sūtra* texts.

In **Prākrit**, Ashokan edicts follow a simple, conversational style, shorn of hyperbole, and with repetition as a device for emphasis. But these texts naturally have no pretensions to the status of literature. In 3.3 above we have suggested that the Buddhist Pāli Canon probably underwent a major process of compilation in Ashoka's time after the Third Council; but the varied constituents of the *Tipiṭaka* ('The Three Baskets') cannot for that reason be ascribed to that time; these must in general have come down from an earlier period, not a small amount from the Buddha's time itself. The major exception is the *Khuddaka Nikāya*, which appears to be the repository of material not included in the initial compilation, though not all of it is necessarily late. The collection includes the celebrated ethical manual, the *Dhaṁmapada*, and the songs of monks and nuns (*Thera-gāthā* and *Theri-gāthā*). The latter typically present the quiet joy and contentment of deliberate destitution. The mundane is not absent: a nun rejoices in her escape from three crooked things, viz. mortar, pestle and a hunch-backed husband.

The Jātakas, the stories of the Buddha in his previous lives or 'births', form a part of the *Khuddaka Nikāya*, but in fact constitute a separate book comprising about 500 stories (formally, 547). These stories are not all about the Buddha, and include tales drawn apparently from folklore and used for didactic purposes with a Buddhist veneer. Some would reappear in the *Pañchatantra*; others have remarkable parallels (or derivatives?) in literatures across the globe. The sculptures at Bharhut and Sanchi (second and first century BC) already have representations of Jātaka stories; and it must, therefore, be assumed that they had not only been composed, but had become a part of the Buddhist sacred lore well before the end of Mauryan times.

3.5 Art and Architecture

To a very large extent it remains true that the history of fine art in India begins with Ashoka and his use of stone for monumental art and architecture.

The most visible Ashokan monuments are the free-standing **pillars** found mainly in the Gangetic basin and at sites near Bhopal in Madhya Pradesh. They are monoliths in that their shafts were originally of single blocks. They are invariably circular, of great length, mildly tapering towards the top and bearing a superb polish, which we cannot today replicate. To take a random example, the shaft of the Allahabad pillar is 10.7 metres in length, 88.8 centimetres in diameter at the bottom and 66 centimetres at the top. Perhaps, the largest of the pillars is the uninscribed pillar at Kolhua (Basarh) in Bihar: it has a height of 12.65 metres, its diameter at a lower level is 1.26 metres and at the top 0.97 metre. The total weight has been estimated at over 50 tons. Over each pillar, there seems originally to have been placed a 'capital', carved out of a separate block of stone but bearing the same polish. Each capital is so carved as to show a bell-shaped, fluted lower part; above it is cut an 'abacus', or platform, with its outer band decorated with animal figures or floral designs; and, finally, at the top is the main capital, composed of a set of lions, a single lion or other single animal. Many capitals have apparently been lost, while

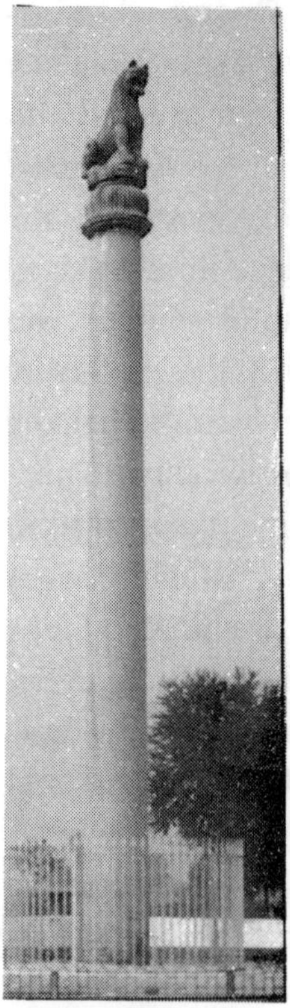

FIG. 3.8 Ashokan pillar, Lauriya Nandangarh. (Photograph: Shamim Akhtar)

others have been recovered near the shafts. It is rare to find the capital still in position at the top of the shaft, as at Lauriya Nandangarh, in northern Bihar (*Fig. 3.8*).

Excluding the Taxila and Amaravati pillar fragments that also bear parts of Ashokan inscriptions, ten of the pillars carry texts of Ashoka's edicts (see above, 2.1). Substantial shafts of uninscribed Ashokan pillars or their capitals have been found at Kolhua (just described) and Rampurwa in Bihar, Gotihwa in Nepalese Terai, Kaushāmbī and Sankisa in Uttar Pradesh, and Besnagar (capital only) and Udayagiri in Madhya Pradesh. In addition, parts of shafts or capitals have been reported from at least six other places. About twenty-five Ashokan pillars are thus known through their physical remains. We must remember that these probably form only a fraction of the pillars he might actually have set up.

In his Minor Rock Edict I, Ashoka says that wherever there was a stone pillar (*silā thaṁbha*), his edict was to be inscribed on it. Had the pillars, then, been put up before his time, by his predecessors? There is evidence that the Pillar Edicts on the Delhi–Topra pillar were engraved while it was standing (the inscribed text is put on all sides of the pillar, and the lower lines of Pillar Edict VII run around it). But Ashoka himself proclaims, in Pillar Edict VII (*Extract 2.7 [A]*), that he had set up *dhaṁma*-pillars (*dhaṁmathaṁbha*), and he also specifically says of the Rummindei pillar that he had it installed. The Lauriya Nandangarh pillar must have been set up under him, for the edicts were engraved on it (confined to one side only) when it was still lying on the ground before erection. Yet, if Ashoka was the builder of some pillars, he must have been the builder of all of them. This is because all the pillars conform to a uniform design, to such an extent that it is impossible to suppose, like J. Irwin, that two or more hands had been involved in envisioning and installing them.

Such being the case, Minor Rock Edict I must be referring to uninscribed pillars set up by Ashoka himself. But this means that, as originally set up, the pillars were not primarily meant to carry inscriptions. It would, indeed, seem that the purpose in setting them up was essentially religious, as is shown by their being installed at Sarnath, Rummindei, Nigali Sagar, Gotihawa, Lauriya Nandangarh and Sanchi, all either sacred sites for Buddhists or in the proximity of *stūpas*, and also at places on the pilgrim route from Pāṭaliputra to Luṁmini (the Buddha's birth-place). If the reason for setting up ten of the pillars can thus be explained fairly reasonably, it might be that each of the others also originally stood near a *stūpa* or monastery. Nor can it be overlooked that Ashoka might also have set up the pillars in towns like Kaushāmbī and Besnagar, and places on the royal highway, such as Sankisa, to do duty as public symbols of both royal majesty and *dhaṁma*. In that sense alone could these be properly called '*dhaṁma*-pillars', as in Pillar Edict VII.

Though some pillars, like the Delhi–Topra pillar with its pinkish sandstone, might have come from the quarries near Mathura, most of the Ashokan pillars are made of the buff-grey, fine, hard-grained sandstone quarried from Chunar, near Varanasi, south of the Ganga. P.C. Pant and V. Jayaswal carried out considerable exploration of the Chunar quarries, but the exact sites from where such long blocks of stone were cut have apparently eluded discovery. None of the old stone blocks found by them have a length of more than 3 metres. While there is some dispute about the period of the short Kharoshṭhī labels found on some of the quarried blocks, it has been claimed that labels of Mauryan Brāhmī too have been found. The quarried blocks were usually cut in cylindrical forms (like the Ashokan pillar-shafts), to assist their being rolled down the slopes and ravines to the bank of the Ganga, where they were put on boats for transportation. One simple example would show what this entailed: the Sanchi pillar being of the Chunar sandstone, a stone block of over 12 metres in length and about 40 tons in weight must have had to be transported on raft up the Ganga, Yamuna and Betwa rivers, and then carried nearly 2 kilometres up the steep Sanchi hillside – a daunting task, perhaps, even for modern engineers.

Since the means of transport available at the time, however efficiently managed, could yet have resulted in damage to the pillar-shafts and capitals, had these been polished and carved near the quarries, such work should usually have taken place at the intended sites of the pillars to which the rough hewn blocks would have been carried. The polishers and stone-carvers must, therefore, have travelled to these sites and not done their work just at some fixed centres. This must be borne in mind when we compare the sculptors' skill shown in one pillar or capital with another: the sculptors were not only possibly different persons, the work too had to be carried out in some cases, at least, under distant supervision.

We shall return to the pillars and their capitals when we consider the features of Mauryan sculpture below; but before we do so, let us first look at two other major aspects of Mauryan architecture, viz. a **pillared hall** and excavated caves.

We have already referred (3.1 above) to the hall with 84 pillars at Kumrahar, Patna (Pāṭaliputra), with each of the pillars 9.3 metres in length. These are of Chunar sandstone and are polished in the same way as the Ashokan pillars. It has long been held that the pillared hall had a magnificent precursor (and, therefore, probably its model) at Persepolis, the Achaemenid capital. But the hall at Pāṭaliputra might not necessarily have been a palace: while the pillars obviously carried wooden roofing, no trace of any walls enclosing the 'hall' has been found. It has been even suggested that Ashoka built the hall for the Buddhist Third Council at Pāṭaliputra. He might have done so, but so long as the very fact of the Council remains a subject of dispute, such speculation is less easy to accept than the description of the hall as a palace.

In the Barabar hills north of Bodh Gaya, Ashoka built three **caves** and gifted them to the Ājīvikas; and in the neighbouring Nāgarjuni hills, one of his successors, Dasharatha, did the same. All the three Ashokan caves are unornamented and functional. Two have a vault-roof hall leading to a domed circular chamber inside; the third only has the hall without the inner chamber. In all the caves the surfaces are highly polished. The caves dedicated by Dasharatha have only one chamber each, with a vault-like roof; but the surfaces are polished throughout. A cave called Lomas Rishi in the Barabar hills has elephants and *stūpas* carved on the archway over the door, leading to a hall with polished surfaces; but the internal circular chamber was left unfinished (*Fig. 3.9*). Probably for this reason, the cave, intended as a retreat for Buddhist monks, has not received a dedicatory inscription. But it otherwise seems to belong to Ashoka's time. Ashoka thus initiated not only the extensive use of stone in Indian architecture, but also the making of rock-cut caves, a tradition that was to endure for a long time.

Before Ashoka's time there is practically no evidence of stone **sculpture**, unless we go back to the Indus Civilization which has left behind small pieces of sculptured stones. With Ashoka we have not

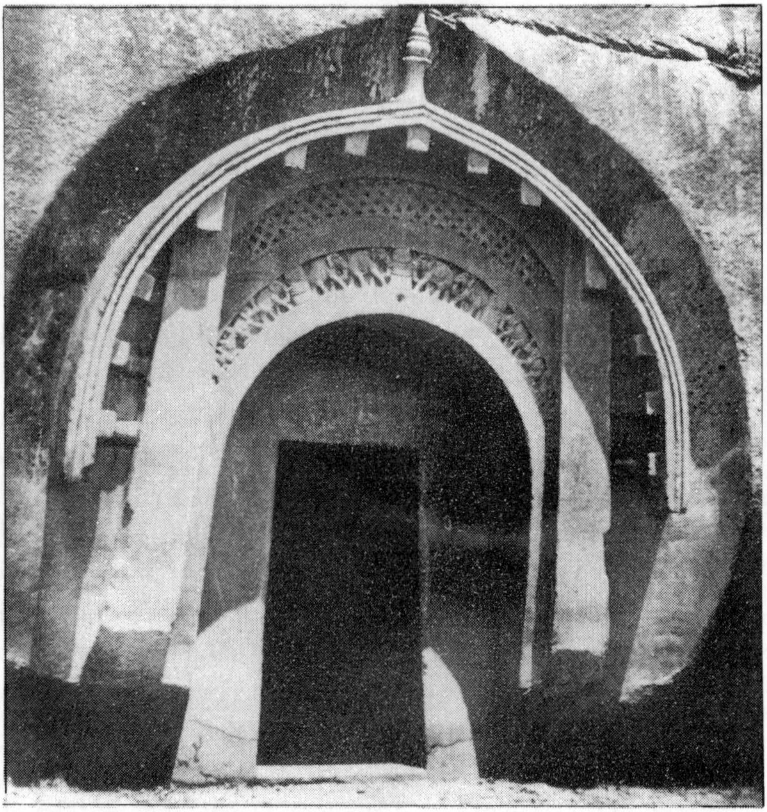

FIG. 3.9 Lomas Rishi cave, Barabar hill. (Courtesy: Archaeological Survey)

only a new tradition in stone sculpture, but also one that is of great skill and exquisite taste.

The major achievements are to be seen in the capitals of Ashokan pillars. Though one's attention is naturally drawn to the statues of animals at the top, those shown in relief in the abacus ought not also to be forgotten. So far, the following animals have been found modelled in three dimensions in the capitals:

Lion (single): Lauriya Nandangarh, Rampurwa, Kolhua, Bansi (forelegs only preserved)

Lion (set of four): Sanchi, Sarnath

Bull: Rampurwa (uninscribed pillar)

Elephant: Sankisa

Crocodile: Besnagar.

FIG. 3.10 (a) Elephant cut into rock, Dhauli. (After A. Cunningham)
(b) Elephant engraved on rock, Kalsi. (After A. Cunningham)

The animals in relief on the abacus rings include the lion, elephant, horse, Bactrian camel, bull and wild geese; there are floral motifs, besides. A mythical winged horse also appears (at Udayagiri).

Besides the animals on the capitals, there are the very interesting life-size elephant cut in rock at Dhauli near the Ashokan inscription (*Fig. 3.10a*), and the elephant outlined on the rock of the Ashokan inscription at Kalsi, with the word *gajatame* ('the best elephant') engraved below (*Fig. 3.10b*).

It has been noted that there is a steady attempt at realism in portraying the animals, both the contours and proportions conforming to the natural form of the animal's body. Niharranjan Ray sees steady progress at each stage in the modelling of the lion, from Kolhua to Lauriya Nandangarh

FIG. 3.11 Lion capital, Sarnath.
(Courtesy: Archaeological Survey)

and, finally, Rampurwa, which he prefers even to the celebrated lions at Sarnath. The great stone wheel whose fragments were found and which originally surmounted the Sarnath pillar might have spoilt its proportions somewhat (the Sanchi pillar had no such wheel at the top despite its similar set of lions). Yet, the Sarnath lions and the bell-shaped base on which they stand (*Fig. 3.11*) deserve, for their design and skill, the highest praise – “unsurpassed”, says John Marshall, “by anything of their kind in the ancient world”.

Elsewhere, too, there is brilliance behind a new realism. At Dhauli, the elephant, necessarily cut in rougher stone, emerges out of solid rock, a picture of power and energy. There is generally both skill and elegance behind secondary representations as well. Floral designs on the abacus rings are stylized, though well-executed; and so too the ‘inverted lotus’ of the bell-capitals.

FIG. 3.12 ***Yakshi*, Didarganj, Patna, first century BC.** (Courtesy: Archaeological Department, Bihar)

It is noteworthy that not a single human form is modelled or shown in relief on any Ashokan sculpture. In view of the exuberance of representations of human figures in subsequent sculpture at Bharhut and Sanchi (where the Buddha, however, is still shown symbolically), the restraint displayed in Ashokan art may possibly have been due to an early Buddhist convention against human representation, textual evidence for which is still lacking. The striking ‘Yakshī’ (semi-divine guardian) from Didarganj (Patna), with its Mauryan polish and display of the standard Greek proportions of the torso (*Fig. 3.12*), datable to the first century BC, probably illustrates what Mauryan art could have achieved had not convention prevented it from sculpturing the human form.

There is one matter that relates purely to taste. The shafts of the Ashokan pillars, superbly polished to smooth glossiness, are scrupulously left unornamented. The ornamentation, never exuberant, is confined to the capitals. This contrast lends grace to the pillars that could have come only from a highly cultivated aesthetic sense. It seems as if Ashoka has left surprises for us in everything he touched.

It does not at all detract from the achievement that there was undoubtedly a certain amount of Achaemenid and Greek inspiration behind it. There was no precedent in India for the extensive use of stone and the lustrous polish, both of which bear the hallmarks of Achaemenid monumental art. The bell-shaped capital too had a model in the bell-shaped pillar base of Achaemenid architecture. The realism of Mauryan animal figures can be plausibly traced to Greek sculpture. There are precedents too for the twisted rope, bead-reed-cable and the honey-suckle designs in Achaemenid and Greek art. While these non-Indian sources of influence are thus fairly definitely established, these do not yet constitute the entire mainsprings of Mauryan art. Buddhism, for example, is manifestly responsible for the lively and sympathetic portraying of animals. It is possible, too, that the Mauryan sculptor drew also on the Indian wood-carver's art, of which unfortunately we know next to nothing, the material having perished. Finally, there are innovations – such as the free-standing pillars themselves, with their smooth cylindrical, not fluted, shafts, and the bell feature, transferred from base to capital – all of which help to reinforce the aura of grace and majesty.

Under the shadows of this art, designed to make an impression on the masses but patronized by the court, existed art at a lower level, pursued by those of lesser means. We have referred to the inscription that an artist (*lupadakha*) from Varanasi has left for us in the Jogimara cave in the Ramgarh hills (3.4 above). The cave apparently contains some of his work as well: on the ceiling, in two shades of red, and yellow, brown, green and black, are paintings of concentric rows of birds, fishes, trees and human beings, and, according to another report, also of a chariot, elephants and attendants. These did not, however, impress the archaeologist who saw them in the mid-1870s: the execution, he said, was coarse, the design stiff.

Terracotta figurines found in considerable numbers at Mauryan sites are products of a widespread folk art. Female deities, animals and toys were made, often perhaps by professional potters, but also possibly by women in their homes. Many figurines were undoubtedly manually shaped, but some were cast from terracotta matrixes, as is

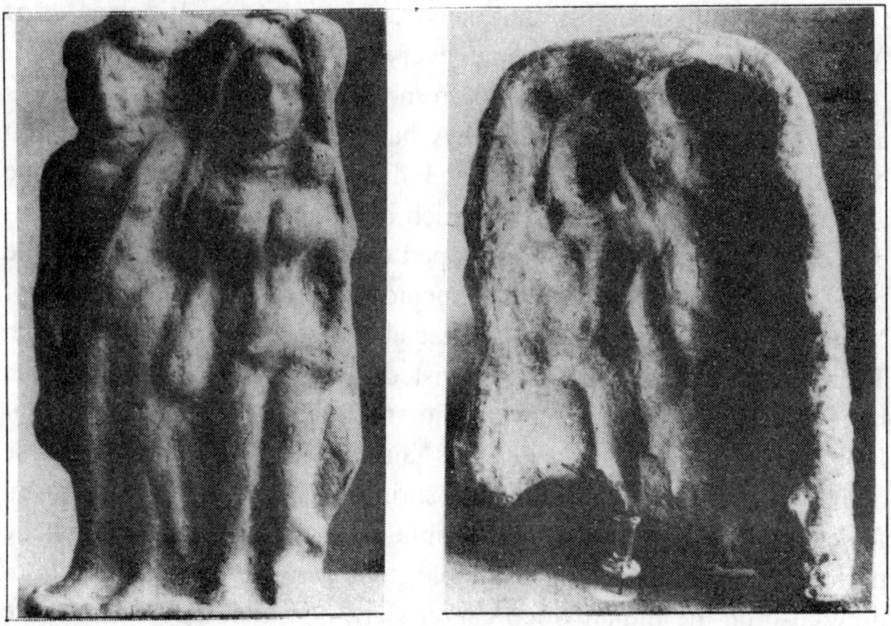

FIG. 3.13 Terracotta plaque with man and woman, and the matrix from which the plaque was cast. Bhir Mound, Stratum II, Taxila. (Reprod. J. Marshall)

illustrated from the many copies of a plaque bearing the figures of a man and woman standing side by side, found along with the matrix, in the Mauryan levels at the Bhir Mound (Taxila) (*Fig. 3.13*). The realism in this plaque is in striking contrast to the crude representations in clay from earlier times: that its cast was made to produce many copies shows that its makers' skill did not remain unappreciated.

TABLE 3.2 Chronology

	BC
Pāṇini, grammarian	*c.* 350
Construction of uninscribed pillars by Ashoka begun	*c.* 262–260
First dated rock-cut caves (Ājīvikas, Barabar hills)	*c.* 258
Kātyāyana, grammarian	*c.* 250
Third Council of Buddhism, Pāṭaliputra	*c.* 244–234
Patañjali, grammarian	*c.* 150

EXTRACTS

Extract 3.1
The Seven Castes

Megasthenes: Paraphrase in Diodorus, II.40–41

The whole population of India is divided into seven castes (*merē*), of which the first is formed by the collective body of the Philosophers (*philosophoi*), which in point of number is inferior to other classes, but in point of dignity pre-eminent over all. For the philosophers, being exempted from all public duties, are neither the masters nor the servants of others. They are, however, engaged by private persons to offer the sacrifices due in lifetime, and to perform the obsequies of the dead: for they are believed to be most dear to the gods, and to be most conversant with matters pertaining to the abode of the dead. In requital of such services they receive valuable gifts and privileges. To the people of India they also render great benefits, when, gathered together at the beginning of the year, they forewarn the assembled multitudes about droughts and wet weather, and also about propitious winds, and diseases, and other topics capable of profiting the hearers. Thus the people and the sovereign, learning beforehand what is to happen, always make adequate provision against a coming deficiency, and never fail to prepare beforehand what will help in a time of need. The philosopher who errs in his predictions incurs no other penalty than bad repute, and he then observes silence for the rest of his life.

The second caste consists of the peasants (*geōragoi*), who appear to be far more numerous than the others. Being, moreover, exempted from fighting and other public services, they devote the whole of their time to cultivation; nor would any enemy coming upon a peasant at work on his land do him any harm, for men of this class being regarded as public benefactors are protected from all injury. The land, thus remaining unravaged, and producing heavy crops, supplies the inhabitants with all that is requisite to make life very enjoyable. The peasants themselves, with their wives and children, live in the country, and entirely avoid going into town. They pay a land-tax to the king, because all India is the property of the Crown, and no private person is permitted to own land. Besides the land-tax they pay into the royal treasury a fourth part of the produce of the soil.

The third caste consists of cattle-herders (*boukoloi*) and shepherds (*poiménes*) and in general all herdsmen who neither settle in towns nor in villages, but live in tents. By hunting and trapping they clear the country of noxious birds and wild beasts. As they apply themselves eagerly and assiduously to this pursuit, they free India from the pests with which it abounds – all sorts of wild beasts and birds which devour the seeds sown by the peasants.

The fourth caste consists of the artisans (*techuitai*). Of these some are armourers, while others make the implements which peasants and others find useful in their different callings. This class is not only exempted from paying taxes, but even receives maintenance from the royal exchequer.

The fifth caste is the military (*polemistai*). It is well organized and equipped for war, holds the second place in point of numbers, and gives itself up to leisure and amusement in times of peace. The entire force – men at arms, war-horses, war-elephants, etc. – are maintained at the king's expense.

The sixth consists of superintendents (*ephoroi*). It is their duty to enquire into and superintend all that goes on in India, and make report to the king, or, where there is not a king, to the magistrates.

The seventh caste consists of councillors and assessors – of those who deliberate on public affairs. It is the smallest class looking to number, but the most respected on account of high birth and wisdom of its members; for from their ranks the advisers of the king are drawn, and the administrators of the state and judges who settle disputes. The army commanders and chief magistrates usually belong to this caste.

Such then are the parts into which society in India is divided. No one is allowed to marry out of his own caste, or to exercise any calling or art except his own. For instance, a soldier cannot become a peasant; or an artisan a philosopher.

(J.W. McCrindle's translation, modified.)

Extract 3.2
The Caste *Dharma*

Arthashāstra, I.3

4. This law (*dharma*) laid down in the Three (Vedas) is beneficial, as it establishes the duties (*svadharma*) according to the four *varṇas* and life's stages (*āshrama*).

5. The Brahman's own *dharma* comprises: to study, perform *yajana* (ritual sacrifice) [for oneself] and to perform it for others (*yājana*), give and receive alms.

6. Of the Kshatriya: to study, perform *yajana* [for oneself], give alms, live by [bearing] arms, and protect living beings.

7. Of the Vaishya: to study, perform *yajana* [for oneself], give alms, pursue agriculture (*krishi*), cattle-rearing and trade (*vāṇijya*).

8. Of the Shūdra: to obey the twice-born, pursue a calling (*vārttā*), work as artisan or actor (*kārukushīlavakarma*).

9. Of the householder: to earn his living according to his own [caste-] *dharma*, marry into families of the same rank [caste], but not within the same *gotra*, [avoid] approaching wife during her periods, offer worship to gods, male ancestors and guests, make gifts to servants (*bhritya*), and partake of food after others have eaten (*sheshabhojana*).

. . .

13. Common to all: to inflict no injury (*ahiṁsā*), and be truthful, upright, free of malice, compassionate and forbearing.

14. One's own *dharma* leads to heaven (*svarga*) and endless bliss.

(Kangle's translation, modified.)

Extract 3.3
Pilgrimage to the Buddha's Birth-place

Rummindei Pillar Edict of Ashoka

The King Devānaṁpiya Piyadasi, anointed twenty years, himself came and offered worship, for here the Buddha was born, the Sakyamuni. He caused a large stone wall to be made and [this] stone pillar to be erected; and made the Luṁmini village (*gāma*) exempt from the *bali* [-tax] (*ubalike*) and liable to pay [only] an eighth portion (*aṭhabhāgiye*) [of the produce].

Note 3.1
Dialects of Ashokan Prākrit

Ashokan inscriptions, through their widespread geographical distribution and by carrying the same substantive texts of edicts, with some linguistic variations, offer us the earliest evidence of regional dialects in Prākrit. By a comparison of their texts, conveniently tabulated (as 'synoptical texts') by E. Hultzsch, R. Basak, D.C. Sircar and others, it has been possible to identify the grammatical and other variations in the texts, and determine areas where similarities are visible. It is clear that throughout we deal with the same language, Ashokan Prākrit, since there is the same sentence structure and the same vocabulary (with rare exceptions), however might the spellings and some grammatical conventions vary. That is why when we identify regional variations, we can speak of only regional dialects and not languages. Moreover, all the dialects show a tendency to avoid combined consonants (present extensively in Sanskrit), though this is strongest in Dialects A and B, as we shall see below, and weaker in Dialects C and D.

Dialect A, which is called Māgadhī by most scholars, is the official standard dialect, in which the original edicts were probably issued from Pāṭaliputra. All

Ashokan inscriptions found in the Gangetic basin and Orissa are in this dialect. The texts of Pillar Edicts I–VI, found in Uttar Pradesh and Bihar, are so closely identical and consistent in their spellings that we can assume that uniform spellings and grammatical rules had been established for this dialect, at least at the official level. Some of the distinctive features of Dialect A are as follows. (1) Compound consonants (e.g., 'ksh', 'ml', 'pr', 'rm', 'st') are extremely rare and are resolved either by omission (e.g., *pajā* for *prajā*) or aspiration (e.g., 'kha' for 'ksha'). (2) Long vowels, though used, tend to be shortened, as in *lāja* for Sanskrit *rājā*. (3) 'r' is not at all used, but is replaced by 'l' throughout, as in *lāja* above. (4) One sibilant alone (usually 's') is used for 's', 'sh' and 'sh' of corresponding Sanskrit words. (5) Of the nasals, only 'n' is used, replacing 'ṇ' and 'ñ' of Sanskrit. (6) There is a tendency towards aspiration, as in *hevaṁ* for Sanskrit *evam*. (7) The nominative singular case-ending of both masculine and neuter genders, in declension in bases of *-a*, is *-e*.

The standard form of the dialect above described is carried by all the Pillar Edicts and other pillar inscriptions (except the Sanchi version of the Schism Edict), the Minor Rock Edict I at Bahapur (Delhi), Bairat, Ahraura, Basaha and Sahasram, the Bairat Rock Edict, and the Barabar and Nagarjuni cave inscriptions. The versions of the Rock Edicts at Kalsi, in Uttarakhand (in Dialect A^1), and the Rock Edicts and Separate Rock Edicts at Dhauli and Jaugada in Orissa (in Dialect A^2), show some minor dialectal differences, whereas the Erragudi and the Sannathi copies of the Rock Edicts are entirely in the standard Dialect A, though the inscriptions are situated in southern Andhra and northern Karnataka. The Mahasthan, Sohgaura, Piprahwa and Jogimara inscriptions also conform to Dialect A.

Dialect B (which may also be called the Ujjaini or Avanti Dialect) is found in Ashokan inscriptions of central and southern India. In its standard form, it is the same as Dialect A, except that both 'r' and 'l' are in use, largely conforming to Sanskrit forms, although by error, as at Sopara, 'l' may be wrongly replaced by 'r' (e.g., *phara* for *phala*). The standard Dialect B is found in the Rupnath, Gujjara and Panguraria versions of Minor Rock Edict I, the Sopara version of the Rock Edicts, and the Sanchi pillar inscription. Further south, the Separate Rock Edicts at Sannathi in Karnataka and Minor Rock Edicts at Erragudi are also in Dialect B. But the versions of the Minor Rock Edicts in other places within Karnataka show stray use of 'sh' and 'ṇ', and so may be supposed to represent a Sub-dialect B^1.

Dialect C, or the Western Dialect, is represented by the Girnar (Gujarat) version of the Rock Edicts. It is the same as Dialect B (like the latter, it uses 'r' regularly), but it has certain special features of its own. For one, the combined consonants occur more frequently: it reads 'Priyadasi', not 'Piyadasi'. For *ksha* and *ksha* of Sanskrit it has *chha*, and only sometimes *khạ*. The long vowel is used in *rājā*. It uses both 'ṇ' and 'ñ'. It has *evaṁ* for *hevaṁ* of Dialects A and B. Finally, the case-ending *-e* is here replaced by *-o*/*-aṁ*. The change of case affects some words also: *rājine* of Dialect B becomes *rāṇo* at Girnar.

The two inscriptions in Kharoshṭhī left by Ashoka are those of the

Fourteen Rock Edicts at Shahbazgarhi and Mansehra in the North Western Frontier Province. These represent Dialect D, which may be regarded as our window to the earliest form of Gāndhārī. Of the latter, the Shahbazgarhi version seems a better representative than Mansehra, which lets many forms of the Dialect-B type remain in its text. The dialect has no long vowels nor the vowels 'ai' and 'au', though, as in Aramaic, readers might have been expected to pronounce these vowels wherever needed. Combined consonants are still more numerous than in Dialect C, with a tendency to be closer to Sanskrit. Thus the dialect has *dhrama*, not *dhaṁma* (compare Sanskrit *dharma*), and 'Priyadrasi' (closer to Sanskrit 'Priyadarshin' than to 'Piyadasi' of Dialects A and B). There is regular use of 'r', 'ṇ', 'ñ', 'sh' and '<u>sh</u>', and, like Dialect C, no tendency towards aspiration (so *evaṁ* throughout). It shares with Dialect C the tendency in declension to end nominative cases of masculine and neuter genders singular (bases in *-a*) in *-o* and *-aṁ* respectively (and not uniformly in *-e* like Dialects A and B).

These details may be found useful for understanding the discussion of Ashokan Prākrit and its dialects in Chapter 3.4.

Note 3.2
Bibliographical Note

Most of the works mentioned in the Bibliographical Notes to Chapters 1 and 2 remain relevant for this chapter.

For Mauryan-period artefacts, John Marshall, *Taxila: An Illustrated Account of Archaeological Excavations*, 3 volumes (Cambridge, 1951), remains the major work of reference, finds at other sites being related to the strata established at the Bhir Mound (Taxila). Numerous Mauryan-period ('NBPW' Culture) artefacts are described and illustrated in R.C. Gaur, *Excavations at Atranjikhera* (Delhi, 1983). G.R. Sharma, *The Excavations at Kauśāmbī, 1957–59* (Allahabad, 1960), has important material, even if the chronology proposed by the author is disputable.

Two works may be consulted for the historical perspective on caste: Ram Sharan Sharma, *Śūdras in Ancient India* (Delhi, 1958), and Suvira Jaiswal, *Caste: Origin, Function and Dimensions of Change* (New Delhi, 1998). For slavery, see Dev Raj Chanana, *Slavery in Ancient India* (New Delhi, 1960).

There is much material of relevance to Mauryan economy, society and culture in V.S. Agrawala, *India as Known to Pāṇini* (Lucknow, 1953). The old edition and translation of Pāṇini's *A<u>sh</u>ṭādhyāyī* by Srisa Chandra Vasu, originally published in 1891–93, has now been reprinted in two volumes (Delhi, 1990).

Practically all works on Ashoka mentioned in our *Note 2.2* deal with the relevant aspects of Buddhism; a recent work, Richard F. Gombrich, *Theravāda Buddhism* (London, 1988; available in paperback), may be found useful. On the Ājīvikas, the standard work is A.L. Basham, *History and Doctrines of the Ājīvikas* (London, 1951; subsequent Indian reprint, Delhi, n.d.). For Vai<u>sh</u>ṇavism, see Suvira Jaiswal, *The Origin and Development of Vaiṣṇavism* (Delhi, 1967).

Maurice Winternitz, *History of Indian Literature*, Vol. I (Calcutta, 1927), deals with the Vedic texts, but includes the epics and Purāṇas in its range, while Vol. II (Delhi, 1983) is concerned with Buddhist and Jain literatures. The development of Sanskrit grammar between Pāṇini and Patañjali is discussed in Winternitz, Vol. III, part 2 (Delhi, 1967), and in Hartmut Scharfe, *Grammatical Literature* (Wiesbaden, 1977). A. Berriedale Keith, *A History of Sanskrit Literature* (Oxford, 1928), is a generally reliable guide to ancient Sanskrit literature, beginning with Pāṇini.

On art, there is a compact survey by Niharranjan Ray, *Maurya and Post-Maurya Art* (New Delhi, 1976). S.P. Gupta, *The Roots of Indian Art* (Delhi, 1980), contains an extensive 'documentation' of the various aspects of Mauryan art. On the sculptures at Bharhut (second century BC), close enough to Mauryan times to be a source for both Buddhism and other aspects of life, see A. Cunningham, *The Stupa of Bharhut* (Calcutta, 1879; reprinted, Varanasi, 1962), and Benimadhab Barua, *Barhut*, 3 volumes (Calcutta, 1934, 1936, 1937). On the sculptures at Sanchi, see John Marshall, Alfred Foucher and N.G. Majumdar, *The Monuments of Sanchi*, 3 volumes (Delhi, 1940; reprinted, Delhi, 1982).

Index

iron, 122, 127; sickles, 112; tools, 122; weapons, 2
irrigation works, 37, 77, 113
Irwin, J., 161
Isfahan in Iran, 3
Isila in Karnataka, 26, 31, 126
Italy, 5
ivory, 110

Jaṁbudīpa, 24
Jain, Canon, 145; monastic establishments, 145; monks, 4, 20, 145, 149; polymath Hemachandra, 13; tradition, 86
Jainism, 94, 138, 145
Jains, 66, 74, 81, 103, 138, 146
Jalauka, 87
Jambai (Viluppuram district, Tamil Nadu), 92
janapada (province, district), 34, 43, 67, 102, 111, 130, 135
Jātakas, stories of the Buddha, 159, 160
jāti, 65, 132
Jaugada, 23, 54
Jayaswal, V. , 162
Jhelum, 8, 9
Jogimara cave inscriptions, 136, 149, 167, 172
judge (*dyn*), 33, 34
Justin, 14, 17, 19

Kabul ('Cophen') river, 6
Kabul, 32
Kalhaṇa, 87; *Rājataraṅgiṇī*, 87
Kalinga, 13, 23, 32, 39, 54, 65, 82
Kalinga War, 46, 71
Kalingas, 22, 42, 43
Kalsi (near Dehra Dun, Uttaranchal), 23, 32, 54
Kāluvākī (Kāruvākī), 26, 59, 86
Kāmbojas, 23, 33, 130, 131
Kandahar, 6, 12, 23, 32, 33, 61, 88, 126, 154
Kandahar bazaar inscription, 83
Kandahar bilingual edict, 54, 63, 69, 72, 78
karma, 68
Karnataka, 23, 32, 52, 53, 92, 145, 172
Kashmir, 23
Kātyāyana, 116, 151, 155, 156
Kaushāmbī, 26, 30, 35, 124, 125, 126, 127, 141, 161, 162
Kaveri delta, 91
Kerala, 23, 92
Keralaputas, 23, 91, 99
Keteus, 3
khaṇḍa (candied sugar), 114
Khāravela, 106
kharif, 114
Kharoshṭhī, 3, 32, 39, 52, 54, 106, 149, 162, 172
Kharoshṭhī inscriptions, 95, 152
Kharoshṭhī script, 148
Khuddaka Nikāya, 159
king, 2, 20, 142
king's officials, 33
kingship, 3
Kirman, eastern Iran, 11
Kirthar Range, 10
koṭavishaya (districts with forts), 25, 27, 28, 82
Koinē, 154
Kolhua (near Vaishali), 128, 161, 164, 165
Konkan, 23
Kosam (Allahabad district), 30
Kosambi, D.D., 47,116
Kosāpagota, 144
Kshatriyas, 3, 40, 131, 133, 170
kumāra Saṁva, 25, 85
Kumrahar, Patna (Pāṭaliputra), 163
Kunāla, 40, 86, 89